LONGMAN SOURCES AND OPINIONS

Tudor England
1485–1603

Roger Lockyer
Dan O'Sullivan

LONGMAN

LONGMAN GROUP UK LIMITED
Longman House, Burnt Mill, Harlow, Essex, CM20 2JE,
England and Associated Companies throughout the World.

© Longman Group UK Limited 1993

First published 1993
Second impression 1994
ISBN 0 582 02202 9

Set in 10/12 point Gill and 10/12 point Palatino (Linotron)
Produced by Longman Singapore Publishers Pte Ltd
Printed in Singapore

The publisher's policy is to use paper manufactured
from sustainable forests.

British Library Cataloguing in Publication Data

Lockyer, Roger
  Tudor England. – (Sources & Opinions
Series)
  I. Title II. O'Sullivan, Dan III. Series
  942.05
  ISBN 0-582-02202-9

Library of Congress Cataloging-in-Publication Data

Lockyer, Roger.
  Tudor England/Roger Lockyer, Dan O'Sullivan.
    p. cm. – (Sources and opinions)
  ISBN 0-582-02202-9
  I. Great Britain – History – Tudors, 1485–1603 – Sources.
2. England – Civilization – 16th century – sources. I. O'Sullivan,
Dan. II. Title. III. Series.
DA310.L814 1993
942.05 – dc20

93-23514
CIP

CONTENTS

ACKNOWLEDGEMENTS

We are grateful to the following for permission to reproduce copyright material:

Ashmolean Museum, Oxford, page 167; Bodleian Library, Oxford, ms 4° R.21. Ant Seld (6), page 100; Bible Society/Bridgeman Art Library, London, page 26; Cambridge University Press, pages 95, 108; from 'The History of the King's Works', volume IV, 1485–1660, reproduced with the permission of the Controller of Her Majesty's Stationery Office, pages 165, 166; Hodder and Stoughton Limited, page 94; The Mansell Collection, page 17; National Portrait Gallery, London, pages 47, 143, 159; Courtesy of The Marquess of Salisbury, page 61; George Weidenfeld & Nicolson Limited, page 5.

Cover: From the National Portrait Gallery, London, Sir Thomas More and his family, painted in 1593.

Picture Research by Sandie Huskinson–Rolfe (PHOTOSEEKERS)

INTRODUCTION

A Level History syllabuses nowadays include more and more source-evaluation and document work, and this trend is likely to continue. It is most important for a student of History to practise the skills of being able to understand, assess and use primary source material, and it is probably also true that such activities are both more enjoyable in themselves and also more educational than that of reading a conventional textbook.

This book presents a wide-ranging collection of documents consisting of extracts taken from a variety of sixteenth-century primary sources. These range from Acts of Parliament and similar official material to anecdotal and private sources such as diaries and letters. The documents are arranged by topic rather than chronologically. Out of the eight chapters, two are on religion, two on government, and one each on foreign policy, economic and social affairs, rebellions and culture. Each chapter is sub-divided into three or four sections, and each section contains a group of documents on a common theme. Every document is preceded by a brief introduction which is intended to put it into context and give some guidance as to how to approach it, but certainly not to answer all the questions and remove all the difficulties it raises. Primary source material should always present a fresh challenge, so that skills of evaluation and interpretation can be applied, and this challenge should never be side-stepped by an excess of editing and explanation. In the same spirit, editing has been kept to a minimum consistent with accessibility. Spelling has been modernised, and omissions from the original text are indicated by spaced dots. Difficult words or phrases are explained, either in the text or in the Glossary at the back of the book. Apart from this, the documents have been left to speak for themselves.

The book is intended both for class or group work and for individual study, and it will be particularly useful for those who are undertaking assignments or personal projects. The thematic approach ought to make it relatively straightforward to find material on a given topic, especially if one looks, not only at the section and chapter headings, but also at the topic index at the back of the book. Equally, one could work right through the book, topic by topic, and achieve in this way a fair understanding of the central themes of sixteenth-century English history. For class work, it is suggested that a particular section could be studied in conjunction with the relevant passage in a narrative textbook.

A teachers' book has been produced to accompany this source book. It contains an historical commentary which attempts to link the documents together, as well as a series of specimen questions on the documents intended to bring out their meaning and significance. The questions are free of copyright and may be photocopied for class use.

Note on the system of references

An asterisk (*) refers the reader to a note at the end of the document concerned. The symbol (†) after a word means that the word is defined in the Glossary at the back of the book. Round brackets ( ) enclose material from the original source itself. Square brackets [ ] enclose editorial explanation: definitions (in italics) and added words (in ordinary type).

Note on sources

After each extract, details of the source from which it was taken are given. In the case of books, the name of the author or editor, the date of publication, the place of publication (unless London) and the page reference(s) are stated.

LIST OF DOCUMENTS

CHAPTER I   CONSERVATIVES AND REFORMERS

This chapter is the first of two on religion, and it presents documents relating to what people believed rather than what central government commanded. There has been much debate recently about the pace of religious change in sixteenth-century England – about the process of conversion of the population from Catholicism to Protestantism. It was one thing for Parliament to pass Acts, or for bishops to issue injunctions[†]; quite another for people's beliefs and attitudes to follow suit, and it now seems that the pace of change was much slower than used to be thought. The first two sections in this chapter are concerned with conservative, or traditional, attitudes. The first section looks at the positive side of the pre-Reformation Church, while the second section is about the position of conservatives after the Reformation had started. The pre-Reformation Church certainly contained glaring abuses and received much criticism, but this did not necessarily imply a desire to sweep away the whole edifice. In fact it could be argued that the volume of criticism, much of it coming from men who were themselves in holy orders, was a sign of health rather than decay.

Henry VIII's Reformation radically altered the relationship between pope, monarch and Church, but it did not affect the common people unduly – it was probably the loss of the monasteries, and later of the chantries[†], that was most keenly felt. Under Edward the pace quickened; by now alterations in services and in the liturgical year would have been noticed by everybody, and resented by many. There is some evidence of popular welcome for Mary, and if she had lived longer, or produced an heir, she and her bishops might have re-established Catholicism on a secure basis. By 1558 England was still, for the most part, a Catholic nation, and the Pope had good reason for hoping that it might return to the papal fold. During Elizabeth's reign a considerable, and largely successful, effort was made to convert the nation, but important pockets of resistance remained in many parts of the country. The missionary priests from the Continent played a major part here, in helping Catholic communities become better organised and determined to survive.

The third and fourth sections are concerned with the Reformers – those who wanted to convert England to Protestantism. There is no doubt that the Reformation in England succeeded because it was imposed from above, but it is also a fact that the State could hardly have imposed the new faith without a significant amount of popular support. An underground, heretical tradition of Lollardy[†] had survived in certain areas ever since the death of John Wycliffe (1384), though it is difficult to know how far this contributed towards the Protestant movement. By about 1530 the surviving elements of Lollardy had begun to merge with, and be reinforced by, new Lutheran ideas from the Continent such as the doctrine of Justification by Faith, which challenged by implication the whole edifice of the Catholic Church. Nevertheless, Protestantism made little headway until given a lead by the State. Henry VIII gave that lead, but he himself was probably conservative in his personal religion, and there was renewed persecution of heretics in his final years. But in the next reign sweeping changes in the direction of Protestantism were enforced, culminating in the reforms of Northumberland and the 1552 Prayer Book.

Mary's reign was too short to allow the restoration of Catholicism to get properly underway. However, the popular reaction against Mary's persecution of Protestants, as well as against her marriage, was skilfully exploited by Protestant exiles, especially the martyrologist John Foxe, and a powerful and lasting myth was created out of the ingredients of patriotism and Protestantism. After the creation of the new Church of England in 1559, the State undertook the gradual consolidation of Protestantism, a process far from complete even by the early seventeenth century. Progress was complicated by the tension between those who wished to push the new Church in the direction of Geneva, and those, such as the Queen, supported by an increasing number of bishops, who were determined that it should adhere to the 'middle way' between the extremes of Presbyterianism[†] and Roman Catholicism. Here, the dogged fight of Elizabeth's third and last Archbishop of Canterbury, John Whitgift, against hard-line Puritans both inside and outside Parliament was crucial, as also were the lucid arguments of Richard Hooker, the best known apologist for the new Church.

Conservatives (1)
The Pre-Reformation Church

1 Piety and church building, 1504, 1515

These first two documents provide evidence that the pre-Reformation Church in England possessed considerable vitality and appeal.

(a) An indenture[†] between King Henry VII and John Islipp, Abbot of St Peter's Monastery, Westminster, and the prior and convent, 16 July 1504.

Whereas it is the King's intent to have there three chantry[†] monks, doctors or bachelors of divinity, to say daily masses and services with the observances specified below...These daily masses and services shall be said perpetually for the good and prosperous estate of the King and prosperity of his realm and for the souls of Elizabeth, late Queen of England, his wife, and their children; Edmund, late Earl of Richmond, his father, and all his other progenitors and ancestors; and of Margaret, Countess of Richmond and Derby, his mother, after her decease; and, after his decease, for the King's soul, together with the aforesaid and all Christian souls. They shall be said at the altar under the lantern place between the choir

From the *Calendar of the Close Rolls, Henry VII*, vol. II, *1500–1509*, HMSO, 1963, no. 389, pp. 139–41.

and the high altar, till the Lady Chapel now begun be fully built and a tomb there made for the interment of the King's body and 'a closure of metall in maner of a Chapel' made thereabouts and an altar enclosed therein... These three monks shall be called 'the Chantry Monks of King Henry VII'.

(b) The building of Louth church spire, 1515.

Memorandum: the fifteenth Sunday after Holy Trinity this year the weathercock was set upon the broach [*spire*] of Holy Rood... there being Will. Ayleby, parish priest, with many of his brother priests there present, hallowing [*consecrating*] the said weather cock and the stone that it stands upon, and so conveyed upon the said broach; and then the said priests singing 'Te deum laudamus' with organs. And then the kirk wardens gart [*did*] ring all the bells and caused all the people there being to have bread and ale. And all to the loving of God, Our Lady and all saints.

From Reginald C. Dudding (ed.), *The First Churchwardens' Book of Louth 1500–1524*, Oxford, 1941, p. 181.

2   A Christian humanist seeks reform, 1522

The Dutch humanist, Erasmus, remained loyal to the papacy whilst strongly attacking church abuses. This extract is from one of his most popular works.

TIMOTHY: Christ commanded us to give to everyone who asks. If I did that, I'd have to beg myself within a month.

EUSEBIUS: I believe Christ means those who ask for necessities. Those who seek, nay demand, or rather extort, large sums to make Lucullan* feasts or – worse yet – to cater to their gluttony and lust, it is charity to refuse. More than that, it's robbery to bestow on those who will use it ill what ought to have relieved the instant distress of our neighbours. Hence those who adorn monasteries or churches at excessive cost, when meanwhile so many of Christ's living temples are in danger of starvation, shiver in their nakedness, and are tortured by want of necessities, seem to me almost guilty of a capital crime. When I was in Britain I saw St Thomas' tomb, laden with innumerable precious jewels in addition to other incredible riches. I'd rather have this superfluous wealth spent on the poor than kept for the use of officials who will plunder it all sooner or later. I'd decorate the tomb with branches and flowers; this, I think, would be more pleasing to the saint.

From *The Colloquies of Erasmus* (1522), translated from the Latin by Craig R. Thompson, Chicago, 1965, p. 70.

*Lucullus was a wealthy Roman, famous for his banquets.

3   Handale Priory, 1536

This is a glimpse of the restricted, almost exclusively female world of a small Yorkshire nunnery. Such houses provided, as well as some local employment, an alternative to the married state for many women. These extracts come from the papers of commissioners appointed to visit the lesser monasteries (those with an income of less than £200) on their dissolution under the Act of 1536.

Handale late priory or house of nuns of the B. V. Mary of Handale or Grendale of the Order of St. Benedict Cistercian.

[*names of the nuns*]
Note that they all be of good living.
Anna Lutton prioress aged 51 years
Joan Scott aged 90 years blind
Alicia Brampton aged 73 years
Margaret Loghan aged 45 years
Isabella Norman aged 29 years
Cicilia Watson aged 31 years
Anna Denyson aged 27 years
Meriall Lumney aged 34 years
Emma Smith aged 32 years.

Servants wages paid
First given in reward to Annys Loghan having
a corrody† there   5s.*
Item given to an old gentlewoman named Eliz. Bryan
in reward   6s. 8d.
Item to John Sawer chief husband servant for his quarter
wages at Lammas [*1 August*] 4s. 3d. and in reward 2s. 5d.   6s. 8d.
Item to John Coverdale mylner for like wages at Lammas
2s. 9d. and in reward 2s. 3d.   5s.
Item to Gilbert Benyson boy for his quarter wage 2s. &
reward 20d.   3s. 8d.
Item to Mathew Carlill a boy for like   3s. 8d.
Item to Mary Lutton butler for her quarter wages at
Lammas 21d. and in reward 3s. 3d.   5s.
Item to Margaret Hodgson cook for her quarter wages
2s. 3d. and reward 2s. 9d.   5s.
Item to Elizabeth Carlill for her quarter wages 21d. and in
reward 3s. 3d.   5s.
Item to Cristabell Boyes for her quarter wages 15d. and
reward 2s. 1d.   3s. 4d.
Item to Thomas Henryson Chaplayne for his quarter
wages 10s. and reward 3s. 4d.   13s. 4d.

The Corrody† of Richard Loggan and Agnes Loggan.

First a house to dwell in yearly *nil quod manet ibidem*
[*nothing, because it remains there*]
Item vii loaves of bread weekly weighing every loaf ii
pounds viz.   xxvis
Item vi gallons of convent ale and i gallon small ale
weekly viz.   xxvis
Item half a cow yearly   vs

Item a whole swine yearly	xx*d*
Item a bushel oats	xii*d*
Item a bushel pese	iiii*d*
Item a bushel and a half salt yearly	viii*d*
Item vii salt fishes yearly	xiiii*d*
Item a C [*100*] herrings white and red	x*d*
Item of every mutton that were killed *1d*	iiii*s*, iiii*d*
Item of every beast that were killed	vi*d*
iiii loads turfs yearly	xx*d*
a load wood	vi*d*
milk of a cow winter and summer	ii*s*
Item from Easter to Martinmass [*11 November*] every week a quart milk	viii*d*
Item every principal feast to dine with the prioress and convent	viii*d*
Every year 1 Ib candles	i*d*
Summa totalis	lxxiii*s* i*d*

From 'Monastic Rentals and Surveys', *Yorkshire Archaeological Society Record Series*, vol. LXXX, 1931, pp. 77–9.

*12 pennies (*d*) = 1 shilling (*s*); 20 shillings = £1.

4   The pattern of monastic property, c. 1530

From Martin Gilbert, *An Atlas of British History*, 1968, p. 43.

A modern map showing the location of monastic houses before the Dissolution in the south-east of England.

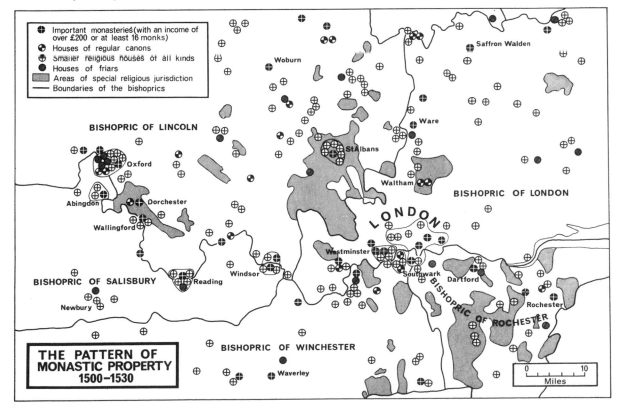

5   A Catholic preamble to a will, 1537

The will of John Mason of York. The wording of the preamble to a will may be an indication of the faith of the testator, although this source must be used with caution.

The original will is in the Borthwick Institute, York (Prob. Reg. 11, f, 250v.). It is printed in W. J. Sheils (ed.), *The Reformation in the North to 1558*, York, 1976, document no. 11.

I John Mason, glover of the City of York, being whole of mind and good remembrance, make and ordain this my testament and my last will in manner and form following. First I . . . commend my soul to Almighty God my creator and to the Blessed Virgin Mary, the mother of mercy, and to all the saints in Heaven, and my body to be buried beside my father and my mother in Saint Thomas' closet within my parish church of the Trinities in Micklegate.

Conservatives (2) After the Reformation

6   The demands of the western rebels, 1549

The religious changes brought about at the beginning of Edward VI's reign were deeply resented by many. In 1549 a group of Cornish rebels moved into Devon and besieged Exeter. At the same time they drew up a list of demands which they sent to Protector Somerset.

1.   First, we will have the general council and holy decrees of our forefathers observed, kept and performed, and whosoever shall gainsay them, we hold them as heretics.

2.   *Item*, we will have the laws of our sovereign lord King Henry the viii concerning the six articles to be in use again, as in his time they were*.

3.   *Item*, we will have the mass in Latin, as was before, and celebrated by the priest, without any man or woman communicating [*taking communion*] with him.

4.   *Item*, we will have the Sacrament† hang over the high altar, and there to be worshipped as it was wont to be. And they which will not thereto consent, we will have them die like heretics against the holy Catholic faith.

5.   *Item*, we will have the Sacrament of the altar but at Easter delivered to the lay people, and then but in one kind [*either the bread or the wine, but not both*].

7.   *Item*, we will have holy bread and holy water made every Sunday, palms and ashes at the times accustomed, images to be set up again in every church, and all other ancient old ceremonies used heretofore by our mother, the holy Church.

8.   *Item*, we will not receive the new service [*the 1549 Prayer Book*], because it is but like a Christmas game. But we will have our old service of mattins, mass, evensong and procession in Latin, as it was before. And so we, the Cornishmen (whereof certain of us understand no English) utterly refuse this new English.

9.   *Item*, we will have every preacher in his sermon, and every priest at his mass, pray specially by name for the souls in purgatory[†], as our forefathers did.

10.   *Item*, we will have the Bible and all books of Scripture in English to be called in again, for we be informed that otherwise the clergy shall not of long time confound the heretics.

12.   *Item*, we think it very meet [*appropriate*], because the Lord Cardinal Pole is of the King's blood, [that he] should not only have his pardon, but also [be] sent for to Rome, and promoted to be of the King's Council.

14.   *Item*, we will that the half part of the abbey lands and chantry[†] lands in every man's possessions, howsoever he came by them, be given again to two places where two of the chief abbeys was within every county... and there to be established a place for devout persons, which shall pray for the King and the commonwealth...

From Frances Rose-Troup,
The Western Rebellion of 1549,
1913, pp. 220–1.

*The Act of Six Articles, 1539, was a restatement of the orthodox Catholic position on doctrinal matters. See **Doc. 30**.

7   Religious changes in Pontefract: a conservative view

The following extract comes from a petition addressed to Cardinal Pole by a leading citizen of the Yorkshire town of Pontefract. It probably dates from 1557–58 but refers to the effects of the dissolution of religious houses under Henry VIII and Edward VI.

May it please your honourable grace... to reduce into your devout memory my old, long and continual suit to your noble grace touching the re-edifying of the church belonging to the college and hospital founded in the honour of the most Blessed Trinity in Pomfret, within the county of York... My lord, as I have said before, we had in that town one abbey, two colleges, a house of friars preachers, one anchoress [*female hermit*], one hermit, four chantry[†] priests, one guild priest. Of all these the inhabitants of the town of Pomfret are neither relieved bodily nor ghostly [*spiritually*]. We have there left an unlearned vicar, which hireth two priests: for indeed he is not able to discharge the cure other ways, and I dare say the vicar's living is under forty marks[†]... My suit to your noble grace at this present is... that you will have compassion of the great misery that this said town of Pomfret is fallen into, both bodily and ghostly, since the godly foundations aforesaid hath been so amiss ordered and misused, and the holy sanctuaries of God so pitifully defiled and spoiled.

From the *Yorkshire Archaeological
Journal*, vol. XXXVII, 1951,
pp. 383–4.

8 Rejoicing at Mary's accession, 1553

From the narrative of Robert Parkyn, curate of Adwick-le-Street near Doncaster.

And so the said Queen Mary was proclaimed there [*York*] on the xxi day of July, and at Pontefract, Doncaster, Rotherham and many other market towns on the 22 of July (*viz.* Saint Mary Magdalen's day), she to be right inheritor and Queen of England and Ireland ... whereat the whole commonalty in all places in the North parts greatly rejoiced, making great fires, drinking wine and ale, praising God. But all such as were of heretical opinions, with bishops and priests having wives, did nothing rejoice, but began to be ashamed of themselves, for the common people would point [at] them with fingers in places when they saw them ...

[By] the beginning of September there was very few parish churches in Yorkshire but mass was sung or said in Latin ... Holy bread and holy water was given, altars were re-edified, pictures or images set up, the cross with the crucifix thereon ready to be borne in procession ... And in conclusion all the English service of late used in the church of God was voluntarily laid away, and the Latin taken up again ... and yet all this came to pass without compulsion of any Act, statute, proclamation or law, but only that the gracious Queen Mary in her proclamation did utter these words: *viz.* Her Majesty did wish and much desire that the same religion which ever she professed from her infancy hitherto, and still was a-minded to observe and maintain the same for herself (through God's grace, during her time), were of all her subjects quietly and charitably embraced. Which words considered, all her loving subjects was very well contented with her godly proceedings and set forward the matter (as is above said) with all speed that might be, to the high honour, laud and praise of Almighty God, the Virgin Mary and all saints in heaven.

Transcribed by A. G. Dickens and printed in the *English Historical Review*, vol. LXII, 1947, pp. 78–80.

9 The Marian Church in 1557

The following extracts come from the visitation returns of Archdeacon Harpsfield, whose jurisdiction covered much of Kent as well as a few adjoining areas. They take the form of orders to the parishioners, mainly concerned with the restoration of Catholic worship.

SANDHURST.
    To provide a fair cross of latten [*brass, or tin plate*], with the images of Mary and John, before Easter.
To provide a fair register book wherein they shall register all christenings, burials and marriages, and also the accounts of the church. The chancel[†] and the church to be repaired in all things before midsummer. The parson is commanded that he do not bury any that do refuse to be confessed or to receive the sacrament[†]. Neither

that he do minister the sacrament at Easter to such as will not creep to the cross*.

Whereas it appeared that Master Finch, in the sale of copes[†], gained in money the sum of 5 marks[†], he is persuaded and hath also promised to deliver the said 5 marks to the use of the church.
And whereas Thomas Pettar and others had in their hands, remaining of the church plate, ll oz. of silver, they are persuaded and have promised to make restitution, and thereof they have delivered to the church a paten of silver [*a paten was a dish used for the administration of the sacraments in the mass*].

STAPLEHURST.
To provide curtains of silk for the holy days, and a front [*frontal*] for the altar above of say [*a fine cloth*] for the working days, with curtains of the same, before the feast of All Saints.
To provide two or three surplices or rochets[†] for the choir before the feast of All Saints.
To provide a grail [*chalice*] before Christmas.
To paint the rood[†], Mary and John, with the patron [*the image of the patron saint*], and to set up the patron decently before Christmas.
Also it is commanded that all those that can sing do serve in the choir upon the Sundays and holy days, and that the churchwardens do make due certificate of them that refuse.
To provide a veil and coverings for the images before Lent.
To provide a convenient light before the rood at this side the feast of All Saints.
To repair the church also in glazing and other reparations before the feast of All Saints.
That the churchwardens do diligently enquire what ornaments, plate, jewels and other goods belonging to the church were sold, and to whom, by whom, and to what use the same was put, and that the said wardens make due certificate thereof.
That the parson bury none that refuse to be confessed or to receive the sacrament.
Neither that he doth minister the sacrament at Easter to such as will not creep to the cross*.
Also it is commanded that one of every house nigh to the church be at procession the Wednesdays and Fridays.

ULCOMBE.
That Elizabeth Post should openly in the parish church upon Sunday next declare that in the sacrament[†] of the altar there is the very body and blood of Christ really, and also that she should confess that all the sacraments and all the ceremonies now used in the church be good and godly; and afterwards to be penitently confessed to the curate, and then reverently to receive the Blessed Sacrament of the altar.

From The Rev. L. E. Whatmore (ed.), *Archdeacon Harpsfield's Visitation, 1557*, Catholic Record Society, 1951, pp. 177, 183, 195, 207.

*A ceremony held on Good Friday, in which clergy and people, kneeling, kiss a crucifix, usually at the altar steps.

10   Catholics in Sussex during Elizabeth's reign

(a) Catholics among office-holding gentry in Sussex.

('Office-holding' means that sometime during the reign a member of the family held the office of either Deputy-Lieutenant, Sheriff or Justice of the Peace.)

I.   The 1560s.
1.   Total number of Catholic families   33
2.   Total number of Protestant families.   18
3.   Total number of families where the religious
     views not known.   34
     Total families.   85

II. Circa 1580.
1.   Total number of Catholic families,   25
     made up as follows:-
     a.   Recusant[†] families.   15
     b.   Heads of Catholic families not returned as
          recusants.   3
     c.   Crypto-Catholics or Catholic sympathisers
          who are heads of families.   7
2.   Total number of Protestant families.   27
3.   Total number of families where the religious
     views not known.   34
     Total families.   86

III. The 1590s.
1.   Total number of recusant families.   16
2.   Total number of families where the head of
     the house harbours recusants or is a Catholic
     sympathiser.   3
3.   Total number of Protestant families.   22
4.   Total number of families where the
     religious views not known (which would
     include those families where the line has
     become extinct).   45
     Total families.   86

From Roger B. Manning, *Religion and Society in Elizabethan Sussex,* Leicester, 1969, Table IV, p. 259.

(b) Catholic survivalism in Sussex, 1569.
A report by Bishop Barlow of Chichester.

In the church of Arundel certain altars do stand yet still to the offence of the godly, which murmur and speak much against the same, and preachers have also spoken against the standing thereof in their sermons of late. They have yet in the diocese in many places images hidden up and other popish ornaments, ready to set up the mass again within 24 hours' warning; as in the town of Battle and in the parish of Lindfield, where they be yet very blind and superstitious. There be schoolmasters who teach without licence and be not of a sound and good religion, as the schoolmaster in the town of

Battle...[In this town], when a preacher doth come and speak anything against the pope's doctrine they will not abide but get them out of the church...The schoolmaster is the cause of their going out, who afterwards in corners among the people doth gainsay the preachers. It is the most popish town in all Sussex.

In some places, because the rood[†] was taken away, they painted there in that place a cross with chalk, and because that was washed away with painting, and the number of crosses standing at graves in the churchyard taken also away, they have since made crosses upon the church walls within and without, and upon the pulpit and communion table, in despite of the preacher...In many places they keep yet their chalices[†], looking for to have mass again, whenas they were commanded to turn them into communion cups...

Many bring to church the old popish Latin primers [*prayer books*] and...pray upon them all the time when the lessons are being read and in the time of the litany. In some places the rood lofts still stand, and those taken down still lie in the churches ready to be put up again.

From William Page (ed.),
The Victoria History of the County of Sussex, vol. 2, 1907, pp. 25–6.

11   A rebellious spirit in the north, 1569

Sir Ralph Sadler reports to Sir William Cecil on 6 December 1569 about Catholic disaffection in the north of England during the Rebellion of the Northern Earls.

There are not 10 gentlemen in all this country that favour her [*the Queen's*] proceedings in the cause of religion. The common people are ignorant, superstitious, and altogether blinded with the old popish doctrine, and therefore so favour the cause which the rebels make the colour of their rebellion that, though their persons be here with us, their hearts are with them. And no doubt all this country had wholly rebelled if, at the beginning, my Lord Lieutenant [*the Earl of Sussex*] had not wisely and stoutly handled the matter. If we should go to the field with this northern force only, they would fight faintly; for if the father be on this side, the son is on the other; and one brother with us and the other with the rebels.

From M. A. E. Green (ed.),
Calendar of State Papers, Domestic Series, of the Reign of Elizabeth, Addenda 1566–1579, 1871, no. 77, p. 139.

12   Recusancy in the north-west, 1591

A report to the Council on the condition of Lancashire and Cheshire.

Small reformation has been made there by the Ecclesiastical Commission*, as may appear by the emptiness of churches on Sundays and holidays, and the multitude of bastards and drunkards; great sums have been levied under pretence of the Commission but the counties are in worse case than before, and the number of those who do not resort to divine service greater. The people lack instruction, for the preachers are few, most of the parsons unlearned, many of those learned not resident, and divers unlearned daily admitted in to very good benefices by the Bishop. The youth are for the most part trained up by such as profess papistry; no examination is had of schools and schoolmasters. The proclamation for the apprehension of seminarists[†], Jesuits, and mass priests, and for calling home children from parts beyond sea is not executed, nor are their Lordships' letters commanding the Justices to call before them quarterly all parsons, vicars, curates, churchwardens, and sworn men, and examine them on oath how the statutes of 1 and 23 Eliz. as to resorting to churches are obeyed ... The people who resort to church are so few that preachers who were determined to preach on Sundays and holidays have refrained, for lack of auditors; the people so swarm the streets and alehouses during service time that many churches have only present the curate and his clerk, and open markets are kept in service time ... The recusants[†] have spies about the Commissioners, to give intelligence when anything is intended against them, and some of the bailiffs attending upon the Commissioners are entertained for that purpose, so that the recusants may shift out of the way and avoid being apprehended.

From M. A. E. Green (ed.), *Calendar of State Papers, Domestic Series, of the Reign of Elizabeth*, vol. CCXL, *1591–1594*, 1867, no. 138, pp. 158–9.

* See **Doc. 37**.

Reformers (1) Before 1559

13   Hunne's case, 1514

This is from the account of Edward Hall, a contemporary City of London official and MP, who wrote a narrative of Henry VIII's reign from a highly anti-clerical point of view.

This year in December there was one Richard Hun, a merchant tailor of London in Lollers Tower [*the Bishop of London's prison*] by the commandment of the Bishop of London, called Richard Fitzjames, and Doctor Horsey, his chancellor, which was a man more of wit to prefer the bishop's jurisdiction and the clergy than the truth of the Gospel; but so it was that the said Hun was found dead hanging by the neck in a girdle of silk within the said tower. The beginning of this matter must be showed for the following of the consequence: for this Hun had a child that died in his house: being an infant, the curate claimed the bearing sheet for a mortuary [*a fee for burying the child*]. Hun answered that the infant had no property in the sheet, whereupon the priest cited him in the spiritual court. He, taking to him good counsel, sued the curate in a praemunire*, and when the priests heard of this, they did so much of malice that they accused him of heresy, and brought him to the Lollers Tower, and there was found dead, as you heard.

From Edward Hall, 'The triumphant reign of Kyng Henry the VIII'; printed in C. H. Williams (ed.), *English Historical Documents*, vol. V, *1485–1558*, 1967, p. 660.

*Hunne attempted to charge the curate with breaching the Statute of Praemunire of 1353, which stated that it was a criminal offence to acknowledge foreign (usually papal) jurisdiction, contrary to the law of the King.

14   Lollards and Protestants, 1528

A Lollard[†] group from Steeple Bumpstead, Essex, meet the Lutheran, Robert Barnes.

Furthermore, he sayeth that at Michaelmas last past was twelve-month, this respondent & Thomas Hilles came to London to Friar Barons [*Barnes*], then being at the Friars Augustines in London, to buy a New Testament in English, as he sayeth. And they found the said Friar Barons in his chamber, where ... there was a merchant man reading in a book, and ii or iii more present. And when they came in, the Friar demanded [of] them from whence they came. And they said, from Bumstead; and so forth in communication they desired the said Friar Barons that they might be acquainted with him, because they had heard that he was a good man, and because they would have his counsel in the New Testament, which they desired to have of him. And he sayeth that the said Friar Barons did perceive very well that Thomas Hilles and this respondent were infected with opinions, because they would have the New Testament. And ... the said Thomas Hilles and this respondent showed the Friar Barons of certain old books that they had: as of [the] iv Evangelists and certain Epistles of Peter and Paul in English. Which books the said Friar did little regard, and made a twyte [*joke*] of it, and said, 'A point for them, for they be not to be regarded toward the new printed Testament in English. For it is of more cleaner English'. And then the said Friar Barons delivered to them the said New Testament in English, for which they paid iiis. iid., and desired them that they would keep it close. For he would be loath that it should be known ... And after the deliverance of the said New Testament to them, the said Friar Barons did liken the New Testament in Latin to a cymbal tinkling, and brass sounding.

From John Strype, *Ecclesiastical Memorials*, vol. I, Oxford, 1882, Part II, no. XVII, pp. 54–5.

15   The interrogation of Anne Askew, 1546

Anne Askew, the daughter of a Lincolnshire knight, was arrested for rejecting the doctrine of transubstantiation, as defined in the Act of Six Articles of 1539 (see **Doc. 30**). She was burnt at the stake in July 1546.

My Lord Mayor, Sir M[artin] Bowes, sitting with the Council, as most meetest for his wisdom, and seeing her standing upon life and death: 'I pray you', quod he, 'my lords, give me leave to talk with this woman'. Leave was granted.

Lord Mayor: Thou foolish woman, sayest thou that the priests cannot make the body of Christ?

Anne Askew: I say so, my lord. For I have read that God made man. But that man can make God I never yet read, nor I suppose ever shall read it.

Lord Mayor: No? You foolish woman! After the words of consecration, is it not the Lord's body?
Anne Askew: No. It is but consecrated bread, or sacramental bread.
Lord Mayor: What? If a mouse eat it after the consecration, what shall become of the mouse? What sayest thou, thou foolish woman?
Anne Askew: What shall become of her say you, my lord?
Lord Mayor: I say that that mouse is damned.
Anne Askew: Alack, poor mouse!
By this time the lords had enough of my Lord Mayor's divinity, and perceiving that some could not keep in their laughing, proceeded to the butchery and slaughter that they intended afore they came thither.

From John Gough Nichols (ed.), *Narratives of the Days of the Reformation*, Camden Society, 1859, pp. 40–1.

16   A Protestant preamble to a will, 1548

The preamble, or introduction, to a will often gave some indication of the testator's faith. (See also **Doc. 5**.)

I Edward Hoppaye of Wakefield doth make this my testament and last will as hereafter followeth. First, I commit me unto God and to his mercy, trusting undoubtedly that by his mercy, grace, and the merits of Jesus Christ, I shall have remission of my sins and resurrection of body and soul. And touching the welfare of my soul, the faith that I have taken and rehearsed is sufficient, as I believe, without any other man's work or works; my belief is that there is but one God and one mediator between God and man, which is Jesus Christ. So that I accept none in Heaven, neither in earth, to be my mediator between God and me, but he only.

The original will is in the Borthwick Institute, York (Prob. Reg. 13, f. 595v.). It is discussed in A. G. Dickens, *Lollards and Protestants in the Diocese of York 1509-1558*, 2nd edn, 1982, pp. 216–17.

17   Anti-Catholic polemics, 1548

This extract is taken from the *Treatise of Certain Things Abused*, by Peter Moone of Ipswich. In the words of Professor A. G. Dickens, who describes Moone as a 'proto-puritan', it 'recalls the old proletarian anti-clericalism as much as the more constructive emphases of the new theology' (*The English Reformation*, p. 247).

This mass, as they [*the priesthood*] supposed, was alone sufficient
To pacify God's wrath for our wretched misery.
Free forgiveness of sins, being never so unpenitent,
Might be received at the mass: this was their doctrine daily.
No small time were we blinded with such popish peltry [*rubbish*],
Making us pay for the holy consecration.
Like thieves that were insatiate, they robbed soul and body,
Without the fear of God's Word, the light of our salvation.

Let us forsake all ceremonies that to Scripture be not consonant,
Traditions of forefathers wherein we have been led,
And with the lively Word of God let us now be conversant,

For therein shall we see with what baggage we were fed,
Wandering in the Pope's laws, forsaking Christ our head,
Heaping upon ourselves the more greater damnation.
Thus were traditions and ceremonies maintained in the stead
Of God's true and sincere Word, the light of our salvation.

From A.G. Dickens, *The English Reformation*, 2nd edn, 1989, pp. 247–8.

18   Schismatics in Colchester, 1556-57

(a) A report by Thomas Tye, an Essex parish priest, to his bishop, Edmund Bonner, 18 December 1556.

Right honourable lord ... these shall be to signify unto your lordship the state of our parts concerning religion. And first, since the coming down of the twenty-two rank heretics dismissed from you, the detestable sort of schismatics[†] were never so bold since the king and queen's majesties' reign as they are now at this present. In Much Bentley, where your lordship is patron of the church, since William Mount and Alice his wife, with Rose Allin her daughter, came home, they do not only absent themselves from the church and service of God, but do daily allure many other away from the same, which before did outwardly show signs and tokens of obedience.

They assemble together upon the Sabbath day in the time of divine service, sometimes in one house, sometimes in another, and there keep their privy conventicles[†] and schools of heresy ... The rebels are stout [*bold*] in the town of Colchester. The ministers of the church are hemmed at in the open streets and called knaves. The blessed sacrament[†] of the altar is blasphemed and railed upon in every ale house and tavern. Prayer and fasting is not regarded. Seditious talks and news are rife, both in town and country.

From *The Acts and Monuments of John Foxe* (1563), ed. The Rev. S.R. Cattley, vol. VIII, 1839, p. 383.

(b) The burning of Rose Allin's hand, 1557.

Rose Allin was burnt at the stake at Colchester in April 1557, along with her mother and stepfather, William and Alice Mount. Such events, as treated by the martyrologist John Foxe, acted as powerful propaganda for the Protestant cause during Elizabeth's reign.

The 7th day of March, anno 1557, being the first Sunday in Lent, and by two of the clock in the morning, one master Edmund Tyrrel (who came of the house of those Tyrrels which murdered King Edward the Fifth and his brother) took with him the bailiff of the hundred[†] ... and the two constables of Much Bentley ... with divers others a great number; and besetting the house of the said William Mount round about, called to them at length to open the door. Which being done, master Tyrrel, with ... certain of his company, went into the chamber where the said father Mount and his wife lay, willing them to rise: 'for', said he, 'you must go with us to Colchester Castle'. Mother Mount, hearing that, being very sick, desired that her daughter might first fetch her some drink; for she was (she said) very ill at ease.

Then he gave her leave and bade her go. So her daughter, the forenamed Rose Allin, maid, took a stone pot in one hand, and a candle in the other, and went to draw drink for her mother. And as she came back again through the house, Tyrrel met her and willed her to give her father and mother good counsel, and advertise them to be better catholic people.

Rose:- 'Sir, they have a better instructor than I. For the Holy Ghost doth teach them, I hope, which I trust will not suffer them to err'.

'Why', said master Tyrrel, 'art thou still in that mind, thou naughty housewife? Marry, it is time to look upon such heretics indeed'.

Rose:- 'Sir, with that which you call heresy, do I worship my lord God, I tell you troth'.

Tyrrel:- 'Then I perceive you will burn, gossip, with the rest, for company's sake'.

Rose:- 'No, sir, not for company's sake, but for my Christ's sake, if so I be compelled. And I hope in his mercies, if he call me to it he will enable me to bear it'.

So he, turning to his company, said 'Sirs, this gossip will burn. Do you not think it?'

'Marry, sir', quoth one, 'prove her, and you shall see what she will do by and by'.

Then that cruel Tyrrel, taking the candle from her, held her wrist, and the burning candle under her hand, burning cross-wise over the back thereof so long till the very sinews cracked asunder . . . In which time of his tyranny he said often to her, 'Why, whore! Wilt thou not cry? Thou young whore! Wilt thou not cry?' Unto which always she answered that she had no cause, she thanked God, but rather to rejoice. He had (she said) more cause to weep than she, if he considered the matter well. In the end, when the sinews (as I said) brake, [so] that all the house heard them, he then thrust her from him violently, and said 'Ah! strong whore! Thou shameless beast! Thou beastly whore!' etc. with suchlike vile words. But she, quietly suffering his rage for the time, at the last said, 'Sir, have ye done what ye will do?' And he said, 'Yea, and if thou think it be not well, then mend it'. 'Mend it!' said Rose. 'Nay, the Lord mend you and give you repentance, if it be his will. And now, if you think it good, begin at the feet and burn to the head also. For he that set you a-work shall pay your wages one day, I warrant you'. And so she went and carried her mother drink, as she was commanded . . .

And this said Rose Allin, being prisoner, told a friend of hers this cruel act of the said Tyrrel; and showing him the manner thereof, she said, 'While my one hand . . . was a-burning, I, having a pot in my other hand, might have laid him on the face with it if I had would, for no man held my hand to let [*stop*] me therein. But, I thank God', quoth she, 'with all my heart, I did it not'.

From *The Acts and Monuments of John Foxe* (1563), ed. The Rev. S.R. Cattley, vol. VIII, 1839, pp. 384–6.

(c) 'The burning of Rose Allins hand, by Edmund Tyrrell, as she was going to fetch drink for her mother, lying sick in her bed.'

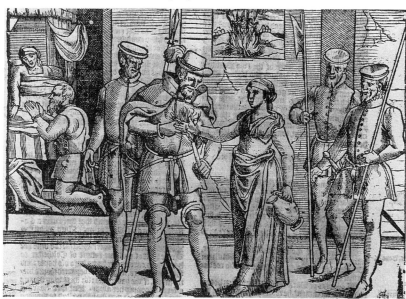

A woodcut from John Foxe, *Acts and Monuments*, alias *Foxe's Book of Martyrs*, first published 1563. This illustration is from the edition of 1965, ed. G. A. Williamson, p. 396.

19   The Marian executions, 1558

The following extract is taken from a letter sent by Thomas Bentham, pastor of an underground Protestant congregation in London, to a friend who was pastor to a group of English Protestants in exile in Switzerland.

There were vii men burned in Smithfield the 28th day of July, altogether; a fearful and cruel proclamation being made that under pain of present death no man should either approach nigh unto them, touch them, neither speak unto nor comfort them. Yet were they so mightily spoken unto, so comfortably taken by the hands, and so godly comforted, notwithstanding that fearful proclamation and the present threatenings of the sheriff and sergeants, that the adversaries themselves were astonished. And since that time the Bishop of London, either for fear or craft, carried seven more, or six at the least, forth of his coal-house to Fulham, the 12th day of this month, and condemning them there the 13th day at one of the clock at afternoon caused them to be carried the same time to Brentford, beside Syon, where they were burned in post haste the same night. This fact purchaseth him more hatred than any that he hath done, of the common multitude.

From John Strype, *Ecclesiastical Memorials*, vol. III, Oxford, 1816, part II, pp. 133–4.

Reformers (2) After 1559

20   The Queen's authority, 1571

The point of view of an uncompromising Puritan[†].

Nevertheless, this is out of doubt, that the Queen's Highness hath not authority to compel any man to believe any thing contrary to God's word, neither may the subject give her Grace the obedience; in case he do, his soul is lost for ever, without repentance. Our bodies, goods and lives be at her commandment and she shall have them as of true subjects. But the soul of man for religion is bound to none but unto God and His holy word . . .

Antichrist, the Pope of Rome, this name is banished out of England. But his body, which be the bishops and other shavelings, do not only remain, but also his tail, which be his filthy traditions, wicked laws and beggarly ceremonies – yea, and the whole body of his pestiferous canon law[†]. And, dearly beloved in the Lord, you go to your parish church and there stand up and say 'I believe in God'. Yet you do but mock with God. So long as you walk in those wicked laws of Antichrist and maintain his knights, the bishops, with such inordinate riches and unlawful authority, so long shall you never banish the monstrous beast, the Pope, out of England.

From a treatise by a member of an English Separatist Congregation, 1567–71?; printed in Albert Peel (ed.), *The Seconde Parte of a Register*, vol. I, Cambridge, 1915, no. 32–3, p. 58.

21   The services of the Church of England, 1577

William Harrison, minister of Radwinter in Essex, and canon of Windsor, produced one of the earliest surveys of the life and habits of the English people, his contemporaries.

And thus do we spend the Sabbath day in good and godly exercises, all done in our vulgar tongue, that each one present may hear and understand the same, which also in cathedral and collegiate churches is so ordered that the Psalms only are sung by note, the rest being read (as in common parish churches) by the minister with a loud voice, saving that in the administration of the Communion the choir singeth the answers, the Creed, and sundry other things appointed, but in so plain, I say, and distinct manner that each one present may understand what they sing, every word having but one note, though the whole harmony consist of many parts, and those very cunningly set by the skilful in that science.

Certes this translation of the service of the church into the vulgar tongue hath not a little offended the Pope almost in every age, as a thing very often attempted by divers princes but never generally obtained, for fear lest the consenting thereunto might breed the overthrow (as it would indeed) of all his religion and hierarchy; nevertheless, in some places where the kings and princes dwelled not under his nose, it was performed maugre [*in spite of*] his resistance...

As for our churches themselves, bells and times of Morning and Evening Prayer remain as in times past, saving that all images, shrines, tabernacles*, rood† lofts, and monuments of idolatry are removed, taken down and defaced; only the stories in glass windows excepted, which, for want of sufficient store of new stuff and by reason of extreme charge that should grow by the alteration of the same into white panes throughout the realm, are not altogether abolished in most places at once but by little and little suffered to decay, that white glass may be provided and set up in their rooms.

*Decorated boxes kept on the altar to contain the Sacrament.

From William Harrison, *The Description of England*, 1577, ed. F. J. Furnivall, vol. I, 1877, pp. 30–2.

22 Whitgift against Cope's Bill and Book, 1587

Anthony Cope's Bill, introduced into the House of Commons, would have abolished the Prayer Book authorised by the Act of Uniformity in 1559 and replaced it by a Presbyterian† form of service. This extract is from Archbishop Whitgift's speech in Parliament against the Bill.

The whole Reformation, begun in King Edward's time and undertaken by her Majesty, consisteth chiefly in the establishment of:
I. A true government of the Church, greatly corrupted and foully usurped by the Bishop of Rome.
II. The pure doctrine of Christ, by a sound reformation and purgation thereof from popery.
III. A godly order for public prayer and administration of sacraments†, with other holy rites and ceremonies, instead of the popish mass, barbarous service, and many other corruptions.

This reformation was made upon most grave consideration by the chief learned doctors and fathers of this Church. It hath...by her Majesty at length [been] brought to such perfection as the profession of this reformed religion in England hath been ever since the chief key and stay thereof in all the reformed churches in Christendom...Among all the assaults made hitherto by sundry sectaries† against this our reformation, there was never any, to my knowledge, comparable to this last Bill and book exhibited here among us...For I pray you, wherein differ these men, in this case, from the papists? The Pope denieth the supremacy of princes; so do, in effect, these...The Pope, where he entereth, doth abrogate [*repeal*] all such laws as any prince hath made in Church matters to his dislike. And so would these men do with all the laws, canons†, constitutions and orders heretofore made in the Church...

From John Strype, *The Life and Acts of John Whitgift*, vol. III, Oxford, 1822, pp. 187–8, 193–4.

23   A hostile image of the Puritan, 1598

By the 1590s the conduct of some of the more extreme Puritans[†] (or 'precisians') had earned them much dislike amongst moderates.

Who would imagine yonder sober man,
That same devout meal-mouth'd precisian,
That cries 'Good brother', 'Kind sister', makes a duck [*bow*]
After the antique grace, can always pluck
A sacred book out of his civil hose,
And at th'op'ning, and at our stomach's close
Says with a turn'd-up eye a solemn grace
Of half an hour; then with silken face
Smiles on the holy crew, and then doth cry,
'O manners! O times of impurity!'

Who thinks that this good man
Is a vile, sober, damned politician [*crafty intriguer*]?
Not I, till with his bait of purity
He bit me sore in deepest usury[†].
No Jew, no Turk, would use a Christian
So inhumanely as this Puritan.

From 'The Metamorphosis of Pygmalion's Image', by W. K., 1598; quoted in G. B. Harrison (ed.), *A Second Elizabethan Journal 1595–1598*, 1931, p. 280.

24   Hooker defends set forms of prayer, 1597

Richard Hooker, a theologian and minister, was stung by Puritan[†] attacks on the Church of England into writing an extended defence of it. The first four books of his *Laws of Ecclesiastical Polity* were published in 1594. The following extract comes from the fifth book, published in 1597 and dedicated to Archbishop Whitgift, who had stoutly defended the established Church against its Puritan critics.

A great part of the cause wherefore religious minds are so inflamed with the love of public devotion is that virtue, force and efficacy which, by experience, they find that the very form and reverend solemnity of common prayer, duly ordered, hath to help that imbecility and weakness in us, by means whereof we are otherwise, of ourselves, the less apt to perform unto God so heavenly a service with such affection of heart and disposition in the powers of our souls as is requisite. To this end, therefore, all things hereunto appertaining have been ever thought convenient to be done with the most solemnity and majesty that the wisest could devise. It is not with public as with private prayer. In this [*i.e. private prayer*], rather secrecy is commended than outward show; whereas that, being the public act of a whole society, requireth accordingly more care to be had of external appearance.

The very assembling of men, therefore, unto this service hath been ever solemn. And concerning the place of assembly ... the gravest of the ancient Fathers seriously were persuaded, and do oftentimes plainly teach, affirming that the house of prayer is a Court beautified with the presence of celestial powers; that there we stand, we pray, we sound forth hymns unto God, having His angels intermingled as our associates; and that with reference hereunto, the Apostle [*St. Paul*] doth require so great care to be had of decency for the angels' sake.

...And as the place of public prayer is a circumstance in the outward form thereof, ... so the person much more with whom the people of God do join themselves in this action, as with him that standeth and speaketh in the presence of God for them. The authority of his place, the fervour of his zeal, the piety and gravity of his whole behaviour, must needs exceedingly both grace and set forward the service he doth ... Is not his very ordination a seal, as it were, to us that the selfsame divine love, which hath chosen the instrument to work with, will, by that instrument, effect the thing whereto He ordained it, in blessing His people and accepting the prayers which His servant offereth up unto God for them?

From *The Works of that Learned and Judicious Divine, Mr Richard Hooker*, ed. Rev. John Keble, vol. II, Oxford, 1888, pp. 118–19.

CHAPTER 2   THE STATE AND RELIGION

This chapter concerns attempts by the State to decide the nation's religion. Behind these lay the assumption, common to everyone at this time, that it was the task of government to ensure the religious unity of a nation, because it was held that non-conformity in religion led directly to non-conformity in politics, in other words, to rebellion.

In the first section the state of the Church before the Reformation is briefly considered, and in the second section the various changes in policy between the 1530s and Elizabeth's settlement of 1559. The changes start with Henry's take-over of the Church and his dissolution of the monasteries, and this first period of the English Reformation ends with the conservative Act of Six Articles in 1539, followed by the fall of Thomas Cromwell. For the rest of Henry's reign doctrinal orthodoxy was strictly enforced. However, the advocates of reform were entrenching themselves at Court as Henry's life drew to a close, and they succeeded in gaining control over the upbringing of the young heir, Prince Edward. This meant that after Henry's death in 1547 the forward thrust of the Reformation was resumed. By the end of Edward's reign the Church had a Calvinist theology and services in English, while at the same time it had kept its traditional structure, including bishops and church courts. After 1553 Mary tried to restore Catholicism but she was unable to persuade the nobles and gentry who dominated Parliament to surrender the former monastic lands which they now owned.

Mary's early death opened the way to the third, Elizabethan, stage of the Reformation. Elizabeth's settlement included an Act of Supremacy making her 'Supreme Governor' of the Church – a change of wording designed to reconcile those who did not like the sound of a woman being 'Supreme Head' as Henry had been – together with an Act of Uniformity imposing a prayer book almost identical with that of 1552.

The third section illustrates the long struggle which the new Church of England fought against the Puritans, those who wanted it to move farther and faster in a Calvinist direction. Here, the first major episode was the Vestiarian Controversy of the early 1560s, and this was followed by the clash over 'Prophesyings', which involved Elizabeth disciplining her own Archbishop of Canterbury, Edmund Grindal, who himself sympathised with some of the Puritans' ideas. Grindal's successor was John Whitgift, a stern disciplinarian who was determined to hold Puritan separatist tendencies in check and impose standards of conformity.

The fourth section is about the English Catholics, that part of the nation which refused to give up its adherence to the old religion. Here, initial toleration, and the attempts by moderates such as Burghley to distinguish an individual's private religion from his politics, were overtaken by international events. After the papal excommunication of Elizabeth there followed increasingly harsh legislation against the Catholics, and especially against the newly arriving seminary priests and Jesuits who sustained them. This campaign succeeded in isolating the Catholic community in England, but failed to defeat the spirit of a community that clung to its faith despite all incentives to do otherwise.

Before the Reformation

25   Neck verses

Benefit of Clergy[†] meant that secular courts could not punish priests, and this privilege had been extended to all laymen who could read. The usual test involved asking the accused to read out in open court one of the following verses from the Latin Bible, known as neck verses because they might save one from the gallows. However, an Act of 1489 laid down that a layman could only enjoy this exemption once. (For examples, see **Doc. 83**.)

Exaudi, Deus, orationem meam, et ne despexeris deprecationem meam: [*Hear my prayer, O God: and hide not thyself from my petition.*]

Psalm 55, verses 1 and 14, from *Biblia Sacra Vulgatae Editionis*, 1977.

Qui simul mecum dulces capiebas cibos: in domo Dei ambulavimus cum consensu. [*We took sweet counsel together: and walked in the house of God as friends.*]

26   Tunstall bans English Bibles, 1526

Cuthbert Tunstall, Bishop of London, equates possession of the scriptures in English with Lutheranism.

Cuthbert, by permission of God bishop of London, unto our well-beloved in Christ, the archdeacon of London, or to his official, health, grace and benediction. By the duty of our pastoral office, we are bound diligently, with all our power, to foresee, provide for, root out, and put away all those things which seem to tend to the peril and danger of our subjects, and especially to the destruction of their souls. Wherefore we, having understanding by the report of divers credible persons, and also by the evident appearance of the matter, that many children of iniquity, maintainers of Luther's sect, blinded through extreme wickedness, wandering from the way of truth and the catholic faith, craftily have translated the New Testament into our English tongue, intermeddling therewith many heretical articles and erroneous opinions, pernicious and offensive, seducing the simple people; attempting by their wicked and perverse interpreta-tions to profanate the majesty of the Scripture which hitherto hath remained undefiled, and craftily to abuse the most holy word of God, and the true sense of the same; of which translation there are many books imprinted, some with glosses and some without, containing in the English tongue that pestiferous and most perni-cious poison, dispersed throughout all our diocese of London in great numbers; which truly, without it be speedily foreseen, without doubt will contaminate and infect the flock committed unto us with most deadly poison and heresy, to the grievous peril and danger of the souls committed to our charge, and offence of God's divine majesty. Wherefore we, Cuthbert...do charge you...that by our authority you warn all and singular...dwelling within your archdeaconries that within thirty days' space...under pain of excommunication and incurring the suspicion of heresy, they do bring in...all...such books as contain the translation of the New Testament in the English tongue.

From *The Acts and Monuments of John Foxe* (1563), ed. The Rev. S.R. Cattley, vol. IV, 1837, pp. 666–7.

27   The Supplication against the Ordinaries, 1532

This is an extract from the *Supplication* drawn up by the House of Commons for presentation to Henry VIII. It consists of a catalogue of grievances against the clergy, and in particular against clerical courts and their canon law[†].

First, the prelates and other of the clergy of this your realm, being your subjects, in their Convocation[†] by them holden...have made and daily make divers fashions of laws and ordinances concerning temporal things; and some of them be repugnant to the laws and statutes of your realm; not having ne [*nor*] requiring your most royal assent to the same laws by them so made, nor any assent or knowl-edge of your lay subjects is had to the same, nor to them published and known in the English tongue... Declaring the infringers of the same laws so by them made not only to incur into the terrible censures of excommunication but also unto the detestable crime and sin of heresy; by the which divers of your most humble and obedient lay subjects be brought into this ambiguity whether they may do and execute your laws according to your jurisdiction royal of this your realm for dread of the same pains and censures comprised in the said laws...

From H. Gee and W. J. Hardy (eds), *Documents Illustrative of English Church History*, 1896, pp. 154–5.

28   The Submission of the Clergy, 1534

An Act for the Submission of the Clergy to the King's Majesty (25 Henry VIII, cap. 19). This Act secured the total surrender of the Church's legislative independence. Here, the 1533 Act of Appeals is confirmed, and Chancery[†] is made the final court of appeal in ecclesiastical causes.

Where the King's humble and obedient subjects, the clergy of this realm of England, have not only [ac]knowledged, according to the truth, that the Convocations[†] of the same clergy is always, hath been, and ought to be assembled only by the King's writ, but also, submitting themselves to the King's Majesty, hath promised . . . that they will never from henceforth presume to . . . enact, promulge [*promulgate*] or execute any new canons[†] . . . unless the King's most royal assent and licence may to them be had to make, promulge and execute the same, and that his Majesty do give his most royal assent and authority in that behalf . . . Be it therefore now [so] enacted by authority of this present Parliament, according to the said submission and petition of the said clergy . . . And be it further enacted by authority aforesaid that . . . no manner of appeals shall be had, provoked or made out of this realm . . . to the Bishop of Rome nor to the see of Rome . . . but that all manner of appeals of what nature or condition soever they be of, or what cause or matter soever they concern, shall be . . . had and prosecuted within this realm . . . And for lack of justice at or in any [of] the courts of the Archbishops of this realm . . . it shall be lawful to the parties grieved to appeal to the King's Majesty in the King's Court of Chancery[†]. And that upon every such appeal a commission shall be directed under the great seal to such persons as shall be named by the King's Highness . . . and that such judgment and sentence as the said commissioners shall make and decree in and upon any such appeal shall be good and effectual, and also definitive, and no further appeals to be had or made from the said commissioners for the same.

From *The Statutes of the Realm*, vol. III, 1817, pp. 460–1.

29   Frontispiece of the Great Bible, 1539

Henry VIII's Great Bible of 1539 made the scriptures officially available in English for the first time. On the title page, Henry, as head of the English Church, is seen handing out copies of the Bible to his archbishops who in turn distribute them to the priests and people.

Changes of Policy

30 The Act of Six Articles, 1539

An Act abolishing Diversity in Opinions (31 Henry VIII, cap. 14). This Act, nicknamed the 'whip with six strings', preceded the fall of Thomas Cromwell and enforced a rigid conservatism in religion for the remainder of Henry's reign.

Where the King's most excellent Majesty is by God's law supreme head immediately under him of this whole Church and Congregation of England, intending the conservation of the same Church and Congregation in a true, sincere, and uniform doctrine of Christ's religion . . . and therefore desiring that such an unity might and should be charitably established in all things touching and concerning the same . . . [he] hath therefore caused and commanded this his most high Court of Parliament . . . to be at this time summoned, and also a synod and convocation[†] of all the archbishops, bishops, and other learned men of the clergy of this his realm [to consider certain articles] . . .

Whereupon, after a great and long, deliberate and advised disputation and consultation had and made concerning the said articles, as well by the consent of the King's Highness as by the assent of the Lords spiritual and temporal, and other learned men of his clergy in their Convocation[†], and by the consent of the Commons in this present Parliament assembled, it was and is finally resolved . . .

First, that in the most blessed sacrament[†] of the altar, by the strength and efficacy of Christ's mighty word, it being spoken by the priest, is present really, under the form of bread and wine, the natural body and blood of our Saviour Jesu Christ, conceived of the Virgin Mary, and that after the consecration there remaineth no substance of bread or wine, nor any other substance but the substance of Christ . . .

Secondly, that communion in both kinds is not necessary *ad salutem* [*for salvation*] by the law of God to all persons, and that it is to be believed, and not doubted of, but that in the flesh under form of bread is the very blood, and with the blood under form of wine is the very flesh, as well apart as though they were both together.

Thirdly, that priests, after the order of priesthood received, as afore, may not marry, by the law of God.

Fourthly, that vows of chastity or widowhood by man or woman made to God advisedly ought to be observed by the law of God . . .

Fifthly, that it is meet [*fit*] and necessary that private masses be continued and admitted in this the King's English Church and Congregation, as whereby good Christian people, ordering themselves accordingly, do receive both godly and goodly consolations and benefits, and it is agreeable also to God's law.

Sixthly, that auricular confession [*verbal confession to a priest*] is expedient and necessary to be retained and continued, used and frequented in the Church and Congregation.

[Any persons affirming contrary opinions, by word or writing] shall be deemed and adjudged heretics, and . . . shall therefore have and suffer judgment, execution, pain and pains of death by way of burning . . .]

From *The Statutes of the Realm*, vol, III, 1817, pp. 739–40.

31   A chantry certificate, 1547

Chantries[†] were endowments for the singing of masses for the souls of the dead. A chantry could be a separate building, a side-chapel within a church, or simply, as here, a legal obligation. In 1547 a national survey of all chantries was made as a preliminary to their abolition the same year. The collegiate church of Ripon was hit particularly badly by this Act which abolished all of its nine chantries so that there were nine fewer priests available for church services.

THE CHANTRIE OF OUR LADY IN THE SAID CATHEDRAL CHURCH [*Ripon*]

William Hamonde, incumbent. Of the foundation of John Fulford and Robert Kendall, priests. To the intent to pray for the souls of the founders and all Christian souls and to be present in the said choir in his habit at mattins, mass, evensong and processions, and in principal and double feasts, and to execute and do service at the high altar as he shall be appointed by the officers of the same choir, as appeareth by a foundation dated the x day of January, in the ix year of the reign of King Henry the iiiith [*1408*].

The same is within the said church. The necessity is to pray, to do divine service in the said church, and to minister sacraments when the vicars be sick and deceased, and the same is used accordingly. There is no land alienated since the statute.

Goods, ornaments and plate pertaining to the same, as appeareth by the inventory, viz. – goods valued at xiis. iii*d*., and plate, nil.

First, xv acres of arable land lying in the fields of Ripon, in the holding of Richard Carlell, xv*s*; one tenement in Northstanley, in the tenure of John Hyrde, v*s*; ii tenements in Alhallogate, in the tenure of Robert Gillowe and Robert Walche, viii*s*; one tenement in Crosgate, in the holding of John Smith, xi*s*; one cottage in Westgate, in the holding of Christopher Warwyke, ii*s*; one cottage there, in the tenure of John Spicer, ii*s*, viii*d*; one tenement there, in the tenure of Percivall Richmonde, v*s*; iii cottages there, in the tenure of [*blank*], x*s*, viii*d*; iii cottages in Skelgate, x*s*; and iii acres of meadow in Elsoynge, v*s*. In all, lxxiiii*s* iiii*d*.

Whereof, payable to the Kings Majesty yearly for the tenths[†], v*s* xi*d*; and to the said sovereign lord the King for a free rent, going forth of the said lands, iiii*s* vii*d*; to the prebendary[†] of Skelton one annual

From *The Certificates of the Commissioners appointed to survey the Chantries, Guilds, Hospitals, etc., in the County of York*, part II, Surtees Society, vol. XCII, 1895, pp. 354–5.

rent, xii*d*; and to the priest of Clotherin, one annual rent, x*s*. In all, xx*s* vi*d q**.

And so remaineth, liiis ix*d ob q**.

$*ob = \frac{1}{2}d, q = \frac{1}{4}d.$

32   The Second Prayer Book of Edward VI, 1552

The following prayer from the Litany and rubrics from the Communion Service represent strongly Protestant elements in this prayer book.

From the *Litany*:

From all sedition and privy conspiracy, from the tyranny of the Bishop of Rome and all his detestable enormities, from all false doctrine and heresy, from hardness of heart and contempt of Thy word and commandment *Good Lord, deliver us.*

From the Communion Service:

To take away the superstition which any person hath or might have in the bread and wine, it shall suffice that the bread be such as is usual to be eaten at the table with other meats; but the best and purest wheat bread that conveniently may be gotten.

Whereas it is ordained in the book of common prayer, in the administration of the Lord's Supper, that the Communicants kneeling should receive the holy Communion: which thing being well meant, for a signification of the humble and grateful acknowledging of the benefits of Christ, given unto the worthy receiver, and to avoid the profanation and disorder which about the holy communion might else ensue. Lest yet the same kneeling might be thought or taken otherwise, we do declare that it is not meant thereby that any adoration is done, or ought to be done, either unto the Sacramental bread or wine there bodily received, or unto any real and essential presence there being of Christ's natural flesh and blood. For as concerning the Sacramental bread and wine, they remain still in their very natural substances, and therefore may not be adored, for that were Idolatry to be abhorred of all faithful christians. And as concerning the natural body and blood of our saviour Christ, they are in heaven and not here. For it is against the truth of Christ's true natural body to be in mo[r]e places than in one at one time.

From *The Book of Common Prayer Printed by Whitchurch 1552. Commonly called The Second Book of Edward VI*, 1844, n.p.

33   A celibate priesthood, 1554

(a) At the start of Mary's reign Archbishop Pole enforces clerical celibacy.

7. *Item*, that every bishop, and all the other persons aforesaid, proceeding summarily, and with all celerity and speed, may and shall deprive, or declare deprived, and amove, according to their learning and discretion, all such persons [*priests*] from their benefices and ecclesiastical promotions, who, contrary to the state of their order and the laudable custom of the Church, have married and used women as their wives ...

8. *Item*, that the said bishop, and all other persons aforesaid, do use more lenity and clemency with such as have married whose wives be dead, than with others whose women do yet remain in life. And likewise such priests as, with the consents of their wives or women, openly in the presence of the bishop do profess to abstain, to be used more favourably: in which case, after penance effectively done, the bishop, according to his discretion and wisdom, may upon just consideration receive and admit them again to their former administration, so it be not in the same place ...

9. *Item*, that every bishop, and all persons aforesaid, do foresee that they suffer not any religious man, having solemnly professed chastity, to continue with his woman or wife; but that all such persons, after deprivation of their benefice or ecclesiastical promotion, be also divorced every one from his said woman, and due punishment otherwise taken for the offence therein.

From H. Gee and W. J. Hardy (eds), *Documents Illustrative of English Church History*, 1896, pp. 381–2.

(b) A married priest renounces his wife (1554).

At which day, hour and place Hewet appeared in person and willingly brought in a certain Margaret Hewet, alias Thomes, his pretended wife. And the same Hewet was asked if he wished to live chastely and apart from his wife henceforth. To which question Hewet replied that he did so wish, and then the said Margaret announced in public her agreement to this order. And then the judge enjoined the following penance on Hewet, that upon Sunday next coming he shall be present in the parish church of Doncaster at the time of procession, bare headed, bare footed, and bare legged, and that he shall proceed before the cross in procession the same day about the church having a sleeveless surplice upon his back, and that he shall kneel before the altar behind the priest all mass time. And that he shall do like penance in the parish church of Kellington the Sunday next after ensuing. And to certify as to the performance of the penance on the morning of the following Friday.

From the 'Act Book of the Archbishop of York's Chancery Court', Chanc. AB, 7, f. 68, Borthwick Institute, printed in W. J. Sheils (ed.), *The Reformation in the North to 1558*, York, 1976, document no. 8.

34   The ownership of ex-monastic lands, 1554

This Act (1&2 Philip & Mary, cap. 8), while repealing the Henrician legislation of the 1530s, specifically provided for the retention by the laity of ex-monastic land and property.

IX. We, the Lords spiritual and temporal and the Commons in this present Parliament assembled, representing the whole body of this realm, reduced and received by your Majesties' intercession to the unity of Christ's Church and the obedience of the See apostolic[†] of Rome and the Pope's Holiness governing the same, make most humble suit unto your Majesties to be likewise means and intercessors that all occasions of contention, hatred, grudge, suspicion and trouble, both outwardly and inwardly in men's consciences, which might arise amongst us by reason of disobedience, may by authority of the Pope's Holiness and by the ministration of the same unto us by the most reverend father in God, the Lord Cardinal Pole...be abolished and taken away...

And finally, where certain acts and statutes have been made in the time of the late schism[†] concerning the lands and hereditaments of archbishoprics and bishoprics, the suppression and dissolution of monasteries, abbeys, priories, chantries[†], colleges, and all other the goods and chattels of religious houses...For the avoiding of all scruples that might grow by any occasions aforesaid or by any other ways or means whatsoever, it may please your Majesties to be intercessors and mediators to the said most reverend father Cardinal Pole...so as all persons having sufficient conveyance of the said lands and hereditaments, goods and chattels...may without scruple of conscience enjoy them, without impeachment or trouble by pretence of any General Council, canons[†], or ecclesiastical laws, and clear from all dangers of the censures of the Church.

From *The Statutes of the Realm*, vol. IV, 1819, p. 248.

35   The Elizabethan Settlement, 1559

(a) The oath from the Elizabethan *Act of Supremacy* (1 Elizabeth I, cap. 1). See also **Doc. 51 (b)**.

All and every archbishop, bishop, and all and every other ecclesiastical person...and all and every temporal judge, justicer, mayor, and other lay or temporal officer and minister, and every other person having your Highness' fee or wages...shall make...a corporal oath upon the evangelist [*swear personally, on the Bible*]...according to the tenor and effect hereafter following, that is to say:

I, A. B., do utterly testify and declare in my conscience that the Queen's Highness is the only supreme governor of this realm and of all other her Highness' dominions and countries, as well in all spiritual or ecclesiastical things or causes as temporal, and that no foreign prince, person, prelate, state or potentate hath or ought to have any jurisdiction, power, superiority, pre-eminence or authority ecclesiastical or spiritual within this realm, and therefore I do utterly renounce and forsake all foreign jurisdictions, powers, superiorities and authorities, and do promise that from henceforth I shall bear faith and true allegiance to the Queen's Highness, her heirs and lawful successors, and to my power shall assist and defend all juris-dictions, pre-eminences, privileges and authorities granted or belonging to the Queen's Highness, her heirs and successors, or united or annexed to the imperial crown of this realm. So help me God and by the contents of this Book.

From *The Statutes of the Realm*, vol. IV, 1819, p. 352.

(b) Church attendance. This is from the *Act of Uniformity* (I Elizabeth I, cap. 2), the other Act which, together with the *Act of Supremacy*, formed the core of the Elizabethan religious settlement.

All and every person and persons inhabiting within this realm ... shall diligently and faithfully, having no lawful or reason-able excuse to be absent, endeavour themselves to resort to their parish church or chapel accustomed ... upon every Sunday and other days ordained and used to be kept as holy days, and then and there to abide orderly and soberly during the time of the common prayer, preachings or other service of God there to be used and ministered; upon pain of punishment by the censures of the Church, and also upon pain that every person so offending shall forfeit for every such offence twelve pence, to be levied by the churchwardens of the parish where such offence shall be done, to the use of the poor of the same parish.

From *The Statutes of the Realm*, vol. IV, 1819, pp. 356–7.

36   The New Prayer Book, 1559

(a) Another extract from the *Act of Uniformity* (I Elizabeth I, cap. 2).

Where at the death of our late sovereign lord King Edward the Sixth, there remained one uniform order of common service and prayer, and of the administration of sacraments[†], rites and ceremonies in the Church of England, which was set forth in one Book ... author-ised by Act of Parliament ... in the fifth and sixth years of our said late sovereign lord ... the which was repealed and taken away by Act of Parliament in the first year of the reign of our late sovereign lady Queen Mary, to the great decay of the due honour of God and discomfort to the professors of the truth of Christ's religion: Be it therefore enacted by the authority of this present Parliament that the said statute of repeal ... shall be void and of none effect ... and that the said Book ... shall stand and be ... in full force and effect.

And further be it enacted ... that all and singular ministers ... be bounden to say and use the matins, evensong, celebration of the Lord's Supper and administration of each of the sacraments, and all their common and open prayer, in such order and form as is mentioned in the said Book...with...the form of the Litany altered and corrected, and two sentences only added in the delivery of the sacrament[†] to the communicants, and none other or otherwise.

(b) The Elizabethan Prayer Book was based upon that of 1552, but, as the following extract shows, at the administration of the communion the minister was required to use a formula which combined the words prescribed in 1552 with those of the First Edwardian Prayer Book of 1549.

And when he [*the minister*] delivereth the Bread, he shall say:

The Body of our Lord Jesu Christ, which was given for thee, preserve thy body and soul into everlasting life and take and eat this in remembrance that Christ died for thee, [and] feed on him in thine heart by faith with thanksgiving.

And the Minister that delivereth the Cup shall say:

The Blood of our Lord Jesu Christ which was shed for thee, preserve thy body and soul into everlasting life. And drink this in remembrance that Christ's Blood was shed for thee, and be thankful.

From The Statutes of the Realm, vol. IV, 1819, pp. 355–6.

From The Book of Common Prayer, Commonly called The First Book of Queen Elizabeth, Printed by Grafton 1559, 1844, fol. 86–86v.

The State and the Puritans

37   The Ecclesiastical Commission, 1559

This commission was issued to a mixed clerical and lay body, consisting of some twenty members, headed by the Archbishop of Canterbury. It developed into the Court of High Commission, which exercised the Queen's disciplinary powers as Supreme Governor of the Church of England.

We do give power and authority to you, or six of you...to enquire, hear and determine all and singular enormities, disturbances and misbehaviours done and committed, or hereafter to be done or committed, in any church or chapel, or against any divine service, or the minister or ministers of the same, contrary to the laws and statutes of this realm: and also to enquire of, search out, and to order, correct and reform all such persons as hereafter shall or will obstinately absent themselves from church and such divine service as by the laws and statutes of this realm is appointed to be had and used.

From G. W. Prothero (ed.), Select Statutes and other Constitutional Documents illustrative of the Reigns of Elizabeth and James I, 4th edn, Oxford, 1946, p. 228.

38   Things indifferent, 1561

John Jewel, Bishop of Salisbury, here affirms that argument about what vestments priests should wear ought not to lead to quarrels within the Church.

Among a few people there is some difference in some vestments and skull-caps. That as I might confess has always been true to some extent, for in this matter our predecessors have always retained some liberty. However, this matter is not in and of itself of such great importance. For we know that neither the apostles nor the prophets were that much concerned about garments, nor do we today place any religion or holiness in them. Our bishops, indeed, without exception one and all use garments similar to one another, such as were used of old in this kingdom; not because we judge this to be necessary or to pertain to religion, but lest any one of those who seek occasion to criticise might complain. And we do it because all signal changes in public worship, those especially which meet the eyes, have always seemed hateful. I know, however, that there are some others a little afraid of this kind of vestments which those men have contaminated with their idolatries and superstitions. And they can scarcely suffer the sacred mysteries to be performed now by pious men in the same garments by which the people of God were fooled for some centuries. Rightly or wrongly, this has nothing to do with the situation at hand . . .

   It has been scarcely two years now since God has restored to us the free and public use of the Gospel. For which reason it should not seem astonishing if our people have scarcely put themselves together again, as after a shipwreck. About the matter itself, there is no disagreement among us. Everybody is enough convinced, even the Prince who commanded these things, that clothing is nothing so far as religion is concerned, that there is in clothing neither any holiness nor any contagion. But why do these people not complain about this too, if there are among us men some of whom are tall, some short, some fat, some thin; that all do not have the same face; that all do not have the same colour or posture of body? . . .

From 'The letter of a certain Englishman [*John Jewel*]. . .,' 1561; translated from Latin in John E. Booty, *John Jewel as Apologist of the Church of England*, 1963. Appendix, pp. 219–21.

39   The Queen forbids prophesyings, 1577

(a) The following letter, addressed by the Queen to the bishops individually, showed her dislike of 'prophesyings', that is the meetings of clergy, with or without a lay audience, which took place in order to discuss scriptural texts. These meetings were a valuable form of education for unlearned clergy, but ministers of Puritan[†] inclination tended to take a leading part in them.

Right reverent father in God, we greet you well. We hear to our great grief that in sundry parts of our realm there are no small numbers of persons, presuming to be teachers and preachers of the church, though neither lawfully thereunto called nor yet [fit] for the same, which, contrary to our laws established for the public divine service of Almighty God and the administration of his holy sacraments[†] within this church of England, do daily devise, imagine, propound and put in execution sundry new rites and forms in the church, as ... by their preaching, reading and ministering the sacraments, as well by procuring unlawful assemblies of a great number of our people out of their ordinary parishes and from place far distant, and that also of some of good calling (though therein not well advised) to be hearers of their disputations and new devised opinions upon points of divinity far ... unmeet of unlearned people, which manner of invasions they in some places call prophesying and in some other places exercises; by which manner of assemblies great numbers of our people, specially the vulgar sort, meet [fit] to be otherwise occupied with honest labour for their living, are brought to idleness and seduced and in a manner schismatically divided amongst themselves into variety of dangerous opinions, not only in towns and parishes but even in some families, and manifestly thereby encouraged to the violation of our laws and to the breach of common order, and finally to the offence of all our quiet subjects that desire to serve God according to the uniform orders established in the church, whereof the sequel cannot be but overdangerous to be suffered ... We therefore, according to [the] authority we have, charge and command you ... to take order through your diocese ... that no manner of public and divine service, nor other form of the administration of the holy sacraments, nor any other rites or ceremonies, be in any sort used in the church but directly according to the orders established by our laws ... And furthermore, considering ... the great abuses that have been in sundry places of our realm by reason of ... assemblies called exercises, and for that the same are not, nor have not been, appointed nor warranted by us or by our laws, we will and straightly charge you that you also charge the same forthwith to cease, and not to be used. But if any shall attempt or continue or renew the same, we will you not only to commit them unto prison, as maintainers of disorders, but also to advertise us or our council of the names and qualities of them, and of their maintainers and abettors, that thereupon, for better example, their punishment may be more sharp, for their reformation ...

Given under our signet[†] at our manor of Greenwich, the 7th of May 1577.

From Edward Cardwell (ed.), *Documentary Annals of the Reformed Church of England*, Oxford, vol. I, 1844, pp. 428–31.

(b) Thomas Wood, an influential Puritan preacher, writes to the Earls of Leicester and Warwick about the suppression of exercises.

It is now come to pass (Right Honourable and my singular good Lords) to the great grief of all that truly fear God, that which your Honours feared long ago, namely, not only the overthrow of Southam exercise, but of all the rest, which is not only a great rejoicing to all God's enemies, but such a service to Satan as, unless the whole religion should be overthrown, a greater could not be done. For surely, if they [*the exercises*] had continued they would in short time have overthrown a great part of his [*Satan's*] kingdom, being one of the greatest blessings that ever came to England. And therefore a heavy account have they to make that have been his instruments in that behalf, of what calling soever they be ...

In the last days of King Edward the godly preachers cried out against the wickedness of those times, and told plainly of the plagues that shortly after came to pass (as some good men do in these days), but no amendment followed ... Mark these words, my Lords, and consider whether these times are not far more dangerous. In this point I am sure it is much worse: for then the faithful ministers might freely tell both Prince and people their faults, but such as would do the like indeed [now] either have their mouths stopped, or cannot be suffered to come in place where it ought chiefly to be done. And therefore ... the number of Papists and Atheists are marvellously increased, and such as be zealous for God's glory, whether they be preachers or professors, are least regarded; so as it may be truly said that for the state of religion, it was better in King Edward's time than now; for then they went forward as knowledge increased (though slowly), but now having greater light, we go most shamefully backward.

From Patrick Collinson (ed.), *Letters of Thomas Wood, Puritan, 1566–1577*, 1960, pp. 22–3.

40   Whitgift's Three Articles, 1583

(a) Archbishop Whitgift drew up these Articles, which were approved by the Queen, as a means of imposing uniformity upon Puritan[†] non-conformists in the Church of England.

That none be permitted to preach, read, catechize, minister the sacraments[†], or to execute any other ecclesiastical function ... unless he first consent and subscribe to these Articles following ...:

I. That her Majesty, under God, hath, and ought to have, the sovereignty and rule over all manner of persons born within her realms ... of what estate ecclesiastical or temporal soever they be ...

II. That the Book of Common Prayer, and of ordering bishops, priests and deacons, containeth nothing in it contrary to the Word of God. And that the same may be lawfully used; and that he himself will use the form of the said book prescribed, in public prayer and administration of the sacraments, and none other.

III. That he alloweth the book of Articles of Religion [*the Thirty-Nine Articles*], agreed upon by the archbishops and bishops in both provinces, and the whole clergy in the Convocation[†] holden at London in the year of our Lord 1562, and set forth by her Majesty's authority. And that he believeth all the articles therein contained to be agreeable to the word of God.

From John Strype, *The Life and Acts of John Whitgift*, vol. I, Oxford, 1822, pp. 229–30.

(b) In a letter to Lord Burghley, Whitgift replies to the criticisms of his proceedings against those ministers of the Church who had refused to subscribe to his Articles.

I have not dealt as yet with any but such as have refused to subscribe and given manifest tokens of contempt of orders and laws... I know your Lordship desireth the peace of the Church. But how is it possible to be procured (after so long liberty and lack of discipline) if a few persons, so meanly qualified as the most of them are, should be countenanced against the whole state of the clergy of greatest account for learning, steadiness, wisdom, religion and honesty? And open breakers and impugners of the laws, young in years, proud in conceit, contentious in disposition, maintained against their superiors and governors [who are] seeking to reduce them to order and to obedience?... For my own part, I neither do nor have done anything in this matter which I do not think myself in duty and conscience bound to do; which her Majesty hath not with earnest charge committed unto me; and the which I am well able to justify to be most requisite for this State and Church.

From John Strype, *The Life and Acts of John Whitgift*, vol. III, Oxford, 1822, pp. 110–11.

41   To abjure the realm, 1593

From *An Act to retain the Queen's subjects in Obedience* ['The Act against Seditious Sectaries[†]'] (35 Elizabeth I, cap. 1).

For the preventing and avoiding of such great inconveniences and perils as might happen and grow by the wicked and dangerous practices of seditious sectaries and disloyal persons: Be it enacted by the Queen's most excellent Majesty, and by the Lords spiritual and temporal and the Commons in this present Parliament assembled, and by the authority of the same, that if any person or persons above the age of sixteen years, which shall obstinately refuse to repair to some church, chapel or usual place of common prayer to hear divine service, established by her Majesty's laws and statutes in that behalf made, and shall forbear to do the same by the space of a month next after, without lawful cause, shall at any time... by printing, writing or express words or speeches advisedly and purposely practise or go about to move or persuade any of her Majesty's subjects... to deny, withstand and impugn her Majesty's power and authority in causes ecclesiastical, united and annexed to the imperial crown of this realm; or to that end or purpose shall advisedly and maliciously move or persuade any other person whatsoever to forbear or abstain from coming to church to hear divine service, or to receive the communion according to her Majesty's laws and statutes aforesaid, or to come to or to be present at any unlawful assemblies, conventi- cles[†] or meetings under colour or pretence of any exercise of religion... That then every such person so offending... shall be committed to prison, there to remain... until they shall conform and yield themselves to come to some church, chapel or usual place of common prayer and hear divine service, according to her Majesty's law and statutes aforesaid ...

If any such person or persons which shall offend against this Act as aforesaid shall not, within three months next after they shall be convicted of their said offence, conform themselves to the obedience of the laws and statutes of this realm in coming to the church to hear divine service, and in making such public confession and submission as hereafter in this Act is appointed ... that in every such case every such offender ... shall upon his and their corporal oath before the Justices of Peace ... or at the Assizes ... abjure [*swear to leave*] this realm of England ... for ever ...

And if any such offender ... shall refuse to make such abjuration as is aforesaid; or, after such abjuration made, shall not ... depart out of this realm according to this present Act, or, after such his departure, shall return or come again into any her Majesty's realms or dominions, without her Majesty's special licence in that behalf first had and obtained: that then, in every such case, the person so offending shall be adjudged a felon, and shall suffer as in case of felony*.

From *The Statutes of the Realm*, vol. IV, 1819, pp. 841–2.

*The penalty for felony was death.

The State and the Catholics

42   Rood lofts and pulpits, 1561

Edmund Grindal, Archbishop of York, attempts to enforce alterations.

These articles following, we, Edmund, by the permission of God Archbishop of York, do command and enjoin to be put in execution within the Archdeaconry of York by the Archdeacon of the same or his official with speed and effect.

Item, that the rood† lofts as yet being at this day aforesaid untransposed shall be so altered that the upper part of the same, with the soller [*gallery chamber*], be quite taken down.

Item, that every parson, vicar, curate and other minister within the said Archdeaconry ... when he readeth morning or evening prayer, or any part thereof, shall stand in a pulpit to be erected for that purpose, and turn his face to the people that he may be the better heard and the people the better edified. Provided always that, where the churches are very small, it shall suffice that the minister stand in his accustomed stall in the choir, so that a convenient desk or lectern, with a room to turn his face towards the people, be there provided at the charges of the parish.

From the Archbishop's Register (Reg. Grindal R. 30 f. 123v–124), Borthwick Institute, York.

43 Elizabeth's excommunication, 1570–71

(a) An extract from the papal Bull *Regnans in Excelsis*, issued by Pius V in 1570.

We do, out of the fullness of Our Apostolic[†] power, declare the aforesaid Elizabeth as being an heretic and a favourer of heretics, and her adherents in the matters aforesaid, to have incurred the sentence of excommunication, and to be cut off from the unity of the Body of Christ. And moreover We do declare her to be deprived of her pretended title to the kingdom aforesaid, and of all dominion, dignity, and privilege whatsoever; and also the nobility, subjects, and people of the said kingdom, and all others who have in any sort sworn unto her, to be for ever absolved from any such oath, and all manner of duty of dominion, allegiance, and obedience; and We also do... deprive the said Elizabeth of her pretended title to the kingdom and all other things before named. And We do command and charge all and every the noblemen, subjects, people, and others aforesaid that they presume not to obey her or her orders, mandates and laws; and those which shall do the contrary We do include them in the like sentence of anathema [*condemnation*].

From William Camden, *The History of the Most Renowned and Victorious Princess Elizabeth, Late Queen of England*, 1688, p. 147.

(b) The government's reaction to the Bull is shown in this extract from *An Act against the bringing in and putting in execution of Bulls and other Instruments from the See of Rome* (13 Elizabeth I, cap, 2), 1571.

Divers seditious and very evil disposed people... have lately procured and obtained to themselves from the said bishop of Rome... divers bulls and writings, the effect whereof hath been and is to absolve and reconcile all those that will be contented to forsake their due obedience to our most gracious sovereign lady the Queen's Majesty, and to yield and subject themselves to the said feigned, unlawful and usurped authority... whereby most wicked and unnatural rebellion hath ensued, and to the further danger of this realm is hereafter very like to be renewed, if the ungodly and wicked attempts in that behalf be not by severity of laws in time restrained and bridled. For remedy and redress whereof, and to prevent the great mischiefs and inconveniences that thereby may ensue, be it enacted... that if any person or persons... shall use or put in ure [*effect*] in any place within this realm... any such bull, writing or instrument... that then all and every such act and acts, offence and offences, shall be deemed and adjudged by the authority of this Act to be high treason.

From *The Statutes of the Realm*, vol. IV, 1819, pp. 528–9.

44   Bloody questions, c. 1570

The so-called Bloody Questions were put to suspected Catholic priests from the 1570s onwards. Those questioned here are William Filbie and James Bosgrave.

1.   *Whether the Bull of Pius V against the Queen's Majesty be a lawful sentence and ought to be obeyed by the subjects of England?*

Filbie. He saith the Pope hath authority to depose any prince; and such sentences, when they be promulgated, ought to be obeyed by the subjects of any prince. But touching the Bull of Pius V, he can say nothing. But if it was such as it is affirmed to be, he doth allow it, and saith that it ought to be obeyed.

Bosgrave. He saith that, in his conscience, as he shall answer before God, he thinketh that the Bull or sentence of excommunication of Pius Quintus against her Majesty was at no time lawful; neither was [it] at any time ... of any of her Majesty's subjects to be obeyed.

2.   *Whether the Queen's Majesty be a lawful Queen and ought to be obeyed by the subjects of England, notwithstanding the Bull of Pius V or any other Bull or sentence that the Pope hath pronounced or may pronounce against her Majesty?*

Filbie. He saith it is a hard question, and therefore he cannot answer it. But upon further advertisement, he answereth as to the first [question].

Bosgrave. He saith that her Majesty is lawful Queen of this realm, and so ought to be taken, notwithstanding any Bull or sentence that the Pope either hath, can, or shall hereafter give.

3.   *Whether the Pope have, or had, power to authorise the Earls of Northumberland, Westmorland, and other her Majesty's subjects, to rebel or take arms against her Majesty?*

Filbie. He knoweth not what to say thereunto.

Bosgrave. He thinketh the Pope had no power or authority to license the Earls of Northumberland and Westmorland or any other of her Majesty's subjects to rebel or to take arms against her Majesty.

4.   *Whether the Pope hath power to discharge any of her Highness's subjects, or the subjects of any Christian prince, from their allegiance or oath of obedience to her Majesty, or to their prince, for any cause?*

Filbie. He saith that so long as her Majesty remaineth Queen, the Pope hath no authority to warrant her subjects to take arms against her or to disobey her. But if he should depose her, then he might discharge them of their allegiance and obedience to her Majesty.

Bosgrave. He saith that the Pope neither hath nor ought to have any authority to discharge any of her Majesty's subjects, or the subjects of any other Christian prince, from their allegiance, for any cause whatsoever; and so he thinketh in his conscience.

6.   *If the Pope do by his Bull or sentence pronounce her Majesty to be deprived and no lawful Queen, and her subjects to be discharged of their allegiance and obedience unto her, and, after, the Pope or any other by his*

From *Dodd's Church History of England*, vol. III, ed. Rev. M. A. Tierney, 1840, Appendix, pp. iv–v, xiv–xvi.

appointment and authority do invade this realm, which part would you take, or which part ought a good subject of England to take?

Filbie. When this case happeneth, then, he saith, he will answer. And if he had been in Ireland [*where a Catholic rising had taken place*] he would have done as a priest should have done: that is, to pray that the right may have place.

Bosgrave. He saith that whatsoever the Pope should do, he would in this case take part with her Majesty against the Pope, what cause soever he would pretend, and this he taketh to be the duty of every good subject . . .

45 Burghley distinguishes religion from politics, 1583

Burghley here attempts to separate a subject's religion from his loyalty to the State, a distinction that in the case of the English Catholics was becoming steadily harder to apply.

And though there are many subjects known in the realm that differ in some opinions of religion from the Church of England and that do also not forbear to profess the same, yet in that they do also profess loyalty and obedience to her Majesty and offer readily in her Majesty's defence to impugn and resist any foreign force, though it should come or be procured from the Pope himself, none of these sort are for their contrary opinions in religion prosecuted or charged with any crimes or pains of treason, nor yet willingly searched in their consciences for their contrary opinions that savour not of treason. And of these sorts there have been and are a number of persons, not of such base and vulgar note as those were which of late have been executed, as in particular some by name are well known and not unfit to be remembered.

The first and chiefest by office was Dr. Heath, that was Archbishop of York and Lord Chancellor of England in Queen Mary's time, who at the first coming of her Majesty [*Elizabeth*] to the crown, showing himself a faithful and quiet subject, continued in both the said offices, though in religion then manifestly differing, and yet was he not restrained of his liberty nor deprived of his proper lands and goods, but, leaving willingly both his offices, lived in his own house very discreetly and enjoyed all his purchased lands during all his natural life, until by very age he departed this world and then left his house and living to his friends, an example of gentleness never matched in Queen Mary's time. The like did one Dr Pole, that had been Bishop of Peterborough, an ancient grave person and a very quiet subject. There were also others that had been bishops and in great estimation . . . Some also were deans . . . and many such others having borne office and dignities in the Church and that had made profession against the Pope, which they only began in Queen Mary's time to change. Yet were these never to this day burdened with capital pains, nor yet deprived of any their goods or proper livelihoods, but only removed from their ecclesiastical offices, which they would not exercise according to the laws. And most of them, and many other of their sort, for a great time were retained in bishops' houses in very civil and courteous manner, without charge to themselves or their friends, until the time that the Pope began by his bulls and messages to offer trouble to the realm by stirring of rebellion.

From William Cecil, *The Execution of Justice in England*, ed. Robert M. Kingdon, Ithaca, New York, 1965, pp. 10–11.

46　Death to be a priest, 1585, 1595

(a) From *An Act against Jesuits, Seminary Priests and such other like disobedient persons* (27 Elizabeth I, cap. 2), 1585.

[Be it enacted] that it shall not be lawful . . . for any Jesuit, seminary[†] priest or other such priest . . . being born within this realm . . . to come into, be or remain in any part of this realm . . . and if he do, that then every such offence shall be taken and adjudged to be high treason; and every person so offending shall for his offence be adjudged a traitor, and shall suffer, lose and forfeit as in case of high treason.

From *The Statutes of the Realm*, vol. IV, 1819, p. 706.

(b) The death of Robert Southwell, S. J., 1595.

Robert Southwell was of a family of good repute, born at St. Faith's in Norfolk, and was sent over young to Douai, where he was for some time alumnus of [*student at*] the English College or Seminary[†] in that university. From thence he went to Rome, and there was received into the Society of Jesus when he was but sixteen years of age . . . In 1584 he was sent upon the English mission, and there laboured with great fruit in the conversion of many souls . . . till the year 1592, when he was betrayed and apprehended in a gentleman's house . . . within seven miles of London, and was then committed to a dungeon in the Tower so noisome and filthy that when he was brought out at the end of the month to be examined, his clothes were quite covered with vermin . . . He was kept in prison three years, and at ten several times most cruelly racked, till at length a resolution was taken on a sudden in the Council to have him executed. Some days before his execution, he was removed from the Tower to Newgate, and there put down into the hole called Limbo, from whence he was brought out to suffer on account of his priesthood, the 21st of February 1595, having been condemned but the day before . . .

[Southwell was taken to Tyburn], drawn on a sled through the streets, and when he was come to the place, getting up into the cart, he made the sign of the cross in the best manner that he could, his hands being pinioned, and began to speak to the people . . .

'I am come to this place to finish my course, and to pass out of this miserable life, and I beg of my Lord Jesus Christ, in whose most precious passion and blood I place my hope of salvation, that He would have mercy on my soul. I confess I am a Catholic priest of the Holy Roman Church, and a religious man of the Society of Jesus, on which account I owe eternal thanks and praises to my God and saviour...As to the Queen, I never attempted nor contrived or imagined any evil against her, but have always prayed for her to our Lord; and for this short time of my life still pray that, in His infinite mercy, He would be pleased to give her all such gifts and graces which He sees in His divine wisdom to be most expedient for the welfare both of her soul and body, in this life and in the next; recommending in like manner, to the same mercy of God, my poor country...In fine, I beg of the Almighty and Everlasting God that this my death may be for my own and for my country's good, and the comfort of the Catholics my brethren'.

Having finished these words, and looking for the cart to be immediately drove away, he again blessed himself and with his eyes raised up to heaven repeated with great calmness of mind and countenance these words of the Psalmist, *In manus tuas*, etc. – 'Into thy hands, O Lord, I commend my spirit' – with other short ejaculations, till the cart was drawn off. The unskilful hangman had not applied the noose of the rope to the proper place, so that he several times made the sign of the cross whilst he was hanging and was some time before he was strangled; which some perceiving, drew him by the legs to put an end to his pain...After he was dead he was cut down, bowelled, and quartered.

From Bishop Richard Challoner, *Memoirs of Missionary Priests* (1741–42), new edn, 1924, pp. 210–12.

CHAPTER 3   PREROGATIVE AND PARLIAMENT

In this chapter we turn to government, and in particular to the role of the monarch, which must include, of course, his or her role as one of the three elements that made up Parliament. The first section is about the monarch's prerogative, meaning those powers which enabled him or her to govern effectively. There is no doubt that there were certain areas, such as foreign policy and religion, in which the monarch's decision was final. However, the question arises as to whether the royal prerogative was superior to the common law or not. For instance, could the sovereign make law merely by issuing a proclamation, as Thomas Cromwell argued? The general consensus, which Henry VIII seems to have shared, was that royal proclamations did indeed have the force of law, but only within certain limits. They could not affect the subject's property rights, nor could they create new felonies or treasons.

Parliament, which is the subject of the second section, consisted of monarch, Lords and Commons. It was not a permanent feature of government, as it met only briefly and irregularly. During Henry VIII's reign there were nine Parliaments (one of which had seven sessions), meeting altogether for a total of 183 weeks; under Elizabeth there were ten, meeting for 126 weeks. Nevertheless, it was generally recognised, especially after the Reformation Parliament (1529–36), that Parliament was a vital part of the constitution, since here, and only here, could the highest form of law, namely statute, be made. Furthermore, Sir Thomas Smith's assertion that Parliament's authority derived from the fact that it represented the entire realm, from the King downwards, was widely accepted.

Within Parliament there was a constitutional equality between the Lords and the Commons. On the whole, the Lords co-operated with the government of the day – their opposition to the religious settlement of 1559 being the major exception. As for the Commons, there has been a tendency to exaggerate the element of conflict between them and the monarch, especially under Elizabeth. It is true that the Commons grew in size during the century and developed into an institution representing the 'political nation' as a whole rather than local interests in the narrower sense. It is also true that the question of freedom of speech was raised frequently during Elizabeth's reign as the Commons constantly sought to discuss issues such as the succession which Elizabeth wanted to keep to herself. But basically the Commons, like the Lords, were co-operative – which is, of course, why Tudor monarchs were willing to work through Parliament, instead of ignoring, by-passing or eliminating it. When conflict did occur, this was, more often than not, a spilling over into Parliament of splits within the Privy Council or differences of opinion between the Council and the sovereign.

The third section focuses on the Court. Because it revolved around the monarch, the Tudor Court was the heart of politics and government, just as it was also the centre of artistic patronage. It was therefore the place to be for anyone seriously on the make. The nearer one could approach to the royal person, the more likely it was that some of the plums might come one's way. At Court, the leading officials were also politicians; a man like Christopher Hatton was courtier, diplomat, statesman, all at the same time. And everyone accepted presents. The modern insistence that administrators should take nothing except their salary was unknown in the sixteenth century. Indeed, salaries were so low that government could hardly have functioned if this principle had been enforced.

The last section is about faction. At the start of Henry VII's reign there were still armies of liveried[†] retainers in attendance upon great lords, largely as a hang-over from the stormy period of the Wars of the Roses. However, in the relative domestic peace of the sixteenth century, faction came to be more important than retaining. A faction was an alliance between a group of courtiers and others for the purposes of obtaining patronage, or pursuing certain policies. They first made their appearance during the divorce crisis in Henry VIII's reign, when a reforming faction, led successively by Anne Boleyn, Thomas Cromwell and Edward Seymour, opposed a conservative group under Norfolk and Gardiner. Factions were at their most powerful under a weak monarch, as during the period of religious wars in France. In England, the nearest approach to factional civil war was the struggle between the Seymours and the Dudleys during Edward VI's reign. Elizabeth quickly learnt how to contain, and even to use, faction; a task made easier because her councillors agreed fundamentally on most issues. It was only over questions of foreign policy that real factional splits occurred. The major issue which divided the Council in the middle of the reign was whether or not to aid the Dutch rebels, but on this, as on all other issues, the ultimate decision lay with the Queen.

The Royal Prerogative

47   A homily on obedience, 1547

Homilies[†] were sermons issued by the government to be used by the clergy. The principle stated here – that the ruler must never be resisted – is central to sixteenth-century political thought.

AN EXHORTATION CONCERNING GOOD ORDER AND OBEDIENCE TO RULERS AND MAGISTRATES

Almighty God hath created and appointed all things in heaven, earth and waters in a most excellent and perfect order. In heaven he hath appointed distinct and several orders and states of archangels and angels. In earth he hath assigned and appointed kings, princes, with other governors under them, all in good and necessary order... Every degree of people in their vocation, calling and office hath appointed to them their duty and order. Some are in high degree, some low; some kings and princes, some inferiors and subjects; priests and laymen; masters and servants; fathers and children; husbands and wives; rich and poor, and every one have need of other. So that in all things is to be lauded and praised the goodly order of God, without the which no house, no city, no commonwealth can continue and endure or last. For where there is no right order, there reigneth all abuse, carnal liberty, enormity, sin, and Babylonical confusion. Take away kings, princes, rulers, magistrates, judges, and such estates of God's order, no man shall ride or go by the highway unrobbed; no man shall sleep in his own house or bed unkilled; no man shall keep his wife, children and possession in quietness; all things shall be common, and there must needs follow all mischief and utter destruction both of souls, bodies, goods and commonwealths.

But blessed be God that we in this realm of England feel not the horrible calamities, miseries and wretchedness which all they undoubtedly feel and suffer that lack this goodly order. And praised be God, that . . . hath sent us his high gift, our most dear sovereign lord King Edward [VI], with a godly, wise and honourable Council, with other superiors and inferiors, in a beautiful order, and godly. Wherefore let us subjects do our bounden duties, giving hearty thanks to God, and praying for the preservation of this godly order. Let us all obey, even from the bottom of our hearts, all their godly proceedings, laws, statutes, proclamations and injunctions[†], with all other godly orders. Let us consider the Scriptures . . . which persuade and command us all obediently to be subject, first and chiefly to the King's Majesty, supreme governor over all, and the next to his honourable Council, and to all other noblemen, magistrates and officers which by God's goodness be placed and ordered. For Almighty God is the only author and provider for this forenamed state and order.

From M. E. Rickey and T. B. Stroup (eds), *Certain Sermons or Homilies*, Gainesville, Florida, 1968, pp. 69–70.

48 Anti-papal propaganda, 1548

In the picture on the right, probably painted in 1548, we see Edward VI enthroned, with the dying Henry VIII on the left and, on the right, the members of the Council, of whom only Somerset (standing) and next to him, John Dudley, Duke of Northumberland, Thomas Cranmer, Archbishop of Canterbury, and John Russell, Earl of Bedford, can be clearly identified.

From Roy Strong, *Tudor and Jacobean Portraits*, vol. 2, HMSO, 1969, plate 678 (National Portrait Gallery 4165).

49 The monarch and the law

Was the royal will superior to the law of the land? In a letter written to Protector Somerset after Henry VIII's death, Bishop Gardiner describes how this question was once put to him by Henry's great minister, Thomas Cromwell.

The Lord Cromwell had once put in the King's our late sovereign lord's head to take upon him to have his will and pleasure regarded for a law; for that, he said, was to be a very king; and thereupon I was called for at Hampton Court. And as the Lord Cromwell was very stout [*bold*], 'Come on, my Lord of Winchester,' quoth he (for that conceit he had, whatsoever he talked with me, he knew ever as much as I, Greek or Latin, and all), 'answer the King here,' quoth he, 'but speak plainly and directly, and shrink not, man! Is not that,' quoth he, 'that pleaseth the King, a law? Have ye not there, in the civil laws,' quoth he, '*quod principi placuit**, and so forth?' quoth he, 'I have somewhat forgotten it now.'

I stood still and wondered in my mind to what conclusion this should tend. The King saw me musing, and with earnest gentleness said, 'Answer him whether it be so or no.' I would not answer my Lord Cromwell, but delivered my speech to the King, and told him I had read indeed of kings that had their will always received for a law; but, I told him, the form of his reign, to make the laws his will, was more sure and quiet. 'And by this form of government ye be established,' quoth I, 'and it is agreeable with the nature of your people. If ye begin a new manner of policy, how it will frame no one can tell; and how this frameth ye can tell; and I would never advise your grace to leave a certain for an uncertain'.

From J. A. Muller (ed.), *Letters of Stephen Gardiner*, Cambridge, 1933, p. 399.

*The reference is to the maxim of Roman, or civil, law: 'What pleases the King hath the force of law'.

50   Ferrers' case, 1542

Henry VIII himself appears to have accepted, on at least one occasion, that his powers when operating through Parliament were superior to his personal power. This admission came when he was upholding the right of a member of the Commons, George Ferrers, who was also a member of the royal household, to freedom from arrest.

First commending their wisdoms in maintaining the privileges of their House (which he would not have to be infringed in any point) he alleged that he, being head of the Parliament and attending in his own person upon the business thereof, ought in reason to have privilege for him and all his servants attending there upon him . . . [He then said] and further we be informed by our judges that we at no time stand so highly in our estate royal as in the time of Parliament, wherein we as head and you as members are conjoined and knit together into one body politic, so as whatsoever offence or injury (during that time) is offered to the meanest member of the House is to be judged as done against our person and the whole Court of Parliament. Which prerogative of the court is so great (as our learned counsel informeth us) as all acts and processes coming out of any other inferior courts must for the time cease and give place to the highest . . .

From *Holinshed's Chronicles of England, Scotland and Ireland*, vol. III, 1808 edn, p. 826.

51   Two supremacies, 1534, 1559

The differences in the wording of the Henrician and Elizabethan Acts of Supremacy indicate that contemporaries perceived differences in the respective positions of the two monarchs. Henry VIII's position as Supreme Head of the Church, which had been 'obscured' by centuries of papal usurpation, was (in theory) merely revealed and acknowledged by parliamentary statute. Elizabeth, as a woman, was only accorded the dignity of Supreme Governor (see also **Doc. 35a**), and even this title derived from parliamentary grant rather than from natural right.

(a) From *The Act of Supremacy* (26 Henry VIII, cap. 1), 1534

Albeit the King's Majesty justly and rightfully is and oweth [*ought*] to be the supreme head of the Church of England, and so is recognised by the clergy of this realm in their convocations[†]; yet nevertheless, for corroboration and confirmation thereof, and for increase of virtue in Christ's religion within this realm of England and to repress and extirpate all errors, heresies and other enormities and abuses heretofore used in the same, be it enacted by authority of this present Parliament that the King our sovereign lord, his heirs and successors Kings of this realm, shall be taken, accepted and reputed the only supreme head in earth of the Church of England, called *Anglicana Ecclesia*, and shall have and enjoy annexed and united to the imperial crown of this realm . . . full power and authority from time to time to visit, repress, redress, reform, order, correct, restrain and amend all such errors, heresies, abuses, offences, contempts and enormities, whatsoever they be . . .

From *The Statutes of the Realm*, vol. III, 1817, p. 492.

(b) From *The Act of Supremacy* (1 Elizabeth I, cap. 1), 1559.

Most humbly beseech your most excellent Majesty your faithful and obedient subjects the Lords spiritual and temporal and the Commons in this your present Parliament assembled, that where in time of the reign of your most dear father of worthy memory, King Henry VIII, divers good laws and statutes were made and established, as well for the utter extinguishment and putting away of all usurped and foreign [*papal*] powers and authorities out of this your realm . . . as also for the restoring and uniting to the imperial crown of this realm the ancient jurisdictions, authorities, superiorities and pre-eminences to the same, of right, belonging and appertaining. By reason whereof we . . . were continually kept in good order . . . until such time as all the said good laws and statutes, by one Act of Parliament made in the first and second years of the reigns of the late King Philip and Queen Mary . . . were all clearly repealed and made void . . . By reason of which Act of Repeal your said humble subjects were eftsoons brought under an usurped foreign power and authority [*the papacy*], and yet do remain in that bondage . . . if some redress, by the authority of this your High Court of Parliament, with the assent of your Highness, be not had and provided.

May it therefore please your Highness, for the repressing of the said usurped foreign power and the restoring of the rights, jurisdiction and pre-eminences appertaining to the imperial crown of this your realm, that it may be enacted by the authority of this present Parliament that the said Act [of Repeal] . . . be repealed and shall from thenceforth be utterly void and of none effect . . .

And that also it may likewise please your Highness that it may be established and enacted by the authority aforesaid that such jurisdictions, privileges, superiorities and pre-eminences spiritual and ecclesiastical as . . . hath heretofore been or may lawfully be exercised or used for the visitation of the ecclesiastical state and persons, and for reformation, order and correction of the same . . . shall for ever, by authority of this present Parliament, be united and annexed to the imperial crown of this realm. And that your Highness . . . shall have full power and authority, by virtue of this Act . . . to assign, name and authorise . . . such person or persons . . . as your Majesty . . . shall think meet, to . . . visit, reform, redress, order, correct and amend all such errors, heresies, schisms, abuses, offences, contempts and enormities whatsoever . . .

From *The Statutes of the Realm*, vol. IV, 1819, pp. 350–2.

52   Authority over war and peace, 1565

One area in which the royal prerogative was never doubted was foreign policy. Sir Thomas Smith, the author of this extract, was a leading administrator and member of the Privy Council. His book on the government, written in 1565 when he was serving as Elizabeth's ambassador to France, is an important contemporary source.

The Prince whom I now call (as I have often before) the Monarch of England, King or Queen, hath absolutely in his power the authority of war and peace, to defy what prince it shall please him, and to bid him war, and again to reconcile himself and enter into league or truce with him at his pleasure or the advice only of his privy council. His privy council be chosen also at the Prince's pleasure out of the nobility or baronry, and of the knights and esquires, such and so many as he shall think good, who doth consult daily, or when need is, of the weighty matters of the realm, to give therein to their Prince the best advice they can. The Prince doth participate to them all, or so many of them as he shall think good, such legations and messages as come from foreign princes, such letters or occurrents [*accounts of events*] as be sent to himself or to his secretaries, and keepeth so many ambassades and letters sent unto him secret as he will.

From Sir Thomas Smith, *De Republica Anglorum*, ed. L. Alston, Cambridge, 1906, pp. 58–9.

Parliament

53   The sovereignty of Parliament, 1565

By the second half of the century political commentators were agreed on the supremacy of the King in Parliament. For details about the author, see the previous document.

(a)

The most high and absolute power of the realm of England consisteth in the Parliament. For as in war, where the King himself in person, the nobility, the rest of the gentility and the yeomanry are, is the force and power of England: so in peace and consultation where the prince is to give life and the last and highest commandment, the Barony for the nobility and higher, the knights, esquires, gentlemen and commons for the lower part of the commonwealth, the bishops for the clergy, be present to advertise, consult and show what is good and necessary for the commonwealth, and to consult together. And upon mature deliberation, every bill or law being thrice read and disputed upon in either House...after[wards] the Prince himself, in presence of both the parties, doth consent unto and alloweth. That is the Prince's and whole realm's deed; whereupon justly no man can complain but must accommodate himself to find it good and obey it...The Parliament abrogateth [*repeals*] old laws, maketh new...changeth rights and possessions of private men, legitimateth bastards, establisheth forms of religion, altereth weights and measures, giveth forms of succession to the crown...appointeth subsidies...taxes and impositions, giveth most free pardons and absolutions, restoreth in blood and name as the highest court, condemneth or absolveth them whom the Prince will put to the trial...The Parliament of England...representeth and hath the power of the whole realm, both the head and the body.

For every Englishman is intended to be there present, either in person or by procuration[†] and attorneys, of what pre-eminence, state, dignity or quality soever he be, from the Prince (be he King or Queen) to the lowest person of England. And the consent of the Parliament is taken to be every man's consent.

From Sir Thomas Smith, *De Republica Anglorum*, ed. L. Alston, Cambridge, 1906, pp. 48–9.

(b)

The Parliament of England, together with the Convocation annexed thereunto, is that whereupon the very essence of all government within this kingdom doth depend; it is even the body of the whole realm; it consisteth of the king and of all that within the land are subject unto him; for they all are there present, either in person or by such as they voluntarily have derived their very personal right unto.

From Richard Hooker, *The Laws of Ecclesiastical Polity*, Book VIII (c. 1595); printed in John Keble (ed.), *The Works of...Mr. Richard Hooker*, Oxford, vol. III, 1888, pp. 408–9.

54   Three readings, c. 1580

Gradually, during the sixteenth century, both Houses of Parliament settled on a uniform procedure for dealing with Bills, as described here by the contemporary scholar and antiquarian, William Lambarde.

Upon the first reading of a bill, the Speaker, taking the bill in one hand, and his cap in the other hand, may say: 'You have heard the bill, the contents whereof are these, etc'. And, after the rehearsal thereof, may read another; without suffering any man, if he may stay him, to speak unto it, but rather to advise thereof until the next reading: which is a means not only to hear effectual speech, but also to save a great deal of time. A bill may not be committed* upon the first reading...At the second reading of a bill, it ought to be either engrossed [*copied on to parchment*], committed, or rejected; and if any shall offer to speak thereto, after that three have spoken all on one side, the Speaker may say, that the bill is sufficiently spoken unto;

'What is your pleasure? Will you have it engrossed, or committed?' And if the more voices will have it engrossed, it must be done accordingly. And if the more voices will have it committed, then the Speaker entreats them to appoint the committees [*the members of the committee*]; and, that done, their names, and the time and place of meeting, and the day of their report shall be endorsed upon it. If the more voices be not apparently discerned, then the Speaker may put the question again still: 'As many as will have this bill engrossed, say "Ay"', And after that voice, 'So many as will not have it engrossed, say "No"'. Again, if the sides seem equal, the Speaker may pray all those that be on the affirmative to go down with the bill, and the rest to sit in their places; and the sides shall be numbered by tellers to be appointed by the Speaker, and the greater number shall prevail . . . When a bill is engrossed, and hath received the third reading, it must either pass, or be rejected by the more voices: if it pass, then it must be endorsed *Soit baillé aux Seigneurs* [*Let it be sent to the Lords*]; and if it be rejected, it must not come any more in the House.

From *The Harleian Miscellany*, vol. V, 1810, pp. 260, 262.

*Sent to a committee for further discussion.

55   'Nipping words'

According to Sir Thomas Smith (see **Doc. 52**), debates were conducted in an orderly fashion, but the *Journal* of the House of Commons reveals that this was not always the case.

(a)

No reviling or nipping words must be used. For then all the House will cry, 'It is against the order'; and if any speak unreverently or seditiously against the prince or the Privy Council, I have seen them not only interrupted but it hath been moved after to the House and they have sent them to the Tower. So that in such a multitude, and in such diversity of minds and opinions, there is the greatest modesty and temperance of speech that can be used.

From Sir Thomas Smith, *De Republica Anglorum*, ed. L. Alston, Cambridge,1906, p. 55.

(b)

[2 December 1584]
This Bill had been much argued upon, before it was committed; and it seems, some arguments being not liked, divers of the House had endeavoured by coughing and spitting to shorten them. Whereupon Sir Francis Hastings made a motion (that as, upon like occasion offered, others had moved that words of note, as Town-Clerk and such like, should not offensively be applied to the persons of such as had formerly spoken) that in like manner it were now to be wished that in respect of the gravity and honour of this House, when any member thereof shall speak unto a Bill, the residue would forbear to interrupt or trouble him by unnecessary coughing, spitting or the like.

From Sir Simonds D'Ewes, *The Journals of all the Parliaments during the reign of Queen Elizabeth*, 1682, p. 335.

56   Freedom of speech

Parliament's capacity to perform its functions depended not only on effective procedures but also on the right of members to speak their minds freely, without fear of punishment. This did not mean, however, that they could discuss any issues they liked, and there was an increasing divergence of views between individual members, on the one hand, and the crown's spokesmen, on the other, about the limits within which the privilege of freedom of speech should be confined.

(a) The first recorded petition by a Speaker for the privilege of free speech in its full sense was made by Sir Thomas More in 1523.

From J. Rawson Lumby (ed.), *Utopia ... together with the life of Sir Thomas More, by his son-in-law, William Roper, reprinted from Hearne's edition 1716,* Cambridge, 1952, pp. xi-xii.

... Therefore (most Gracious Sovereign) considering that in all your high courts of Parliament is nothing intreated but of matters of weight and importance concerning your Realm, and your own Royal estate, it could not fail to let [*prevent*] and put to silence from the giving of their advice and counsel many of your discreet Commons except they were utterly discharged of all doubt and fear how any thing that should happen them to speak, should happen of your Highness to be taken ...

It may therefore like your most abundant Grace (our most gracious King) to give to all your Commons here assembled your most gracious licence and pardon freely, without doubt of your dreadful displeasure, every man to discharge his conscience, and boldly in every thing incident among, declare his advice; and whatsoever happeneth any man to say, it may like your noble Majesty of your inestimable goodness to take all in good part, interpreting every man's words, how uncunningly soever they be couched, to proceed yet of a good zeal towards the profit of your Realm and honour of your Royal person, the prosperous estate and preservation whereof (most excellent Sovereign) is the thing which we all your most humble loving subjects, according to the most bounden duty of our natural Allegiance, most highly desire and pray for.

(b) In 1587 Peter Wentworth, an outspoken and far from typical member of the Commons, made a claim for freedom of speech without any limitations in a number of questions he put to the House.

3.   *Item,* whether free speech and free doings or dealings be not granted to every one of the Parliament House by law.

4.   *Item,* whether that great honour to God and those great benefits may be done unto the Prince and state without free speech and doings in this place, that may be done with them.

5.   *Item,* whether it be not an injury to the whole state, and against the law, that the Prince or Privy Council should send for any member of this House in the Parliament time, or after the end of the Parliament, and to check, blame or punish them for any speech used in this place, except it be for traitorous words ...

7.   *Item,* whether it be not against the orders and liberties of this House to receive messages either of commanding or prohibiting, and whether the messenger be not to be reputed as an enemy to God, the Prince and state.

8.   *Item,* whether it be not against the orders and liberties of this House to make anything known unto the Prince that is here in hand, to the hurt of the House; and whether the tale-carrier be not to be punished by the House and reputed as an enemy unto God, the Prince and state.

Printed by J. E. Neale in the *English Historical Review*, vol. 39, 1924, p. 48.

(c) Elizabeth made her views known, via the Lord Keeper, in 1593.

...Her Majesty granteth you liberal but not licentious speech, liberty therefore but with due limitation. For even as there can be no good consultation where all freedom of advice is barred, so will there be no good conclusion where every man may speak what he listeth, without fit observation of persons, matters, times, places and other needful circumstances. It shall be meet therefore that each man of you contain his speech within the bounds of loyalty and good discretion, being assured that as the contrary is punishable in all men, so most of all in them that take upon them to be counsellors... of the commonwealth. For liberty of speech her Majesty commandeth me to tell you that to say 'Yea' or 'No' to bills, God forbid that any man should be restrained or afraid to answer according to his best liking, with some short declaration of his reason therein, and therein to have a free voice, which is the very true liberty of the House; not, as some suppose, to speak there of all causes as him listeth, and to frame a form of religion or a state of government as to their idle brains shall seem meetest. She saith no king fit for his state will suffer such absurdities...

Printed by J. E. Neale in the *English Historical Review*, vol. 31, 1916, pp. 136–7.

57   Conflict over the succession, 1566

The element of conflict between monarch and Parliament, particularly during Elizabeth's reign, has been exaggerated. Many of the alleged confrontations between Elizabeth and her Commons were in fact the outcome of campaigns orchestrated by her Council in order to try to force her to alter course. This is true, for instance, of events in 1566, when the Queen reacted angrily to the Commons' draft preamble to the subsidy Bill, which included a request for her to name a successor. The preamble was subsequently scrapped.

(a) The draft preamble.

...Thirdly, we cannot but also thankfully remember to your Majesty that it pleased the same to signify unto us that you did not mislike of us for our desire in this Parliament to have the succession of the crown declared, for that you rightly conceived the same our desire to proceed from us (as indeed it did) of mere duty and love towards your Highness, your realms and countries, and not of any other disposition or pretensed purpose. And signified further of your godly disposition and natural love towards us, to our great comfort, that rather than your realm should threat ruin for lack of declaration of succession – which you trusted Almighty God would show of your own body in due time after your marriage – you would by God's help, though it should appear some peril to yourself (which God defend), declare the succession in such convenient time as your Highness, with the advice of your Council and assent of your realm, should think most meet . . . to the joyful comfort of us all.

(b) Elizabeth's comments.

. . . I know no reason why any my private answers to the realm should serve for prologue to a subsidies-book. Neither yet do I understand why such audacity should be used to make without my licence an act of my words. Are my words like lawyers' books, which nowadays go to the wire-drawers* to make subtle doings more plain? Is there no hold of my speech without an act compel me to confirm? Shall my princely consent be turned to strengthen my words that be not of themselves substantives? I say no more at this time; but if these fellows were well answered, and paid with lawful coin, there would be fewer counterfeits among them.

*Those who will 'draw out' the words by excessive analysis.

From J. E. Neale, *Elizabeth I and her Parliaments 1559–1581*, 1953, pp. 163–4.

58   Conflict in the Lords, 1559

In their preoccupation with the Commons, historians have until quite recently underestimated the significance of the Lords, whose institutional authority, as well as the individual standing of its members, gave it great prestige and influence. The same qualities meant that the Lords could on occasion be formidable opponents of royal policy – as was shown in 1559, when Catholic peers strongly resisted the Supremacy Bill.

(a) Viscount Montagu's speech.

In changing of religion we condemn all other nations, of whom some be our friends and many our enemies, open and ancient, who long time have, and no doubt do expect, an opportunity to annoy us. If the pope hearing us by schism[†] divided from the Church do proceed to the excommunication of the realm . . . how enjoyeth the king of Spain . . . And thereby authority given to him to possess the same that could by strong hand obtain it? This . . . may be of right feared in ourselves, being environed [*surrounded*] and, as it were, set about in one of two so potent enemies, who as you know would be loath to lose such opportunity . . .

(b) Archbishop Heath's speech.

From T. E. Hartley (ed.), *Proceedings in the Parliaments of Elizabeth I*, Leicester, 1981, pp. 7, 10.

Her Highness, being a woman by birth and nature, is not qualified by God's words to feed the flock of Christ . . . Therefore it appeareth, that like as your honours have not His authority to give her highness this second point of spiritual government, to feed the flock of Christ, so by [Saint] Paul's doctrine her highness may not intermeddle herself with the same. Therefore she cannot be supreme head of Christ's Church here in this realm... To preach or minister the holy sacraments[†] a woman may not; neither may she be supreme head of the Church of Christ.

From John Strype, *Annals of the Reformation*, vol. I, Oxford, 1824, part ii, pp. 399–407.

59   Private Bills, 1572

From the Council's point of view the problem with the Commons was not so much political as managerial. One aspect of this was the mass of private Bills put forward by particular interest groups or cities, which held up essential government legislation. Here, an anonymous member advocates a tactful selection process.

If her Majesty's meaning be to have the session short, then is it good to abridge the things that lengthen the session which, amongst others, are these.
1.   The number of private Bills of singular persons.
2.   The Bills of occupation, mysteries[†] and companies and specially the Bills of London...

For the first matter I think good that a choice be made of Bills, wherein this I note, that it is not good... that anything for choice or admitting or rejecting of Bills... be delivered by the Speaker or any Councillor or other, as by her Majesty's commandment. For so would by and by be raised by some humorous [*difficult*] body some question of the liberties of the House and of restraining their free consultation, perhaps offensive to her Majesty and assuredly with long speeches to the troublesome prolonging of the session...

I wish a motion to be made presently that sithence [*since*] her Majesty hath so graciously made us partakers of her pleasure for shortness of the session, it shall be good for us to take our benefit of this warning for well spending and sparing our time. And therefore to pray that there may be committees of the House to consider of Bills offered, to prefer the forwarding of the most necessary before the other, but in no wise to make mention of rejecting of any (although indeed it amounteth to a rejecting of those that be of small importance); for private Bills ever be eagerly followed and make factions...

From Michael A. R. Graves, *Elizabethan Parliaments 1559–1601*, 1987, pp. 110–11.

The Court

60   Patronage in Henry VIII's reign

(a) The Tudor Court was the centre of a web of patronage, and those nearest the sovereign were constantly besieged with requests and flooded with gifts. For example, after about 1527 it was known that Anne Boleyn had gained Henry VIII's favour and she herself immediately became a source of patronage.

Howbeit, after she knew the king's pleasure, and the great love that he bare her in the bottom of his stomach, then she began to look very hault and stout [*proud and bold*], having all manner of jewels, or rich apparel, that might be gotten with money. It was therefore judged by-and-by through all the court of every man, that she, being in such favour, might work masteries with the king, and obtain any suit of him for her friend.

From George Cavendish, *The Life of Cardinal Wolsey*, 1827, pp. 130–1.

(b) In 1537, after receiving a series of presents from Lady Lisle in Calais, Anne Boleyn finally agreed to take one of the Lisle daughters to be brought up at Court. This news was reported to Lady Lisle by John Hussee, Lord Lisle's agent, on 17 July 1537.

My bounden duty promised unto your ladyship. These shall be signifying the same that the Queen's Grace heartily thanketh your ladyship for the quails I brought, and they came very well. Those that your ladyship shall hereafter send, let them be very fat, or else they are not worth thanks ... Madam, upon Thursday last the Queen being at dinner, my Lady Rutland and my Lady Sussex being waiters on her Grace, her Grace chanced, eating of the quails, to common [*speak*] of your ladyship and of your daughters; so that such communication was uttered by the said two ladies that her Grace made grant to have one of your daughters; and the matter is thus concluded that your ladyship shall send them both over, for her Grace will first see them and know their manners, fashions and conditions, and take which of them shall like her Grace best; and they must be sent over about six weeks hence, and your ladyship shall not need to do much cost on them till time you know which of them her Grace will have. But two honest changes [*two respectable changes of dress*] they must have, the one of satin, the other of damask ... And for as much as they shall now go upon making and marring, it shall please your ladyship to exhort them to be sober, sad [*grave*], wise and discreet and lowly above all things ... For your ladyship knoweth the Court is full of pride, envy, indignation and mocking, scorning and derision, therefore I would be sorry but they should use themselves according unto the birth and state that God hath called them ...

From Muriel St. Clare Byrne (ed.), *The Lisle Letters*, vol. 4, Chicago, 1981, no. 887.

61   Essex as a patron, 1594

Elizabeth's favourite, the Earl of Essex, attempted to procure the post of Solicitor-General for his protégé, Francis Bacon, but without success. The following letter, written by the Earl to Bacon on 26 March 1594, casts a vivid light on his methods, and perhaps also on the reasons for his failure.

I find the Queen very reserved, staying herself from giving any kind of hope, yet not passionate against you till I grew passionate for you. Then she said that none thought you fit for the place but my Lord Treasurer and myself: 'Marry! The others must, some of them, say so before us, for fear or for flattery'. I told her the most and wisest of her Council had delivered their opinions, and preferred you before all men for that place...Yet if they had been never for you, but contrarily against you, I thought my credit, joined with the approbation and mediation of her greatest Councillors, might prevail in a greater matter than this, and urged her that though she could not signify her mind to others, I might have a secret promise; wherein I should receive great comfort, as in the contrary great unkindness. She said she neither was persuaded, nor would hear of it till Easter, when she might advise with her Council (who were now all absent); and therefore in passion bade me go to bed if I would talk of nothing else. Wherefore in passion I went away, saying while I was with her I could not but solicit for the cause and the man I so much affected, and therefore I would retire myself till I might be more graciously heard. And so we parted. Tomorrow I will go hence of purpose, and on Thursday I will write an expostulating letter to her. That night, or upon Friday morning, I will be here again and follow on the same course, stirring a discontentment in her, etc.

From *The Letters and the Life of Francis Bacon*, ed. James Spedding, vol. I, 1890, p. 289.

62   Being noticed at Court, 1600

For an ambitious young man, such as the seventeen-year-old Edward Herbert from Wales, a major step on the career ladder was to attract the monarch's attention.

About the year of our Lord 1600 I came to London, shortly after which the attempt of the earl of Essex, related in our history, followed...Not long after this, curiosity rather than ambition brought me to court; and, as it was the manner of those times for all men to kneel down before the great Queen Elizabeth, who then reigned, I was likewise upon my knees in the presence chamber when she passed by to the chapel at Whitehall. As soon as she saw me she stopped and, swearing her usual oath ['*God's Death!*'], demanded, 'Who is this?' Everybody there present looked upon me, but no man knew me, until Sir James Croft, a pensioner [*member of the Queen's bodyguard*], finding the Queen stayed, returned back and told who I was and that I had married Sir William Herbert of St. Gillian's daughter. The Queen hereupon looked attentively upon

From *The Life of Edward Lord Herbert of Cherbury*, written by himself, 1826 edn, pp. 92–3.

me and, swearing again her ordinary oath, said, 'It is pity he was married so young;' and thereupon gave her hand to kiss twice, both times gently clapping me on the cheek.

63   The royal presence, 1595

No matter where the monarch happened to be, there was little variation in the ritual and geography of the Court. The following description was sent to the Duke of Wurttemberg by his envoy, Breuning von Buchenbach.

General Norris, who had but recently come from France and soon after was sent against the insurgents in Ireland, came with ten stately gentlemen* who then led me into the Presence Chamber. There I was detained with all sorts of talk until the Lord Chamberlain came, received me, and led me into the Privy Chamber, where also all my followers were admitted. Both the Privy Chamber and the Presence Chamber were full of Mylords, Grandees, Earls, Lords, and of very grand Countesses and Ladies, who were all without exception beautiful. As soon as I descried Her Majesty I made my first courtesy. Thereupon Her Majesty with arms outstretched came half-way up the room to meet me, where I with due reverence kissed her hand. Her Majesty then turned back and seated herself upon a chair under a canopy of cloth and gold. I was about to kneel before her, but Her Majesty would not suffer it. I then submissively addressed Her Majesty... in Italian; which language, I had been told, would sound sweetest to her ears.

From Victor von Klarwill (ed.), *Queen Elizabeth and some foreigners*, 1928, p. 363.

*Gentlemen pensioners who formed the Queen's bodyguard.

64   The cult of Elizabeth, 1573

A new factor in the life of the Court during Elizabeth's reign was the cult of the Queen, of which Sir Christopher Hatton, later to be Lord Chancellor, was a major exponent. The following extract comes from a letter he wrote to Elizabeth on 5 June 1573, during a brief stay abroad.

Madam, I find the greatest lack that ever poor wretch sustained. No death, no, not hell, no fear of death shall ever win of me my consent so far as to wrong myself again as to be absent from you one day. God grant my return. I will perform this vow. I lack that I live by. The more I find this lack, the further I go from you ... My spirit and soul (I feel) agreeth with my body and life, that to serve you is a heaven, but to lack you is more than hell's torment unto them. My heart is full of woe. Pardon (for God's sake) my tedious writing. It doth much diminish (for the time) my great griefs. I will wash away the faults of these letters with the drops from your poor Lids [*her nickname for him*] and so enclose them. Would God I were with you but for one hour. My wits are overwrought with thoughts. I find myself amazed. Bear with me, my most dear sweet Lady. Passion overcometh me. I can write no more ...

From Sir Harris Nicolas (ed.), *The Life and Times of Sir Christopher Hatton*, 1847, pp. 25–6.

65 Portraits of Elizabeth

Throughout Elizabeth's reign there was a continuous and growing demand for portraits of the Queen. This led to concern that uncontrolled demand might lead to the production of inferior images by hack artists. Consequently several attempts were made to control royal portraiture.

(a)

... Therefore her Majesty, being herein as it were overcome with the continual requests of so many of her Nobility and Lords, whom she cannot well deny, is pleased that for their contentations [*contentment*] some coning [*expert*] person mete thereof shall shortly make a portrait of her person or visage to be participated to others for satisfaction of her loving subjects, and furthermore commandeth all manner of persons in the meantime to forbear from painting, graving, printing or making of any portrait of her Majesty until some special person that shall be by her allowed shall have first finished a portraiture thereof, after which finished, her Majesty will be content that all other painters, printers or gravers, that shall be known men of understanding, and so thereto licensed by the head officers of the places where they shall dwell (as reason it is that every person should not without consideration attempt the same), shall and may at their pleasures follow the said patron [*pattern*] or first portraiture. And for that her Majesty perceiveth that a great number of her loving subjects are much grieved and take great offence with the errors and deformities already committed by sundry persons in this behalf, she straightly chargeth all her officers and ministers to see to the due observation hereof, and as soon as may be to reform the errors already committed, and in the meantime to forbid and prohibit the showing or publication of such as are apparently deformed, until they may be reformed which are reformable.

Part of a draft of a proclamation written in 1563 (but never in fact issued); printed in *Archaeologia*, vol. II, 1773, p. 170.

(b) From the records of the Privy Council, July 1596.

A warrant for her Majesty's Serjeant Painter and to all public officers to yield him their assistance touching the abuse committed by divers unskilful artisans in unseemly and improperly painting, graving and printing of her Majesty's person and visage, to her Majesty's great offence and disgrace of that beautiful and magnanimous Majesty wherewith God hath blessed her, requiring them to cause all such to be defaced and none to be allowed but such as her Majesty's Serjeant Painter shall first have sight of.

From J. R. Dasent (ed.), *Acts of the Privy Council*, New Series, vol. XXVI, AD 1596–1597, 1902, p. 69.

(c) The Ermine Portrait (opposite). This is one of the most famous portraits of Elizabeth. It was painted in 1585 and is now exhibited at Hatfield House. The ermine on the Queen's left arm symbolised virginity, the sword, justice, and the olive branch (held in her right hand), peace.

From Roy Strong, *Tudor and Jacobean Portraits*, HMSO, 1969, plate 202.

66   Seeking vain shadows, 1579

Spenser's jaundiced view of the Court was probably written in 1579 when his friend and patron, Sir Philip Sidney, tried to oppose Elizabeth's apparent determination to marry Francis, Duke of Alençon.

Full little knowest thou that hast not tried,
What hell it is, in sueing long to bide:
To lose good days, that might be better spent;
To waste long nights in pensive discontent;
To speed today, to be put back tomorrow;
To feed on hope, to pine with fear and sorrow;
To have thy Prince's grace, yet want her peers';
To have thy asking, yet wait many years;
To fret thy soul with crosses and with cares;
To eat thy heart through comfortless despairs;
To fawn, to crouch, to wait, to ride, to run,
To spend, to give, to want, to be undone.
Unhappy wight [*man*], born to disastrous end,
That doth his life in so long [at]tendance spend.
Who ever leaves sweet home, where mean estate
In safe assurance, without strife or hate,
Finds all things needful for contentment meek;
And will to Court for shadows vain to seek,
Or hope to gain, himself will a daw try [*will prove a fool*]:
That curse God send unto mine enemy.

From Edmund Spenser, 'Mother Hubberds Tale', lines 892–913, in *Spenser's Poetical Works* (1912), Oxford, 1985, p. 504.

Faction

67   Retaining, 1504, 1554

(a) In the interests of law and order Henry VII passed several Acts attempting to restrict the right of great lords to maintain their own retainers. The following extract is from 19 Henry VII, cap. 14, 1504.

And over that our said Sovereign Lord the King ordayneth...that no person of what estate or degree or condition he be...give any livery[†] or sign or retain any person other than such as he giveth household wages unto, without fraud or colour, or that he be his manual servant or his officer or man learned in the one law or in the other [*the common law or the civil (Roman) law*]...and if any do the contrary, that then he run and fall in the pain and forfeiture for every such livery and sign, badge or token, 100 shillings...

   And also it is ordained...that no person, of what estate or condition he be...name or cause himself to be named servant, or retained to or with any person, or buy or cause to be bought or wear any gown as a livery gown, sign or token of the suit or livery of any

From *The Statutes of the Realm*, vol. II, 1816, p. 658.

person, or any badge, token or sign of any person, upon pain of forfeiture for every day and time that he doth, 40 shillings, and also to have imprisonment by the discretion of the judges . . .

(b) Apart from times of special crisis, the great lords of the realm gradually ceased to pose a physical threat to government. Nevertheless, the practice of retaining went on, although more as a matter of display and prestige on certain ceremonial occasions. The opening of Mary's second Parliament was such an occasion. The following account comes from a letter written to the Emperor Charles V by his ambassador, Simon Renard, in November 1554.

The service concluded, the gathering made its way to the Parliament-house where the Speaker, as he is called, read his speech in presence of the assembled Estates. This lasted a good two hours and, I am told, dealt mainly with the religious question and demanded the approval of Parliament for the agreements made by the marriage articles; though I am informed that it also contained much other matter. Present was a great concourse of lords and members for the country, more than have ever attended any other Parliament. Besides the great lords already mentioned, there were the Earl of Rutland and the Earl of Pembroke, who was accompanied by about 300 retainers, among them being 44 of his gentlemen clothed in black velvet cloaks with gold tassels or other ornaments and each one wearing his gold chain, and the rest attired in blue cloth with a device representing a serpent on one sleeve. These last also wore some velvet garments. Then my Lord Talbot [*Earl of Shrewsbury*] came out very brave with a great following, but not nearly as sumptuously dressed as Pembroke's.

From Royall Tyler (ed.), *Calendar of Letters, Despatches, and State Papers relating to the Negotiations between England and Spain*, vol. XIII, *Philip and Mary July 1554–November 1558*, 1954, no. 97, p. 82.

68   The Netherlands question, 1576, 1582

During the 1570s and '80s, the overriding issue, which divided the Council into a 'war' and a 'peace' faction, was whether to give open aid to the Dutch rebels in their struggle against Spain.

(a) The following extract comes from a letter written by William Herle to Lord Burghley on 14 March 1576.

It is given out very maliciously amongst gentlemen and soldiers and those of good sort who profess the [Protestant] religion, that his lordship [*Burghley*] has been the only let and overthrow of this Holland service, by dissuading her Majesty from that enterprise, where otherwise the Earls of Leicester and Sussex were earnest furtherers of it. They judge very hardly that they* have been, contrary to her promise, by indirect dealing so long delayed here to their utter undoing at home and abroad. They say Mr. Walsingham dealt justly with them in that he assured them from the beginning that they would obtain nothing here, but lose their time. They say these unworthy proceedings with foreign nations make the English

From Allan James Crosby (ed.), *Calendar of State Papers, Foreign Series, of the Reign of Elizabeth, 1575–77*, 1881, no. 668, pp. 269–70.

the most hated men in the world and to be condemned for mere abusers, as those who put on religion, piety and justice for a cloak to serve humours withal and please the time, while policy only is made both justice, religion and God with them.

*The members of a Dutch delegation in England to seek the Queen's support.

(b) The second extract reflects a foreign view. It comes in a despatch written to Philip II of Spain by Bernardino de Mendoza on 25 April 1582.

Leicester, Hatton and Walsingham have endeavoured to persuade the Queen that it is desirable for her to openly take the States under her protection, as she could then settle with your Majesty on better terms, whereas if she lets this opportunity pass she can only look for ruin; because, if either your Majesty, or Alençon and the French, get possession of the country, neither one nor the other could be trusted. This view they have enforced by many arguments, but they have been opposed by Cecil and Sussex when the matter was discussed in the Council, and the question therefore remained undecided. When it was referred to the Queen, I understand that she complained greatly, saying what a miserable state was hers, since the death of a single person* made all her Councillors tremble and her subjects lose their courage.

From Martin A. S. Hume (ed.), *Calendar of Letters and State Papers relating to English Affairs, preserved principally in the Archives of Simancas*, vol. III, *Elizabeth 1580–1586*, 1896, no. 252, p. 346.

*The falsely rumoured death of William of Orange.

69   Elizabeth's control of factionalism

It was not in Elizabeth's interests to allow any one faction, or politician, to monopolise her favour or dominate her policies. This, at least, is what Robert Naunton, who grew up during the reign, believed.

Her ministers and instruments of state, such as … bare a great part of the burthen, were many, and those memorable, but they were only favourites, not minions; such as acted more by her own princely rules and judgments than by their own wills and appetites … The principal note of her reign will be, that she ruled much by faction and parties, which herself both made, upheld and weakened, as her own great judgment advised. For I disassent from the common received opinion that my Lord of Leicester was absolute and above all in her grace. [*Naunton then recounts the story of a dispute involving Leicester, at the end of which the Queen told him*] 'My lord, I have wished you well, but my favour is not so locked up for you that others shall not partake thereof. For I have many servants unto whom I have and will at my pleasure bequeath my favour, and likewise resume the same. And if you think to rule here, I will take a course to see you forthcoming. I will have here but one mistress and no master' … From whence, and in more instances, I conclude that she was absolute and sovereign mistress of her graces, and that all those to whom she distributed her favours were never more than tenants-at-will, and stood on no better ground than her princely pleasure and their own good behaviour.

From Sir Robert Naunton, *Fragmenta Regalia* (c. 1633), ed. Edward Arber, 1870, pp. 16–18.

70   Above faction, 1592

Robert Beale, Walsingham's chief assistant, advised the Secretary to remain outside any factions.

Take heed you do not addict yourself to any faction that you may find among the Councillors. You shall find they will only use you for their own turns and that done set little by you afterwards. Many times also men have been in danger without due desert and undone by suspicion of such men and matters. And the jealousy of princes is such that they cannot abide any councillor should depend on any other than themselves, neither is it convenient. Seek therefore by all the means you can to deserve well of them all and suffer yourself to be rather carried with the matter than with the man, as shall be most meetest for the service of God and her Majesty.

If there arise any partialities and factions, do you endeavour rather to compound than to increase them or to have them continued to the hurt of the state, for by such means neither good came to any prince or sound advice in council given where they were maintained…Remember touching England the wise and politique [*moderate*] discourse of Philip de Comines how Queen Margaret, wife to King Henry VI, by maintenance of such debate between the Duke of Somerset and the Earl of Warwick, overthrew her husband, her son, herself and almost the whole realm. Although, God be thanked, there be no such strong parties now, yet considering our enemies, which attend any occasions, it is better they were suppressed than continued.

Robert Beale, 'A Treatise of the Office of a Councillor and Principal Secretary to Her Majesty' (1592). Printed in Conyers Read, *Mr Secretary Walsingham and the policy of Queen Elizabeth*, vol. I, Oxford, 1925, Appendix, p. 441.

CHAPTER 4   GOVERNMENT AND THE GOVERNED

This chapter is about the techniques and problems of governing Tudor England. In the first section we start with the Council which, under the monarch, actually ran the country. Henry VII's Council had a large nominal membership, though most of its work was done by an inner core of bishops, nobles, and officers of the royal household. In 1526 Wolsey tried to eliminate the outer ring of the Council, and although nothing came of this during his lifetime, following his fall from power an inner or Privy Council of some twenty members emerged which, by 1540, had acquired its own clerk, charged with keeping an official record of its proceedings. Under Mary, the nominal membership of the Council increased, but the core of regular attenders was round about the Henrician figure. Elizabeth held membership down to a maximum of nineteen, and numbers tended to shrink as the reign went on.

The Council's most important role was to advise the monarch on policy – although such advice was not included in the minutes recorded by the clerk, which are today our main source for its activities. What does appear in the minutes is evidence of the remarkable scope and variety of the Council's administrative work. Technically, it was not a law court, although it could carry out investigations, make decisions, and even commit offenders to prison. However, most Council members also sat in the Court of Star Chamber which, like the Privy Council, had emerged out of the undifferentiated 'Council sitting in Star Chamber' of Henry VII's reign, and subsequently became a separate institution.

The second and third sections are about local government. One of the Council's most important functions was to act as the link between central and local government. A constant flow of messages, orders and reports passed between it and the JPs who controlled the localities. The status and work-load of these amateur, unpaid Justices steadily increased during the century. They became responsible for licensing alehouses, checking on recusants[†], overseeing the poor law, fixing wage rates, and many other things. The government did not have as much control over them as it would have liked, but if dissatisfied with a particular JP's performance it could always leave his name off the Commission of the Peace for the following year. The Quarter Sessions, a combination of law court and administrative meeting held four times a year in county towns, was the JPs' main arena, but they also did much work singly, or in smaller meetings that eventually acquired the name of Petty Sessions. As judges, they dealt with breaches of the peace and misdemeanours; more serious crimes (felonies) were passed on to the Assize courts held twice yearly in larger towns.

The smallest unit of local government was the parish, which in the sixteenth century was taking over the role formerly played in this sphere by the manor. Like JPs, parish officials – churchwardens, constables, and overseers of the poor – were unpaid and amateur. To be a parish constable was a troublesome, possibly dangerous, task, and one to be avoided if at all possible. The office of churchwarden conferred more prestige and might well be passed round among the prosperous yeomen of the parish. It is important to remember that most people would have come into contact far more with these minor officials than with anyone representing the central government.

One of the major ways in which the royal government affected the citizen was through taxation, which is the subject of the last section. The crown's income can be divided into 'ordinary' and 'extraordinary', the latter being sanctioned by Parliament. The most important of the 'ordinary' sources were the crown lands, which formed the basis of Henry VII's restoration of the royal finances after the troubles of the fifteenth century. The dissolution of the monasteries greatly increased this source but much of the newly acquired land had been sold off by the end of the Tudor period. Other sources included customs duties and also feudal dues, much exploited by Henry VII. Of these feudal revenues, purveyance (see **Doc. 92**) acquired special importance under Elizabeth, as did wardship – the crown's right to act as guardian of an under-age heir, with all the opportunities for profit that this entailed.

At the close of the Middle Ages the main parliamentary tax was the 'Fifteenth and Tenth', which had originally been levied on movable goods but had by this date become frozen into a standard charge yielding about £30,000. Wolsey established a new tax, the Subsidy, based upon up-to-date assessments of individual wealth, but unfortunately for the crown the same process occurred again, and the yield of the Subsidy steadily declined, not least because local gentry were unwilling to assess themselves and their friends too realistically. Various other efforts to increase revenue were tried, such as the so-called 'Amicable Grant' of 1525 which nearly provoked rebellion. Another expedient, later in the century, which aroused intense resentment was the crown's practice of granting monopoly rights in the sale or manufacture of certain articles to favoured individuals. These were desperate measures on the part of impoverished governments and they caused more ill-will than they were worth. What was really needed was a re-endowment of the crown, but this was not forthcoming under the Tudors.

The Council

71   Henry VII's Council in session, 1486

At this fairly typical meeting, the King was present, along with Lord Chancellor Morton (at that time Bishop of Ely) and three other bishops. Five other clerics attended, as well as thirteen lay peers, including Lord Treasurer Dynham, and twelve household officials, of whom the most notable were Sir Reginald Bray and Sir Thomas Lovel.

£6000... to be paid to the province of Biscay, so that the provinces of Biscay and Guipuzcoa [*in Spain*] keep to us firm peace and amity.

A truce to be taken with Brittany for [the] term of both Princes' lives, and one year after as touching the intercourse of merchandise.

Proclamation to be made against Richard Michell of the County of Northampton.

Thomas Green enjoined [on a] *subpoena* [of] 1000 marks[†] to appear on Thursday next, and to endeavour himself to bring forth the four persons that were at the slaying of [Sir Richard] Delabere's man at Westminster Bridge.

The Lord Grey of Ruthen and Thomas Greene enjoined to bring in surety for their good habearing [*behaviou*r], hanging [*pending*] the discussing of the riot.

The Lord Mautravers and Delawarr to bring in their bills [*written statements*] tomorrow, upon their riots.

It is concluded and agreed that every lord and gentleman, if any of his servants make a riot or other excess, the master of the same trespasser shall have in commandment to bring forth the same servant; and if he so do not, to abide such direction and punition [*punishment*] as by the King and his Council shall be thought convenient. And over that, if the same riot or excess arise because... of any quarrel or displeasure concerning the master of him that so exceedeth, the same master shall answer for the same excess such wise as shall be thought to the King and his Council expedient.

From G.C. Bayne and W.H. Dunham (eds), *Select Cases in the Council of Henry VII*, 1958, p. 11.

72   The new Privy Council, 1540

Twelve days after the execution of Thomas Cromwell a 'Privy Council' of nineteen members met and resolved henceforth to provide itself with a professional bureaucracy. Whether this reform came about as a conscious and deliberate act of administrative reform by Cromwell, or in a more pragmatic manner, is uncertain.

The 10th day of August in the 32nd year of the reign of our sovereign lord King Henry VIII... an order was taken and determined by his Majesty by the advice of his Highness' Privy Council... That there should be a clerk attendant upon the said Council to write, enter and register all such decrees, determinations, letters and other

From Sir Harris Nicolas (ed.),
*Proceedings and Ordinances of the
Privy Council of England*, vol. VII,
1837, pp. 3–4.

such things as he should be appointed to enter in a book, to remain always as a ledger, as well for the discharge of the said councillors touching such things as they should pass from time to time, as also for a memorial unto them of their own proceedings; unto the which office William Paget, late the Queen's secretary, was appointed by the King's Highness and sworn in the presence of the said Council the day and year abovesaid.

73   The categories of Council business, 1600

The outstanding characteristic of the Council was its all-pervasiveness. John Herbert, one of its clerks, made the following analysis of Council business.

Memorandum: That all causes to be treated on in Council and resolved are either only for her Majesty, or betwixt party and party, or betwixt some party (either subject or stranger) and the Queen's Majesty.

The first doth handle principally questions and consultations of state, growing from foreign advertisements or some extraordinary accidents within the realm.

The second (between party and party) are very seldom heard particularly, but rather ended by overruling an obstinate person who is made to acknowledge his fault, or else the parties are remitted to some court of justice or equity[†], or recommended by some letters to some justices [*of peace*] in the country to compound the differences either by consent of the parties or by direction. Or, if the cause be great, then to write letters to some principal persons to have some circumstances better understood and examined concerning matter of fact, whereof the Council cannot be so well informed when they have only the suggestions of one party against another; upon which report it often happeneth that quarrels and differences are taken up by the Council when it appears clearly who is in default.

When there is anything in question wherein the Queen is a party, it is commonly either by the breach of peace or for some other title. If there be breach of peace the lords do either punish the offender by commitment [*imprisonment*], or do refer the matter to be further proceeded in in the Star Chamber, where great riots and contempts are punished. If it be matter of title [*property-rights*], then the lords refer it to the Queen's learned counsel, and recommend the same to the judges' care.

If there be some suits to the Queen of poor men, then do the lords endorse their petitions with their opinions, and recommend the dispatch to the secretary, or for the poorer sort to the master of the requests*.

From G.R. Elton, *The Tudor
Constitution*, 2nd edn,
Cambridge, 1982, pp. 105–6.

*The Court of Requests was a prerogative court, intended especially for the poor.

74   The Court of Star Chamber, 1565

The Council exercised a major influence on the whole machinery of justice in England, but its members also acted as judges in their own right when they dealt with matters affecting public order and state security. During Wolsey's period in office, when the Council's role in government declined, its judicial activities became formalised, and the Councillors sitting to do justice in Star Chamber developed into the Court of Star Chamber. After the creation of the Privy Council, the two bodies were formally separate, but all Privy Councillors were *ipso facto* judges of the Court of Star Chamber. (For details about the author of this extract, see **Doc. 52**.)

There is yet in England another court, of the which that I can understand there is not the like in any other country. In the term time . . . every week once at the least (which is commonly on Fridays and Wednesdays, and the next day after that the term doth end), the Lord Chancellor and the lords and other of the Privy Council, so many as will, and other lords and barons which be not of the Privy Council and be in the town, and the judges of England, specially the two chief judges, from nine of the clock till it be eleven do sit in a place which is called the Star Chamber, either because it is full of windows or because at the first all the roof thereof was decked with images of stars gilted. There is plaints heard of riots. Riot is called in our English term or speech, where any number is assembled with force to do anything . . . If the riot be found and certified to the King's Council, or if otherwise it be complained of, the party is sent for, and he must appear in this Star Chamber, where seeing (except the presence of the Prince only) as it were the majesty of the whole realm before him, being never so stout [*bold*] he will be abashed; and being called to answer (as he must come, of what degree soever he be) he shall be so charged, with such gravity, with such reason and remonstrance, and of those chief personages of England, one after another handling him on that sort, that, what courage soever he hath, his heart will fall to the ground, and so much the more when if he make not his answer the better, as seldom he can so in open violence, he shall be commanded to the Fleet [jail], where he shall be kept in prison in such sort as these judges shall appoint him, lie there till he be weary as well of the restraint of his liberty as of the great expenses which he must there sustain, and for a time be forgotten, whiles after long suit of his friends he will be glad to be ordered by reason. Sometimes, as his deserts be, he payeth a great fine to the Prince, besides great costs and damages to the party, and yet the matter wherefor he attempteth this riot and violence is remitted to the common law. For that is the effect of this court, to bridle such stout noblemen or gentlemen which would offer wrong by force to any manner men, and cannot be content to demand or defend the right by order of law.

This court began long before, but took great augmentation and authority at that time that Cardinal Wolsey, Archbishop of York, was Chancellor of England, who of some was thought to have first devised the court because that he, after some intermission by negligence of time, augmented the authority of it, which was at that time marvellous necessary to do, to repress the insolency of the noblemen and gentlemen of the north parts of England, who being far from the King and the seat of justice made almost as it were an ordinary war among themselves and made their force their law . . .

From Sir Thomas Smith, *De Republica Anglorum*, ed. L. Alston, Cambridge, 1906, pp. 115–18.

75 Examples of Council business, 1565–74

These are some illustrations of the wide-ranging work of the Elizabethan Council taken from the Council minutes.

(a)

At Greenwich, the viiith of July, 1565.

German miners
  A letter to the mayor and other officers of Newcastle that where there be presently certain Almaynes [*Germans*], to the number of xl or l, looked for to arrive at that town within these x days, they are willed to cause the said Almaynes to be for their money courteously received and used, and by their good order guided and conducted from Newcastle to Keswick in Cumberland, the place where they are appointed to rest and work.

(b)

At Westminster, the xiith of January, 1566/67. [*In Tudor England the old, Julian, calendar was still in use, and the new year began on 25 March instead of 1 January. This means that 12 January 1566 was, in modern usage, 1567. Hence, the convention of giving such dates as 1566/67.*]

A warrant to Sir Frauncys Knolles, knight, Treasurer of the Chamber, to deliver, by way of the Queen's Majesty's reward, to Sebastian Westcote, Master of the Children of Powles [*St. Paul's*], for presenting two plays before her Highness at Christmas last past, the sum of xiii*li* vi*s* viii*d*, that is to say, vi*li* xiii*s* iiii*d* for every play.

(c)

At Oatelandes [*in Surrey*], the xxth of June, 1570.

A letter to Justice Southcoote to cause one Thomas Androws, presently prisoner in the Marshalsey, to be brought to the Tower and offered the torture of the rack there, and examine him of his knowledge touching a very heinous murder lately committed in Somerset shire, whereof the said Androws is vehemently suspected, and will hitherto confess nothing, although he hath been divers times examined thereupon; and after he shall have taken his confession, the said Mr Southcote is willed to return him to the Marshalsey again, to be further proceeded withall according to the order of the law.

(d)

At Greenwich, the xiiith of March, 1572/73.

A warrant to the Treasurer of the Chamber to deliver to Jeffrey Hall, Keeper of the gaol in the town of Sandwich, for charges in sending up letters to the Council and prisoners, the sum of vi*li* xiiis iiii*d*.

(e)

At Greenwich, the xith of May, 1573.

A letter to the Lord Cobham to take order with the town of Hastings for sending up of certain persons that intended to pass the seas, and were before examined by the Bailiffs and Jurattes there and thereupon stayed.

(f)

At Hampton Court, the xxist of February, 1573/74.

Three letters to the Justices of Peace and Sheriffs of the counties of Berks, Bedford and Hertford at their next Sessions to call in all licences granted to badgers [*corn dealers*], who inordinately, by procuring hands [*letters*] from one Justice of Peace to another, bought up corn to sell it dearer again; and there to admit only so many and such as they should think convenient, and in the shire town to set up their names that it might be known who were admitted, and for how long; and generally to have good regard that neither by forestalling, regrating [*buying up and re-selling at a higher price*] or other deceitful and corrupt dealings the price of corn be enhanced; with a postscript to communicate these with the Justices of Assizes* and to take their advice therein.

*See **Doc. 83**.

(g)

At Bristowe [*Bristol*], the xvith of August, 1574.

Two letters, one to the Earl of Bedford and the other to the Lord President of Wales, to send out of each of their provinces a hundred soldiers, most part of them shotte [*musketeers*], of those numbers which they were appointed by her Majesty's letters to be put in a readiness for her Majesty's service in Ireland; the said ii c to be embarked in place most convenient to be transported to Waterford, to enter into wages at the day of their embarking, and from thenceforth their victuals to be defalked [*deducted*] upon their wages.

(h)

At Hampton Court, the xxiind of November, 1574.

A letter to the Earl of Derby and the Bishop of Chester in answer of a letter from the said Bishop of this present touching their proceedings against certain obstinate persons in the county of Lancashire for matters of religion, and that their Lordships should have now some conference together to take order for the redress thereof, as by the Commission sent unto them of late for that purpose they be directed; and further that they should cause, by all means possible they can, such Popish persons to be apprehended as are suspected to have reconciled themselves to the Pope, that they may be particularly examined as well upon the said point of reconciliation as any other their behaviour or doings that shall be found contrary to her Majesty's laws, and to proceed to the punishment thereof as is appointed by their said commission.

From J.R. Dasent (ed.), *Acts of the Privy Council of England*, New Series, vol. VII, AD 1558–1570, 1893, (a) p. 229, (b) p. 322, (c) p. 367; vol. VIII, AD 1571–1575, 1894, (d) p. 89, (e) p. 105, (f) p. 197, (g) p. 282, (h) p. 317.

76   'Like so many kings', 1603

The Venetian agent, Scaramelli, reporting back to the Doge and Senate on 7 April 1603, describes an audience with the Council at the very end of Elizabeth's reign when the Queen was on her deathbed.

I accordingly went down to Richmond, although it was Easter Day, and found all the Palace, outside and in, full of an extraordinary crowd, almost in uproar, and on the tip-toe of expectation. I was immediately introduced into the Council Chamber. There I found sitting on long benches, on each side of a table, the Lord Chancellor, the Treasurer, the High Admiral, the Equerry, the Lord Chief Justice of England, the Treasurer and the Controller of the Royal Household, the Chancellor of the Exchequer, and others not Peers but Knights. They numbered eleven in all, and no one was missing except the Archbishop of Canterbury, who is Primate of England and President of the Council as well. I was received with every mark of respect for your Serenity, although, as I have already reported, these Lords of the Council behave like so many kings. They compelled me to sit down on a brocaded chair at the head of the table, and listened to me with gracious and friendly mien.

After touching slightly on the Queen's illness, I set forth as briefly as I could the instructions given me in your Serenity's dispatch of the fifteenth of February about the ship *Veniera*, seized by William Piers with all its cargo, to the value of a hundred thousand ducats. I dwelt on the insult offered to the person of the Consul da Mosto, the Republic's representative, and through him to your Serenity yourself; and I insisted on the continued mischief wrought by English subjects and pointed out that unless these grave excesses were vigorously remedied here serious consequences for the subjects of both nations must inevitably follow ... They all with one voice declared that should it please God to send the stolen goods and the thief into their hands, your Serenity would be fully satisfied ... My demands ... seemed reasonable to the Lords of the Council. They promised to give the matter every attention and to send their decision to my lodging, and with this they gave me courteous leave.

From Horatio F. Brown (ed.), *Calendar of State Papers ... in the Archives ... of Venice*, vol, IX, 1592–1603, 1897, no. 1171, pp. 567–8.

Justices of the Peace and Assize Judges

77 The right to appeal against JPs, 1489

Henry VII's concern for justice in the countryside is shown in this Act (3 Henry VII, cap. 12) passed early in his reign.

The King our Sovereign Lord considereth that by the negligence, misdemeaning, favour and other inordinate causes of the Justices of Peace in every shire of this his realm, the laws and ordinances made for the politique weal [*welfare*], peace and good rule of the same, and for the profit, surety and restful living of his subjects of the same, be not duly executed according to the tenor and effect that they were made and ordained for. Wherefore his subjects be grievously hurt and out of surety of their bodies and goods, to his great displeasure; for to him is nothing . . . more joyous than to know his subjects to live peaceable under his laws and to increase in wealth and prosperity . . .

For repressing and avoiding of the said mischiefs, sufficient laws and ordinances [have been] made, by authority of many and diverse parliaments holden within this realm, to the great cost of the King, his Lords and Commons of the same. And [there] lacketh nothing but that the said laws be not put in due execution, which laws ought to be put in execution by the Justice of Peace in every shire of this realm, to whom his Grace hath put and given full authority so to do since the beginning of his reign. And now it is come to his knowledge that his subjects be little eased of the said mischiefs by the said Justices, but by many of them rather hurt than helped. And if his subjects complain to these Justices of Peace of any wrongs done to them they have thereby no remedy . . .

[Therefore] he chargeth and commandeth all manner of men, as well the poor as the rich, which be to him all one in due ministration of justice, that is hurt or grieved in anything that the said Justice of Peace may hear or determine or execute in any wise, that he so grieved make his complaint to the Justice of Peace that next dwelleth unto him, or to any of his fellows, and desire a remedy. And if he then have no remedy, if it be nigh such time as his [*the King's*] Justices of Assizes* come into that shire, that then he so grieved show his complaint to the same Justices. And if then he have no remedy, or if the complaint be made long after the coming of the Justices of Assizes, then he so grieved come to the King's Highness or to his Chancellor for the time being, and show his grief. And his said Highness then shall send for the said Justices, to know the cause why his said subjects be not eased and his laws executed. Whereupon, if he find any of them in default of executing of his laws in these premises according to this his high commandment, he shall do [*cause*] him so offending to be put out of the Commission [of Peace], and further[more] to be punished according to his demerits.

From *The Statutes of the Realm*, vol. II, 1816, pp. 537–8.

*See **Doc. 83**.

78   Petty Sessions, 1574

By this date Norfolk justices were finding it convenient to hold, in addition to the Quarter Sessions, frequent divisional meetings which were beginning to assume a regular pattern.

Upon the Wednesday, being market day there [*Acle, near Norwich*], the Bishop, with certain gentlemen and chief yeomen thereabouts, do meet once in three weeks or a month, at ix of the clock, when they first repair to the church there and spend one hour in prayer and preaching, the chief effect whereof is to persuade love, obedience, amity, concord, etc. That done they return to their inn, where they dine together at their own charges, observing the law for Wednesday [*a fish day*]. In the meanwhile, between sermon ended and dinner, they go to the said house of Bridewell [*the town jail*] to consider and examine how all things there are provided and ordered, as well for their due punishment and reasonable work as for their meat and necessaries, without which often sight and overseeing the said house and orders would come quickly to nothing. After dinner, if any chief constable there prove of any disorder or misdemeanour within their Hundreds[†], redress whereof belongeth to the Justices of Peace, which else would require the said constables further travel to some Justice's house, if he will complain of it there, the offender is either openly punished or other order taken as the cause requireth. And if, besides all this, there be any private controversies between poor neighbours, whereof the Hundred court had wont to be full, they bestow the rest of the day in entreating them to peace one with another, by accord between themselves or by arbitrament of their nearest neighbours.

From A. Hassell Smith,
County and Court: Government and Politics in Norfolk 1558–1603,
Oxford, 1974, p. 104.

79   The Quorum, 1565

The increase in the Justices' work raised questions of organisation. One answer was the provision for a Quorum[†], to ensure that important matters should not be considered without the presence of at least one of a small nucleus in each county of trusted or legally trained members. (For details about the author of this extract, see **Doc. 52**.)

The justices of peace be men elected out of the nobility, higher and lower, that is the dukes, marquises, barons, knights, esquires and gentlemen, and of such as be learned in the laws, such and in such number as the prince shall think meet, and in whom for wisdom and discretion he putteth his trust, inhabitants within the county; saving that some of the high nobility and chief magistrates for honour's sake are put in all or in the most of the commissions of all the shires of England. These have no time of their rule limited but by commission from the Prince alterable at pleasure.

At the first they were but 4, after 8, now they come commonly to 30 or 40 in every shire, either by increase of riches, learning, or activity in policy and government. So many more being found which have either will or power or both, are not too many to handle the affairs of the commonwealth in this behalf. Of these in the same commission be certain named which be called of the Quorum[†], in whom is especial trust reposed, that where the commission is given to 40 or 30, and so at the last it cometh to 4 or 3, it is necessary for the performance of many affairs to have likewise divers of the Quorum. The words of the commission be such, *Quorum vos A.B., C.D., E.F. unum esse volumus* [*of whom we wish you . . . to be one*].

From Sir Thomas Smith, *De Republica Anglorum* (1583), ed. L. Alston, Cambridge, 1906, pp. 85–6.

80   Wiltshire justices in Quarter Sessions, 1578

This extract gives some idea of the variety of the justices' work.

Warminster, Sessions of the Peace held Tuesday after the close of Easter, 8 April 20 Elizabeth, before John Zouche, Walter Hungerford, James Mervyn, John Danvers and Thomas Wroughton, knights; John Eyre, Giles Escourt, William Hussey, Christopher Dodington, William Brouncker, Giles Thistlethwaite and Jasper More, esquires, Justices of the Peace.

Travers. Edward Meryvale the elder and John Meryvale . . . yeomen[†], plead not guilty to an indictment[†] for trespass . . .

[*Alehouse*]. Edward Charlton of Warminster, yeoman, bound in £5, and his sureties, William Brent, alias Martin, husbandman[†], and John Carpenter, yeoman . . . each in 5 marks[†] . . .

The fine of the inhabitants of Laverstock tithing[†] for not repairing the Queen's highway is taxed at 2s. 6d . . .

Constables elected. William Barter and John Moore for Dunworth Hundred[†] . . .

Ordo. It is ordered at this court that William Poton, gentleman, shall pull up the hedge which he hath made . . .

Pro Pace [*for the peace*]. Peter Polden of Chittern, yeoman, bound in £10, and his sureties, Walter Miles of the same, husbandman, and William Moulton of Maiden Bradley, chapman [*a small trader*], each in £5, for his appearance at the next Sessions, and for his keeping the peace, particularly towards Katherine Spender . . .

It is ordered at this court that Charles Sandell and Joan Long, whom he begat with child, shall be whipped . . .

Warrant of the peace granted against William Vernall of Deverell Langbridge, weaver . . .

Pro Bene Gerendo [*for good behaviour*]. John Gawen of Tynhed, husbandman, bound in £20, and his sureties, Robert Blackborow, clothier, and Richard Glover, baker, both of the same, each in £10, for his appearance at the next Sessions, for beating a tithingman[†], for which he stands indicted . . .

Pro Pace. Katherine Spender of Imber, widow, bound in £10, and

From H. C. Johnson (ed.), *Wiltshire County Records. Minutes of Proceedings in Sessions, 1563 and 1574–1592*. Wiltshire Archaeological and Natural History Society, 1948, pp. 38–40.

her sureties[†], Walter West, yeoman, and Peter Saw, husbandman, both of the same, each in £5 for her keeping the peace, particularly towards Peter Butcher . . .

Memorandum. That Peter Polden hath promised the court that he will not disturb the quiet possession of Katherine Spender, widow, until he hath recovered the same by law; and that the said Spender shall pay the said Polden one bushel of wheat.

Memorandum. The said bushel of wheat is paid in court.

81   Menaced by vagrants, 1596

Edward Hext, a Somerset JP, writes to Burghley in September 1596 of the threat posed by organised gangs of vagrants at a time of dearth and disorder in the countryside.

Of this sort of wandering idle people, there are three or four hundred in a shire: and though they go by two or three in a company, yet all or the most part of a shire do meet, either at fairs or markets, or in some alehouse, once a week . . . And they grow the more dangerous in that they find they have bred that fear in Justices and other inferior officers that no man dares call them into question. And at a late Sessions, a tall man, a man sturdy and ancient traveller, was committed by a Justice, and brought to the Sessions and had judgement to be whipped. He present at the bar, in the face and hearing of the whole bench, swore a great oath that if he were whipped it should be the dearest whipping to some that ever was. It struck such a fear in him that committed him as he prayed he might be deferred until the Assizes, where he was delivered [*freed*] without any whipping or other harm; and the Justice glad he had so pacified his wrath. And they laugh themselves at the lenity of the law and the timorousness of the executioners of it.

From John Strype, *Annals of the Reformation*, vol. IV, Oxford, 1824, pp. 410–11.

82   Justices of the Peace: a less favourable view, 1587

Edwin Sandys, Archbishop of York, in a letter to Lord Treasurer Burghley, gives his opinion of the Justices of the Peace in Yorkshire and Nottinghamshire.

I have noted in a paper, herein enclosed, such as in mine opinion may be well put out of the commission [of the peace], and given some reasons why . . . I deal with no knights, lest I should be noted to follow affection; but I assure you some of them be of the baddest sort, unworthy to govern, being so far out of order themselves. One man hath brought in the most part, who will be offended if any be brought in without him. And to speak the truth, although there be many gentlemen in Yorkshire, yet it is very hard to choose fit men for that purpose. And if none should be in commission but such as are rated at £20 for the subsidy, you should put out half of those that be in, as I suppose.

Robert Lee. He is a notable open adulterer, one that giveth great offence and will not be reformed. He useth his authority as well to work private displeasure as to serve other men's turns. A very bad man, and one that doth no good. Better put out than kept in.

Peter Stanley. A man noted to be a great fornicator. Of small wisdom, and less skill. One that is little in subsidy, but in only to serve turns. Ever at commandment without further respect. A man of none account.

Thomas Wentworth. A very senseless blockhead, ever wronging, and wronging his poor neighbours, being a great grain-man himself. He bought grain in the beginning of last year in every market, so much as he could, and heaped it up in his houses to sell at the dearest. He dependeth wholly upon him that brought him in, and will serve all turns. If you look into the subsidy book, you shall find him little there.

Francis Alford. This man liveth much at London. He hath no wife. A man of small living, less skill, of no countenance. One that may be very well spared.

Brian Lascelles. He is a man full of quarrels and contentions, one that maketh divisions, maintaining evil causes, bolstering out evil matters, ever in law, and one that only liveth by other men's losses.

From John Strype, *Annals of the Reformation*, vol. III, Oxford, 1824, part II, pp. 463–4.

83   The Assize Judges at work, 1576

The Assize Courts were higher courts held twice a year in county towns. They were staffed by judges of the central law courts from London whose role was to try difficult and important cases and also to survey local administration.

Kingston Assizes, July 1576. Before John SOUTHCOTE, J, and Thomas GAWDY, J.

LUXFORD, William, of London, labourer, indicted[†] for grand larceny[†]. On 15 April 1576 at Godstone he stole a cow (26s. 8d.) from John Bedyll. *Guilty. Allowed [benefit of] clergy*[†].

HOLLYDAY, William, of Croydon, labourer, indicted for highway robbery. On 31 March 1576 he assaulted Robert Ware in the highway at Lambeth and stole from him 15s. in money, a black cloak (7s.) and a dagger (3s. 4d.). *Guilty. To hang.*

PARKER, Robert, and BETTS, Thomas, labourers of Southwark, indicted for grand larceny. On 22 July 1576 at Southwark they stole 2 cows (£2) and a calf (5s.) from an unknown man. *Not guilty.*

TAYLOR, Robert, of Guildford, yeoman[†], indicted for grand larceny. On 12 February 1576 at Guildford he stole £6 in money and a silver ring (5s.) from Abraham Parvys. *Guilty. Allowed clergy.*

SURE, Joan, of Battersea, spinster, indicted for grand larceny. On 14 May 1576 at Penge in Battersea she stole a shirt (1s.), a smock

(1s.), a green woollen carpet (1s.), 2 linen aprons (1s.), a hat (1s.) and a pair of woman's hose (8d.) from William Trewe. On 14 May 1576 at Battersea she stole 3s. 1d. in money from William Mouncker. *Guilty. Remanded because pregnant, and pardoned by general pardon in 1581.*

FOYLE, John, LEVENSON, Robert, and WALLE, Richard, hatmakers of Southwark, indicted for infringing the statute regulating the making of hats. On 1 July 1576 they engaged more than two apprentices each, contrary to the Act 8 Eliz. cap. 11. *Verdict unknown.*

BROCKHALL, George, of Betchworth, clerk, indicted for witch-craft. On 19 July at Betchworth he bewitched to death a bull (£2) belonging to William Ponder. *At large. Tried in February 1577 and found Not guilty.*

TARRENTEN, Simon, of London, silkweaver, indicted for murder. By an inquisition held at St. Saviour, Southwark, 26 June 1576, before Thomas Agar, coroner, on the body of Joan Smith, aged 15 years, a jury ... found that on 20 December 1575, in Golden Lane, Middlesex, Tarrenten assaulted Smith, his servant, with a bedstaff and a bobbin, inflicting injuries to several parts of her body. She was taken to the house of Helen Hudson, her mother, in St. Saviour, and then to St. Thomas's Hospital, Southwark, where she died on 15 June 1576. *Not guilty. Pardoned by general pardon.*

From J. S. Cockburn (ed.), *Calendar of Assize Records, Surrey Indictments, Elizabeth I,* 1980, pp. 147–8.

Parish Officials

84   The oath of a constable

The form of oath to be taken by a new parish constable shows how demanding were the duties of this office, at any rate in theory.

The Form of the Oath concerning the office of a Constable.

You shall swear, that you shall well and truly serve our Sovereign Lord the King in the office of a Constable. You shall see and cause his Majesty's peace to be well and duly kept and preserved according to your power. You shall arrest all such persons as in your sight and presence shall ride or go armed offensively, or shall commit or make any riot, affray, or other breach of his Majesty's peace. You shall do your best endeavour (upon complaint to you made) to apprehend all felons[†], barrators [*brawlers*], and rioters, or persons riotously assembled. And if any such offender shall make resistance (with force) you shall levy hue and cry[*], and shall pursue them until they be taken. You shall do your best endeavour that the watch in and about your town be duly kept for the apprehending of rogues, vagabonds, night-walkers, eavesdroppers, scouts [*spies*], such as go armed, and the like; and that hue and cries be duly raised and pursued ... against murderers, thieves, and other felons. And that the statutes made for the punishment of rogues and vagabonds, and such other idle persons, coming within your bounds and limits, be duly put in execution. You shall have a watchful eye to such persons as shall maintain or keep any common house or place where any unlawful game is or shall be used; as also to such as shall frequent or use such places, or shall use or exercise any unlawful games there, or elsewhere, contrary to the statutes. At your Assizes, Sessions of the Peace, or Leet [*manor court*] you shall present all and every the offences done contrary to the statutes made to restrain the inordinate haunting and tippling in inns, alehouses, and other victualling houses, and for repressing of drunkenness. You shall there likewise true presentment make of all blood-sheddings, affrays...and other offences committed or done against the King's Majesty's peace within your limits. You shall once every year, during your office, present at the Quarter Sessions all popish recusants[†] within your parish, and their children above 9, and their servants...And you shall have a care for the maintenance of archery according to the statute. You shall well and duly execute all precepts and warrants to you directed from the Justices of Peace of this county. And you shall well and duly, according to your knowledge, power and ability, do and execute all other things belonging to the office of a Constable, so long as you shall continue in this office. So help you God.

From Michael Dalton, *The Countrey Justice*, 1635, pp. 363–4.

*See **Doc. 86**.

85   Setting the watch

In *Much Ado About Nothing* Shakespeare makes fun of Constable Dogberry's instructions to the town watch before they start their night patrol.

DOGBERRY: You are thought here to be the most senseless and fit man for the constable of the watch; therefore bear you the lantern. This is your charge: you shall comprehend all vagrom men; you are to bid any man stand, in the prince's name.

SECOND WATCH: How if a' will not stand?

DOGBERRY: Why, then, take no note of him, but let him go; and presently call the rest of the watch together, and thank God you are rid of a knave.

VERGES: If he will not stand when he is bidden, he is none of the prince's subjects.

DOGBERRY: True, and they are to meddle with none but the prince's subjects. You shall also make no noise in the streets; for the watch to babble and talk is most tolerable and not to be endured.

FIRST WATCH: We will rather sleep than talk: we know what belongs to a watch.

DOGBERRY: Why, you speak like an ancient and most quiet watchman; for I cannot see how sleeping should offend: only, have a care that your bills [*billhooks*] be not stolen. Well, you are to call at all the ale-houses, and bid those that are drunk get them to bed.

FIRST WATCH: How if they will not?

DOGBERRY: Why, then, let them alone till they are sober: if they make you not then the better answer, you may say they are not the men you took them for.

FIRST WATCH: Well, sir.

DOGBERRY: If you meet a thief, you may suspect him, by virtue of your office, to be no true man; and, for such kind of men, the less you meddle or make with them, why, the more is for your honesty.

FIRST WATCH: If we know him to be a thief, shall we not lay hands on him?

DOGBERRY: Truly, by your office, you may; but I think they that touch pitch will be defiled: the most peaceable way for you, if you do take a thief, is to let him show what he is, and steal out of your company.

From William Shakespeare, *Much Ado About Nothing*, Act III, Scene iii.

86 The hue and cry

A major duty of the parish constable was the catching of criminals. William Harrison, writing in the 1570s, describes the workings of the system, and its defects.

For the better apprehension also of thieves and man-killers there is an old law in England very well provided, whereby it is ordered that if he that is robbed or any man complain and give warning of slaughter or murder committed, the constable of the village where-unto he cometh and crieth for succor is to raise the parish about him and to search woods, groves and all suspected houses and places where the trespasser may be or is supposed to lurk; and not finding him there he is to give warning unto the next constable, and so one constable, after search made, to advertise another from parish to parish till they come to the same where the offender is harboured and found. It is also provided that if any parish in this business do not her duty but suffereth the thief (for the avoiding of trouble sake), in carrying him to the jail if he should be apprehended or other letting of their work, to escape, the same parish is not only to make fine to the King but also the same, with the whole hundred[†] wherein it standeth, to repay the party robbed his damages and leave his estate harmless. Certes, this is a good law; howbeit, I have known by my own experience felons[†], being taken, to have escaped out of the stocks, being rescued by other for want of watch and guard; that thieves have been let pass because the covetous and greedy parishioners would neither take the pains nor be at the charge to carry them to prison, if it were far off; that when hue and cry have been made even to the faces of some constables, they have said, 'God restore your loss! I have other business at this time.' And by such means the meaning of many a good law is left unexecuted, malefactors emboldened, and many a poor man turned out of that which he hath sweat and taken great pains for toward the maintenance of himself and his poor children and family.

From William Harrison, *Description of England* (1577), ed. George Edelen, Ithaca, New York, 1968, pp. 194–5.

87   City administration, 1547

The sixteenth-century records of larger towns show a proliferation of officials, appointed by the city council, exercising vigilant supervision over every aspect of urban life. The following extracts are from the records of Ipswich.

I. E. VI, Monday after Candlemas [*7 February 1547*].

The 12 Headburrows shall go quarterly about the town . . . and they shall view the annoyances of the town. And they shall be warned thereto by a serjeant, and all defaulters warned shall forfeit 5s., and at such a day as the Headburrows shall bring in their books (which shall be within 8 days after enquiry) the Chamberlains shall deliver them 5s. towards their charges. And the Bailiffs shall quarterly levy all the amercements [*fines*] before the next quarter after the presentment shall be brought in.

I. E. VI. Wednesday ye 12 of Octob. [*1547*].

Constables nominated; three to each ward. All muck shall be carried out of the houses, yards, and streets into such common places as are appointed, or other places, provided that it be no nuisance to the town nor the people inhabiting there or repairing there . . . The Headburrows shall give order to every of the inhabitants to pathe the streets, every one against their own houses, gardens, and yards, by a certain day, and under a certain pain [*fine*] by them limited. And they shall present the defaulters that shall suffer their hogs to go abroad in the streets, and every person that is owner of such hogs shall for such default forfeit 4d.

The Constables are allowed to licence victuallers within the town and all offenders without their licence shall forfeit 12d. for every day's transgression.

No person shall keep open his shop or shop window upon Sunday after 8 of the clock in the morning under the forfeiture of 12d. for every offence. Nor shall any beer brewer carry beer on that day, under the like penalty for every offence.

From Nathaniel Bacon, *The Annals of Ipswich* (1654), ed. William H. Richardson, Ipswich, 1884, pp. 226, 228–9.

88   Churchwardens' accounts, 1599

The office of churchwarden was an ancient one, but the Elizabethan Poor Law gave churchwardens important new secular duties.

The accounts of the churchwardens and overseers of the poor in the parish of Staplegrove [Somerset] for the year last past. This account stood before her Majesty's Justices on the 11th day of April in Anno Domini 1599.

A note what every man hath paid to this collection this whole year that was set weekly to the poor.

George Poyre	11s.
John Wuse	18s.

. . . .

William Hit before he had his apprentice	8s. 4d.
Thomas Perrett before he had his apprentice	5s.
Wat Gale before he had his apprentice	6s. 8d.
John Chattocke before he had his apprentice	6s. 8d.

. . . .

A note of every man's name that keep any poor body and them that hath taken apprentices.

Roger Smith keepeth William Harvy, *Impot.* ['*impotent*', *or unable to look after himself*].
Walter Knight keepeth Christine Fort, *Impot.*
Nicholas Cornishe keepeth Harry Gale as apprentice
William Hit keepeth Mamwell Brice as apprentice

. . . .

The names of all them that have received collection and every one of them have received as follows.

first Jone Cole have received	29s.
Richard Rison & his wife received	57s.

. . . .

To Christian Fort in her sickness and for wood	3s. 9d.
To John Gould's burial	12d.
To the tithingman[†] for relieving the poor strangers that were brought to him	12d.
We have laid out before Christmas for clothes for the poor & for wood and apparel for the apprentices	38s.

. . . .

Churchwardens	Hugh Portman
	John Colles
	John Frances
	Thomas Beaton
	Thomas Perett & Bartholmew Sindercomb.
Overseers	Richer Smyth, Water Knight
	Nicholas Cornish & John Chattocke.

From E. M. Leonard, *The Early History of English Poor Relief,* Cambridge, 1900, pp. 327–30.

The Income of the Crown

89   A forced loan, 1492

Henry VII raised considerable sums by demanding loans from prosperous subjects. These included Sir Henry Vernon, to whom the following letter was sent.

Trusty and well-beloved, we greet you well, letting you witte [*know*] that, as well by our spies that we have in the parts beyond the sea, as otherwise, we understand that our enemies of France prepare themself to do all the hurt and annoyance that they can compass and devise to this our realm and subjects of the same; for the resisting and subduing of whose malicious purpose we shall, with God's grace, sufficiently provide and put us with a good multitude of our subjects in defensible readiness for the same intent, which can in no wise be done without great substance of good. Wherefore we, holding for undoubted that ye bear a singular tenderness to such things as concern the surety and universal weal and tranquillity of our said realm and subjects, desire and heartily pray you that ye will lend unto us the sum of £100, and to send it unto our Treasurer of England by some trusty servants of yours, to the intent that they may receive bills of him for contentation [*satisfaction*] thereof again. And we faithfully promise you by these our letters that ye shall have repayment or sufficient assignment upon the half quinzame [*Fifteenth*[†]] payable at Martinmass [*11 November*] next coming, whereunto ye may verily trust, wherein you shall not only do unto us [a] thing of great and singular pleasure, but also cause us to have you therefore more specially recommended in the honour of our grace in such things as ye shall have to pursue unto us hereafter. Given under our signet[†] at our manor of Greenwich the 26th day of April.

From *Historical Manuscripts Commission*, 12th Report, Appendix, part IV, *The Manuscripts of the Duke of Rutland*, 1888, pp. 13–14.

90   'Persons by His Grace wronged', 1509

Towards the end of his reign Henry VII's careful budgeting turned into avarice and rapacity. This was admitted by Edmund Dudley before his execution by Henry VIII.

The petition of me Edmund Dudley, the most wretched and sorrowful creature, being a dead man by the King's laws, and prisoner in the Tower of London, there abiding life or death at the high pleasure of my Sovereign Lord (to whom I never offended in treason or thing like to it to my knowledge, as my sinful soul be saved)... And forasmuch as the mind and last will of the said late King was especially that restitution should be made to all persons by his grace wronged, contrary to the order [of] his laws, which things would in my poor mind be specially regarded: I have perused my books touching all such matters as I was privy unto, and in this quire [of paper] hereafter have written such persons as I think were hardly intreated and much more sorer than the causes required... And also the pleasure and mind of the King's grace, whose soul God pardon, was much set to have many persons in his danger at his pleasure, and that as well spiritual men as temporal men; wherefore divers and many persons were bound to his grace... in great sums of money... It were against reason and good conscience [that] these manner of bonds should be reputed as certain debts, for I think verily his inward mind was never to use them. Of those there are very many...

Item, one obligation of my lord [Bishop] of London for £500 to be had at the King's pleasure, and a recognizance[†] of £300 to be paid at certain days. He was hardly dealt withal herein, for he said unto me, by his priesthood the matter laid against him was not true...

Item, Sir Thomas Bucler of Lancashire made a recognizance of 1000 marks[†] to hang at the King's pleasure for an old outlawry, over and besides 300 marks which he is bound to pay for his pardon for the same.

Item, the King's grace had of one Hubbard for the office of weighing of wools at Hampton 50 marks; which Hubbard never had the office, but one Troyes had it...

Item, the Earl of Northumberland was bound to the King in many great sums. Howbeit, the King's mind was to have payment of £2000 and of no more, as his grace showed me. Yet that was too much for ought that was known.

Item, the Lord Abergeny [*Abergavenny*] had a very sore end, for any proof that was against him to my knowledge.

Item, the Bishop of Salisbury paid 1000 marks for a very light cause...

Item, the order of Cistercians paid £5000, which was too much for the matter laid against them...

Item, Peter Centurion, a Genenois, was evil intreated and paid much money and upon malicious ground, in my conscience...

Item, the King had the substance of Nicolas Nives' goods, by reason of another man's obligation given unto his grace, for his wife and his creditors had nothing...

Item, one Hastewood was kept long in prison and paid a great sum of money, upon a light ground...

Item, one Curl, a poor man, paid £50 for wools at Calais, to his utter undoing, upon a light surmise only...

Item, a poor gentleman of Kent called Roger Appleton paid 100 marks upon an untrue matter...

Item, the King had of the Prior of Eysborne [*Easebourne, Sussex*] threescore pounds or thereabout, without any good ground...

From C. J. Harrison, 'The Petition of Edmund Dudley', *English Historical Review*, vol. 87, 1972, pp. 86–9.

91 Objections to the 'Amicable Grant', 1525

To finance the war with France Wolsey attempted to raise what was in effect a forced loan or benevolence.

When this matter was opened through England, how the great men took it was marvel: the poor cursed, the rich repugned [*opposed*], the light wits railed, but in conclusion all people cursed the Cardinal and his co-adherents as subversor of the laws and liberty of England. For, they said, if men should give their goods by a commission, then were it worse than the taxes of France, and so England should be bond and not free.

It happened at Reading, in Berkshire, that the commissioners sat for this money to be granted, and the people in no wise would consent to the sixth part: but of their own mere mind, for the love they bore to the king, they granted the twelfth part, that is, 20d. of the pound. The commissioners hearing this, said they would send to the Cardinal, desiring him to be content with this offer, and so the Lord Lisle wrote the letter, so that Sir Richard Weston would bear it; the which letter, at the request of the gentlemen of the country, the said Sir Richard took upon him to carry, and rode to the Cardinal: which therewith was sore grieved, and said, but because that the Lord Lisle wrote that the matter was but communed of and not concluded, it should cost the Lord Lisle his head, and his lands should be sold to pay the king the values that by him and you foolish commissioners he had lost, and all your lives at the king's will. These words sore astonished Sir Richard Weston, but he said little.

Then the Cardinal wrote letters to all commissioners of the realm that they should keep their first instruction, and in no wise to swerve one jot, upon pain of their lives ... But for all that could be persuaded, said, lied and flattered, the demand could not be assented to, [the people] saying that they that sent forth such commissioners were subverters of the law and worthy to be punished as traitors.

From Hall's *Chronicle*; printed in Charles Wibley (ed.), *The Lives of the Kings: Henry VIII*, 1904, vol. II, pp. 36–7.

92 Purveyance, 1594

'Purveyance' was the term used to describe the crown's right to requisition food supplies for the Court at lower than market prices. This applied mainly to the counties near London, but the system was widely abused and aroused intense resentment.

Articles of agreement and composition had and made the 4th day of April, *anno* 35 Elizabeth, between the right honourable the Lords of her Majesty's most honourable Privy Council ... and the worshipful George More [etc.] ... being authorized to compound and conclude for the delivery of certain provisions towards the expenses of her Majesty's most honourable house[hold] out of the county of Surrey, as hereafter follows:

First, that one hundred fat and great veals of the age of six weeks and upwards shall be delivered at the court gate...at 6s. 8d. the piece.

Item, that ten good flitches of bacon, without gammons...be delivered at the court gate upon Good Friday, at 12d. the piece.

Item, that fifty fat and good lambs shall be delivered at the court gate...at 12d. the piece.

Item, that 16 doz. capons at 4s. the doz.; 10 doz. hens, at 2s. the doz.; 30 doz. pullets, at 18d. the doz.; 5 doz. geese, at 4s. the doz.; and 100 doz. chickens, at 12d. the doz. shall be delivered at London or elsewhere upon one month's warning given to the compounders, or to any two justices of peace of the said shire...

Item, that ready money shall be paid for the said veals, bacon, lambs and poultry, immediately upon the receipt of the same.

Item, if any person or persons inhabiting within the said shire shall wilfully refuse to pay and contribute towards these provisions...that then...a pursuivant shall be sent down to apprehend and bring before their honours all such persons so refusing, to answer their contempt.

From Alfred John Kempe (ed.), *The Losely Manuscripts*, 1836, pp. 272–3.

93   The debate on monopolies, 1601

Monopolies were royal grants allowing one or more individuals the sole right to import, sell or manufacture a particular commodity. During the war years, when Elizabeth's government was under acute financial pressure, it vastly increased the number of monopolies, much to the discontent of the public.

[20 November]

Mr. Lawrence Hide said: 'To end this controversy, because the time is very short, I would move the House to have a very short Bill read, entitled "An act of explanation of the common law, in certain cases of letters-patents[†]." ' And all the House cried, 'I,I,I' ...

Mr Francis Bacon said, ' ... For the prerogative-royal of the Prince, for my own part I ever allowed of it; and it is such as I hope I shall never see discussed. The Queen, as she is our sovereign, hath both an enlarging and restraining liberty of her prerogative: that is, she hath power by her patents to set at liberty things restrained by statute law or otherwise. And by her prerogative she may restrain things that are at liberty...The use hath been ever by petition to humble ourselves to her Majesty, and by petition to desire to have our grievances redressed – especially when the remedy toucheth her so nigh in prerogative...I say, and I say again, that we ought not to deal, or meddle with, or judge of her Majesty's prerogative. I wish every man, therefore, to be careful in this point' ...

Doctor Bennet said, 'He that will go about to debate her Majesty's prerogative royal must walk warily. In respect of a grievance out of that city for which I serve, I think myself bound to speak that now which I had not intended to speak before. I mean, a monopoly of salt. It is an old proverb, *Sal sapit omnia* [*salt flavours everything*]. Fire and water are not more necessary. But for other monopolies, of cards (at which word Sir Walter Rawleigh blushed), dice, starch, etc. they are (because monopolies) I must confess very hateful, though not so hurtful. I know there is a great difference in them' . . .

Mr Francis Moore said 'Mr Speaker, I know the Queen's prerogative is a thing curious to be dealt withal. Yet all grievances are not comparable. I cannot utter with my tongue, or conceive with my heart, the great grievances that the town and country for which I serve suffer by some of these monopolies. It bringeth the general profit into a private hand, and the end of all is beggary and bondage to the subject . . . And to what purpose is it to do anything by Act of Parliament when the Queen will undo the same by her prerogative? Out of the spirit of humility, Mr Speaker, I do speak it: there is no act of hers that hath been, or is, more derogatory to her own majesty, or more odious to the subject, or more dangerous to the commonwealth, than the granting of these monopolies'.

Mr Martin said, 'I speak for a town that grieves and pines, and for a country that groaneth under the burthen of monstrous and unconscionable substitutes [*deputies*] to the monopolitans of starch, tin, fish, cloth, oil, vinegar, salt, and I know not what – nay, what not? The principal commodities both of my town and country are ingrossed into the hands of these bloodsuckers of the commonwealth' . . .

[25 November]

Mr. Speaker, after a silence (and every one marvelling why the Speaker stood up), spake to this effect: 'It pleased her Majesty to command me to attend upon her yesterday in the afternoon. From whom I am to deliver unto you all her Majesty's most gracious message, sent by my unworthy self. She yieldeth you all hearty thanks for your care and special regard of those things that concern her state and kingdom . . . She said that, partly by intimation of her Council, and partly by divers petitions that have been delivered unto her, both going to chapel and also walking abroad, she understood that divers patents that she had granted were grievous unto her subjects, and that the substitutes of the patentees had used great oppression. But, she said, she never assented to grant anything that was *malum in se* [*evil in itself*]. And if in the abuse of her grant there be anything that is evil, which she took knowledge there was, she herself would take present order for reformation thereof'.

From Heywood Townshend, *Historical Collections, or An exact Account of the Proceedings of the Four last Parliaments of Q Elizabeth of Famous Memory*, 1680, pp. 230–4, 248.

94   The grant of tonnage and poundage, 1509–10

During the Tudor period a life grant of the customs duties known as tonnage and poundage was made to every sovereign by the first Parliament of his or her reign.

We, your poor Commons, by your high commandment come to this your present Parliament for the shires, cities and boroughs of this your noble realm, by the assent of all the Lords spiritual and temporal in this present Parliament assembled, grant by this present indenture[†] to you our sovereign lord, for the defence of this your said realm, and in especial for the safeguard and keeping of the sea, a subsidy called tonnage, to be taken in manner and form following: that is to say, 3s. of every tonne of wine coming into this your said realm. And of every tonne of sweet wine coming into the same your realm, by every merchant alien . . . 3s. over the said 3s. afore granted; to have and to perceive [*receive*] from the first day of this present Parliament for time of your life natural.

And over that, we your said Commons . . . grant to you our sovereign lord, for the safeguard and keeping of the sea, another subsidy called poundage: that is to say, of all manner merchandises of every merchant denizen [*native*] and alien . . . carried out of this your said realm or brought into the same by way of merchandise, of the value of every 20s., 12d . . . To have and perceive yearly the said subsidy of poundage from the first day of your most noble reign during your life natural.

Printed in *The Statutes of the Realm*, vol. III, 1817, p. 21.

95   Parliamentary subsidy, 1571, 1598

(a) Although the subsidy was devised in the early Tudor period as a substitute for the customary Fifteenth and Tenth[†] (which now yielded a mere £30,000 or so, and took no account of changes in the distribution of wealth), in practice the older tax continued to be granted at the same time as the subsidy, thereby increasing the total yield to the crown. The following extract is from the Subsidy Act of 1571 (13 Elizabeth I, cap. 27).

Considering your Majesty's both careful travail and happy success, by the great providence of God, in government of this your realm (most mighty and redoubted sovereign), whereby not only we have been so long time kept in peace with foreign realms, and quiet within ourselves, more happily than in any former time we can find to have been; and that the same most happy estate hath been of late attempted by certain evil-disposed, unnatural and unkind subjects of your Majesty, enemies to God and to your Highness, to be interrupted*; which evil, unnatural, popish and rebellious attempt, although by the great grace of God . . . and your Highness' great providence and inestimable charges, was and hath been soon brought to an end, yet it hath been discomfort to us, your loving subjects, grief to your Highness, and great waste unto your treasure. Therefore we, most humble, loving and obedient subjects, the Lords spiritual and temporal and the Commons in this present Parliament assembled, have thought it – for those and other many great and urgent occasions – no less than our duty to offer to your Highness for part of a supply of that your Majesty hath borne and is like to bear, not only in repressing the said rebels but also in providing against foreign attempts which in and after such cases are not wont to be unready, one little and small present, the which most humbly and on our knees we pray your most excellent Majesty to accept in good part, not weighing the smallness thereof, but the goodwill of our minds: that is, Two Fifteenths and One Subsidy ... to be paid, taken and levied of the movable goods, chattels and other things usual to such Fifteenths ... And the said Two Fifteenths ... to be paid in manner and form following: that is to say, the first whole Fifteenth ... to be paid to your Highness ... before the twentieth day of October which shall be in the year of our Lord God one thousand five hundred threescore and twelve [1572] ...

From *The Statutes of the Realm*, vol. IV, 1819, p. 568.

*The reference is to the Rebellion of the Northern Earls at the end of 1569.

(b) The yield of the subsidy, for reasons which are made apparent in the following document, steadily declined after Henry VIII's reign, and did not even keep pace with inflation.

[*A letter from the Council to the Commissioners for the first payment of the Subsidy, 26 July 1598*]

Whereas you are appointed Commissioners for the assessment of the first Subsidy granted by the last Parliament ... we have thought good also to put you in mind (as heretofore we have done) of that care we think meet you should use in the performance and furtherance of this service, considering therefore the excessive charge her Majesty is daily put unto for the necessary defence of her realm and loving subjects, both by sea and land, far greater than any her predecessors have sustained. And yet these Subsidies, of later times, have come to far less sums than those of former ages; which cannot grow but by the remiss and neglectful dealing of such as are the Commissioners for the assessment of the same ... You cannot perform the trust reposed in you, nor your duties towards her Majesty and your country, if you proceed not in this service with great care and endeavour to advance the sums and assessments as much as may be, in assessing all men indifferently that are of ability, without regard of any favour. For it hath been noted heretofore that this burden is laid on the meaner sort, who, though they contribute small sums, yet they are less able indeed to bear the burthen; and the wealthier and best able to spare the same are too favourably dealt withal, the Commissioners (for the most part) bearing one with another, and every of them bearing with their own private friends and followers. Which fault it is looked for at this time that

From J. R. Dasent (ed.), *Acts of the Privy Council of England*, new series, vol. XXVIII, *AD 1597–98*, 1904, pp. 625–7.

you will carefully redress, and not slightly peruse (as ordinarily you do) your former books and rates, to ease yourselves of trouble and keep one rate and rule, but inform yourselves of the true ability [to pay] of every man, and to see them assessed in some good proportion as they ought to be . . . Herein if you would perform your duties with that sincerity and care as you ought to do, and give good example in not sparing yourselves, no doubt the sum of this necessary contribution would be greatly increased, and her Majesty should not need to require so often Subsidy.

CHAPTER 5   ECONOMY AND SOCIETY

This chapter looks at various aspects of economic and social life in sixteenth-century England. The first section is about the growth of population, and also about inflation, which was possibly the highest in English history before the twentieth century. By 1520 the wage and price stability typical of the previous century was over; from now on both wages and prices climbed steeply, especially during the mid-century, and again in the 1590s. Among the causes of this inflation were the increased pressure on resources brought about by a growing population, and the severe debasements of the coinage by Henry VIII after 1544 and subsequently by Protector Somerset. The population of England went up from something over two million in 1500 to about four million by 1600. This may have been due to a decline in mortality; there were fewer major epidemics such as plague or 'sleeping sickness' (a virulent form of influenza) than previously. It is also likely that the average age of marriage was coming down slightly, resulting in a higher birth-rate. Such tentative statements can only be made owing to the fact that parish registers started to be kept from 1538 onwards.

The second section concerns vagrancy and poverty. The main element in price inflation was the rise in food prices which kept ahead of wage increases and naturally most affected the landless poor. Contemporaries' growing concern about beggars and vagrants resulted in a series of poor laws being passed between 1531 and 1601. These set up an increasingly sophisticated system, based on the parish, for dealing with the different categories of pauper. Many of the government's measures, such as the levying of a compulsory poor rate and the provision of work for the 'able-bodied' poor, were copied from cities like London and Norwich which had earlier pioneered local systems of poor relief. The comprehensive Elizabethan poor law, given its final form in the Acts of 1598 and 1601, was undoubtedly one of the major achievements of the Tudors, and was to last almost unchanged until the nineteenth century.

The great Statute of Artificers (1563), which is the focus of the third section, was another major legislative achievement, although it was basically a conservative rather than an innovative measure, concerned with preserving the socio-economic status quo. It was passed partly as a reaction to higher wage demands caused by temporary labour shortages resulting from the economic dislocation of the 1550s. This Act greatly increased the workload of JPs, who were expected not only to regulate local wages, but also to prevent those who had not been apprenticed from pursuing a craft, and to direct unemployed men into husbandry and unemployed women into domestic service.

The last section is about farming, and in particular the question of enclosures. One major effect of price inflation was to reward with higher profits the enterprising farmer who could succeed in improving productivity or enlarging his landholding. Many middling gentry and yeomen did just this, and one of the techniques they used was enclosure. This meant either amalgamating landholdings previously held in the form of separate strips, or actually 'enclosing' such holdings with fences or hedges, while also extinguishing the communal rights of others over the land so that more intensive methods of cultivation could be followed. There was much opposition to such measures, on the part of intellectuals, the poor and dispossessed themselves, and governments, which were worried about the military implications of 'depopulation'. However, authors like Thomas Tusser were right to stress the increased productivity often brought about by enclosure. The effects were to be felt in the next century when England ceased to suffer from periodic nation-wide famine.

Population and Inflation

96   Cromwell's Injunctions, 1538

The Injunctions[†] issued by Thomas Cromwell in 1538 required all parish priests to keep a register in which to record births and deaths. Not all priests complied, and those who did so varied in efficiency. Yet the surviving parish registers, however unsatisfactory from the point of view of present-day historians, are the basis on which estimates of population have to depend.

This extract is from the Second Royal Injunctions of Henry VIII, 1538, drawn up by Cromwell and issued by Archbishop Cranmer to all archdeacons.

Item, that you, and every parson, vicar, or curate within this diocese, shall for every church keep one book or register, wherein ye shall write the day and year of every wedding, christening, and burying made within your parish for your time, and so every man succeeding you likewise; and also there insert every person's name that shall be so wedded, christened, or buried; and for the safe keeping of the same book, the parish shall be bound to provide of their common charges one sure coffer with two locks and keys, whereof the one to remain with you, and the other with the wardens of every such parish, wherein the said book shall be laid up; which book you shall every Sunday take forth, and in the presence of the said wardens, or one of them, write and record in the same all the weddings, christenings, and buryings made the whole week before, and that done, to lay up the book in the said coffer as before; and for every time that the same shall be omitted, the party that shall be in the fault thereof shall forfeit to the said church three shillings and fourpence, to be employed on the reparation of the same church.

From Henry Gee and William John Hardy (eds), *Documents Illustrative of English Church History*, 1896, p. 279.

97   Population estimates and plague

(a) The following estimates, drawn up by two modern demographers, show that population was increasing at an average rate of 1 per cent a year between 1540 and 1590, with the exception of the late 1550s, and also the 1590s.

		Percentage increase since last total	*Compound annual percentage growth rate since last total*
1541	2,773,851		
1546	2,853,711	2.88	0.56
1551	3,011,030	5.51	1.08
1556	3,158,664	4.90	0.96
1561	2,984,576	−5.51	−1.13
1566	3,128,279	4.81	0.94
1571	3,270,903	4.56	0.90
1576	3,412,722	4.34	0.85
1581	3,597,670	5.42	1.06
1586	3,805,841	5.79	1.13
1591	3,899,190	2.45	0.49
1596	4,011,563	2.88	0.57
1601	4,109,981	2.45	0.49

From E. A. Wrigley and R. S. S. Schofield, *The Population History of England 1541–1871*, 1981. Table 7.8, pp. 208–9.

(b) The inhabitants of Tudor England were always at risk from plague, influenza, and the vagaries of the weather which could lead to a series of harvest failures. When all these came together, the strains on the social system were enormous, as were the risks of political upheaval. The following table indicates the months and also the years – notably 1557–59 and 1597 – when the Tudor State was in crisis.

A month without an asterisk indicates a death-rate at least 25 per cent above what was usual. One asterisk implies a rate 50–99 per cent above average; two asterisks +100 per cent.

1542	Dec
1543	Jan–Feb* April – May* Oct
1544	July Oct* Nov – Dec
1545	Jan Sept – Oct* Nov
1546	May June – July*
1547	Feb May June*
1550	July
1551	July** Aug Dec
1556	Sept Dec
1557	June – July Aug – Oct* Nov** Dec*
1558	Jan – Feb* March – April July Aug – Dec**
1559	Jan – April** May*
1560	March May – June
1563	April – May June – July* Aug – Oct
1564	Oct
1566	April

1570   Sept – Oct
1571   Jan
1573   March
1574   Feb
1578   March
1579   Jan
1580   May   July
1584   Sept
1587   Aug – Sept
1588   Jan – Feb*   May
1590   Aug*   Oct
1591   March – April   Aug
1592   Sept   Dec
1593   Jan – Aug
1597   Jan   March   May*   June   July*   Sept – Dec
1598   Jan – Feb
1603   May – July   Aug – Oct*   Nov

From E. A. Wrigley and
R. S. Schofield, *The Population
History of England 1541–1871*,
1981. Table 8.13, pp. 338–9.

98   Wheat prices and wage rates

(a) Agricultural day wage rates in southern England. These are median
rates for ordinary day-to-day agricultural operations performed by male
workers – for example, hedging, ditching, spreading dung. Seasonal tasks –
for example, haymaking – were normally paid at higher rates.

Decade	d.*	Decade	d.*
1470–79	4.00	1540–49	4.66
1480–89	3.75	1550–59	6.33
1490–99	4.00	1560–69	7.00
1500–09	4.00	1570–79	8.17
1510–19	4.00	1580–89	8.00
1520–29	4.17	1590–99	8.66
1530–39	4.33	1600–09	8.66

Adapted from Peter Bowden,
'Statistical Appendix', in Joan
Thirsk (ed.), *The Agrarian History
of England and Wales*, vol. IV,
1500–1640, 1967, p. 864.

*d. = pennies. See note to **Doc. 3**.

(b) Movement of wheat prices in England, 1480–1625.

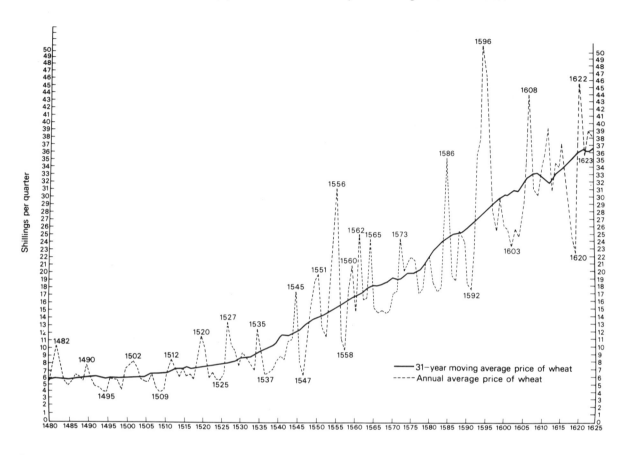

From W. G. Hoskins, *The Age of Plunder*, 1976, Appendix II, p. 246.

99   The causes of inflation

This extract is from a treatise probably written by John Hales in 1549 but first printed – with appropriate amendments to bring it up to date – in 1581.

Knight   If this [*the debasement of the coinage*] were the chiefest cause of the dearth [*dearness*], as of very good probability (by you, master Doctor) heretofore alleged, it should seem to be; how cometh it to pass (where as you say, if the cause be removed the effect is also taken away) that the prices of all things fall not back to their old rate, whereas now long since our English coin (to the great honour of our noble Princess, which now reigneth) hath been again thoroughly restored to his former purity and perfection?

Doctor ... I find therefore two special causes, in mine opinion, by means of the which, notwithstanding that restitution made in our coin, the aforesaid dearth of things (in respect of the former age) remaineth yet among us. The first is, that whereas immediately after the baseness of our coin in the time of King Henry the eight, the prices of all things generally among all sorts of people rose: it must needs happen here withall (as ye know) that our gentlemen which lived only upon the revenues of their lands were as near or nearer touched (as is before proved) with the smart hereof than any other, of what order or estate soever. This therefore being taken as most true, the gentlemen, desirous to maintain their former credit in bearing out the porte [*style of life*] of their predecessors, were driven of necessity as often as when soever any leases devised for term of years, by themselves or their ancestors, were thoroughly expired and fell into their hands, not to let them out again for the most part, but as the rents of them were far racked [*raised*] beyond the old: yea, this racking and hoisting up of rents hath continued ever since that time, until this present day: hereupon the husbandman[†] was necessarily enforced, whereas his rent was now greater than before (and so continueth unto this day), to sell his victuals dearer, and to continue the dearth of them: and likewise other artificers[†] withall to maintain the like proportion in their wares.

. . . Another reason I conceive in this matter to be the great store and plenty of treasure which is walking in these parts of the world, far more in these our days than ever our forefathers have seen in times past. Who doth not understand of the infinite sums of gold and silver which are gathered from the Indies and other countries, and so yearly transported unto these coasts? As this is otherwise most certain, so doth it evidently appear by the common report of all ancient men living in these days. It is their constant report that in times past, and within the memory of man, he hath been accounted a rich and wealthy man and well able to keep house among his neighbours which (all things discharged) was clearly worth xxx or xl pounds; but in these our days the man of that estimation is so far (in the common opinion) from a good housekeeper, or man of wealth, that he is reputed the next neighbour to a beggar. Wherefore these ii reasons seemed unto me to contain in them sufficient probability for causes of the continuance of this general dearth.

From E. Lamond (ed.), *A Discourse of the Common Weal of this Realm of England*, 1893, pp. 186–8.

Vagrancy and Poverty

100 'An Act against vagabonds and beggars', 1495

The wording of this Act (2 Henry VII, cap. 21) reveals that the problem of vagrancy exercised governments well before the sixteenth century.

For as much as the King's grace most entirely desireth amongst all earthly things the prosperity and restfulness of this his land and his subjects of the same, to live quietly and surefully to the pleasure of

God and according to his laws, willing and always of his pity intending to reduce them thereunto by softer means than by such extreme rigour therefore provided in a statute made in the time of King Richard the second . . . his Highness will [that] by the authority of this present Parliament it be ordained and enacted that . . . constables and petty constables and all other governors and officers of cities, burghs, towns, townships, villages and other places, within three days after this Act proclaimed, make due search, and take or cause to be taken all such vagabonds, idle and suspect persons living suspiciously, and them so taken to set in stocks, there to remain by the space of three days and three nights and there to have none other sustenance but bread and water; and after the said three days and three nights to be had out and set at large, and then to be commanded to avoid the town . . . And if any person or persons give any other meat or drink to the said misdoers being in stocks in form aforesaid, or the same prisoners favour in their misdoing, that then they forfeit for every time so doing twelve pence.

And also it is ordained by the said authority that all manner of beggars not able to work, within 6 weeks next after proclamation made of this Act, go rest and abide in his hundred[†] where he last dwelt, or there where he is best known or born, there to remain or abide without begging out of the said hundred, upon pain to be punished as is beforesaid.

From *The Statutes of the Realm*, vol. II, 1816, p. 569.

101   Municipal poor relief, 1547, 1570

The main features of the Elizabethan poor law were anticipated by local schemes, in London and other cities.

(a) In 1547 a compulsory poor rate was levied in London.

It is . . . this day by the Lord Mayor, aldermen and commons in this present Common Council assembled, and by authority of the same, ordained . . . that the citizens and inhabitants of the said city shall forthwith contribute and pay towards the sustentation, maintaining and finding of the said poor personages by the space of one whole year now next ensuing the moiety or half deal of one whole Fifteenth[†]. And that the said weekly collection of the devotion of the people [*the previous voluntary collection*] for that intent and purpose shall from henceforth utterly cease and be discharged . . . And it is also enacted and agreed by the said authority that it shall be lawful for all and every the petty collectors of the said moiety or half deal of the said Fifteenth to distrain all and every person and persons that shall refuse or deny to content and pay all such sum and sums of money as he or they shall be assessed at towards the said payment.

From the *Guildhall Journal of the City of London*, printed in John Pound, *Poverty and Vagrancy in Tudor England*, 2nd edn, 1986, p. 100.

(b) In 1570, Norwich took a census revealing details of more than 2300 paupers in the city. This was followed by measures forbidding begging and setting the able bodied to work.

These being the names of the poor within the said city as they were viewed in the year of our Lord God 1570.
In the time of Mr John Alldereche, mayor . . .
The Ward of South Consforthe.
Names of the poor to be relieved weekly.
In St Peters of Southgate.

In the house of Robert Susling. No alms and very poor but able to work. Richard Bitche of the age of 35 years, a husbandman[†] which worketh with Mrs Cantrell and keepeth not with his wife (but at times) and helpeth her a little. And Margarit his wife of the age of 40 years she spins white warp and Jone her daughter, of the age of 12 years, that spins also the same. And Simond her son of the age of 8 years that go to school. And Alice and Faithe the eldest of the age of 8 years and the other of the age of 3 years. And have dwelt here two years and since Whitsuntide and have dwelt most part at Banham where they were married and since at Swanton next Norwaltham and Amringall . . .

From the 'Mayor's Book for the Poor', Norwich; printed in E. M. Leonard. *The Early History of English Poor Relief*, 2nd edn, 1965, p. 308.

102 Rogues and vagabonds, 1567

(a) One type of vagabond depicted in Thomas Harman's rogues' gallery was the so-called 'upright man'.

Of these ranging rabblement of rascals, some be serving men, artificers[†], and labouring men, traded up in husbandry[†]. These not minding to get their living with the sweat of their face, but casting off all pain, will wander after their wicked manner through the most shires of this realm: as Somersetshire, Wiltshire, Berkshire, Oxfordshire, Hertfordshire, Middlesex, Essex, Suffolk, Norfolk, Sussex, Surrey and Kent, as the chief and best shires of relief. Yea, not without punishment by stocks, whippings and imprisonment in most of these places abovesaid. Yet, notwithstanding, they have so good liking in their lewd, lecherous loitering, that full quickly all their punishments be forgotten . . .

These unruly rascals . . . disperse themselves into several companies, as occasion serveth, sometime more and sometime less. As, if they repair to a poor husbandman's[†] house, he will go alone, or one with him, and stoutly [*boldly*] demand his charity, either showing how he hath served in the wars and there maimed, [or] that he seeketh service, and saith he would be glad to take pain for his living (although he meaneth nothing less). If he be offered any meat or drink, he utterly refuseth scornfully, and will [have] nought but money. And if he espy young pigs or poultry, he well noteth the place, and then, the next night or shortly after, he will be sure to have some of them, which they bring to their . . . tippling houses ... For you must understand, every tippling alehouse will neither receive them or their wares; but some certain houses, in every shire, especially for that purpose, where they shall be better welcome to them than honester men, for by such have they most gain. And [they] shall be conveyed either into some loft, out of the way, or other secret corner ... And thither repair at accustomed times their harlots ... not with empty hands, for they be as skilful in picking ... and filching as the upright men, and nothing inferior to them in all kind of wickedness ...

If they ask at a stout yeoman[†] or farmer's house his charity, they will go strong, as three or four in a company; where, for fear more than goodwill, they often have relief ... If any search be made, or they suspected for pilfering clothes off hedges, or breaking of houses – which they commonly do when the owners be either at the market, church, or otherways occupied about their business – [or] rob some silly [*simple*] man or woman by the highway, as many times they do, then they hie them into woods, great thickets, and other rough corners, where they lie lurking three or four days together, and have meat and drink brought them by their ... doxies [*women*].

From Thomas Harman, *A Caveat or Warning for Common Cursetors, vulgarly called Vagabonds*, 1567, reprinted 1814, pp. 13–15.

(b) The frontispiece of Thomas Harman's book.

From A. V. Judges, *The Elizabethan Underworld*, 1930, facing p. 61.

103 'An Act for the setting of the poor on work', 1576

(a) This Act (18 Elizabeth I, cap. 3) was the first which required the parish to make provision for compulsory work for the unemployed.

Also, to the intent youth may be accustomed and brought up in labour and work, and then not like to grow to be idle rogues, and to the intent also that such as be already grown up in idleness, and so [be] rogues at this present, may not have any just excuse in saying that they cannot get any service or work . . . and that other poor and needy persons being willing to work may be set on work, be it ordained and enacted by the authority aforesaid, that in every city and town corporate . . . and . . . likewise in every other market town or other place . . . where, to the Justices of Peace . . . shall be thought most meet and convenient, a . . . competent store and stock of wool, hemp, flax, iron, or [such] other stuff as the country is most meet for . . . shall be provided. The said stores and stocks [shall] be committed to the hands and custody of such persons as shall by the mayor, bailiff, justices or other head officers . . . be appointed. Which said persons so appointed . . . shall from henceforth be called the Collectors and Governors of the Poor, to the intent every such poor and needy person, old or young, able to do any work, standing in necessity of relief, shall not (for want of work) go abroad either begging or committing pilferings or other misdemeanour . . . Which Collectors and Governors of the Poor from time to time (as cause requireth) shall and may of the same stock and store deliver to such poor and needy person a competent portion to be wrought into yarn or other matter . . . for which they shall make payment to them which work the same, according to the desert of the work, and of new deliver more to be wrought; and so from time to time to deliver stuff unwrought and receive the same again, wrought, as often as cause shall require. Which hemp, wool, flax or other stuff wrought from time to time, shall be sold by the said Collectors and Governors of the Poor either at some market or other place, and at such time as they shall think meet; and with the money coming of the sale, to buy more stuff, in such wise as the stock or store shall not be decayed in value. And if hereafter any such person able to do any such work shall refuse to work, or shall go abroad begging, or live idly . . . he, she or they . . . shall be received into such House of Correction, there to be straightly kept, as well in diet as in work, and also punished from time to time . . .

From *The Statutes of the Realm*, vol. IV, 1819, p. 611.

(b) An item from the Essex Quarter Sessions records shows how certain parishes had attempted to implement the Act of 1576, and the problem they faced in so doing.

Note from Roger Harlakinden [JP] reciting that the parish of Earls Colne and divers other parishes thereabouts being much charged with great numbers of poor people, the said people have of a long time been set on work by spinning wool of Dutchmen which they have delivered to the said poor people weekly at the town of Earls Colne aforesaid, and there received the same from them again being spun, whereby many of the said poor people have been and yet are relieved and maintained in good sort; but now of late certain evil disposed persons... having received some of the said Dutchmen's wool to spin, have sold and conveyed away the same to certain persons... so that the said Dutchmen have made complaint that unless the said offenders may be by some good and lawful course punished, and they themselves have some reasonable relief and restitution for their losses, which they say is very great to them, being poor men, they shall be forced to leave off their former course, and then it is to be feared the said poor people, being already very ill disposed, will grow to be out of all government and order.

From Alan Macfarlane (ed.), *Records of an English village: Earls Colne 1400–1750*, vol. 2, microfiche, 1980, item no. 204.00388.

104   Causes of poverty, 1594

The scholar William Lambarde here speculates as to some of the causes of contemporary poverty.

The dearth [*dearness*] of all things maketh likewise many poor, and that cometh either by the excessive enhancement of the rents of land, which hath now invaded the lands both of the church and Crown itself, or by that foul and cancerous sore of daily usury[†], which is already run and spread over all the body of the commonwealth, or by our immoderate use, or rather abuse, of foreign commodities, the which we (breaking all symmetry and good proportion) do make as vile and common unto us as our own domestical. But whether these only, or chiefly, or they with some other be the true causes of dearth, that is a disputation for another time, place and assembly. These I note that every man may have a conscience in them, lest through his fault dearth grow and consequently the number of the poor be increased by it.

   Lastly, the poor are exceedingly much multiplied because for the most part all the whole children and brood of the poor be poor also, seeing that they are not taken from their wandering parents and brought up to honest labour for their living but, following their idle steps... as they be born and brought up, so do they live and die, most shameless and shameful rogues and beggars.

   And to the increase of these evils, we have, as I said, a sort of poor lately crept in amongst us and not before known to our elders: I mean poor soldiers... when not only our gaols are scoured and our highways swept but also the channels of our streets be raked for soldiers, what marvel is it if after their return from the wars they do either lead their lives in begging or end them by hanging. Nevertheless we are by many duties most bound to help and relieve them, considering that they fight for the truth of God and defence of their country...

From Conyers Read (ed.), *William Lambarde and Local Government*, Ithaca, New York, 1962, pp. 182–4.

105   A begging licence, 1590

The war against Spain produced numbers of disabled soldiers and sailors for whom the government made no provision except permission to beg.

Charles Lord Howard, Baron of Effingham ... To all and singular viceadmirals, justices of peace, mayors, sheriffs, bailiffs, constables ... greeting. Whereas this bearer William Browne, of London gunner, lately served in her Majesty's service against the Spaniards, in the *Barke* of Feversham, and in that service was shot through his body, and grievously wounded in sundry places, and by means of the same maimed for ever: In consideration whereof, and for that I understand he is greatly indebted to his surgeons in the curing of his wounds, and otherwise brought to extreme poverty thereby. I have thought good to grant him these presents, and by authority hereof, in her Majesty's name do require [you] ... to help and relieve him with your charitable benevolence and alms towards the supplying of [his] great want, and to permit, suffer and assist [him] to gather and ask the same in all churches and chapels, and of all well disposed people ... wherein you shall do a deed very acceptable in the sight of God, and greatly comfortable to him, his said wife and children in this extremity, wherein we require you not to fail. This presents to endure for the space of twelve months, from the date hereof ...

From H. W. Hodges and E. A. Hughes, *Select Naval Documents*, Cambridge, 1927, pp. 30–1.

106   Poverty and death in Elizabethan London, 1593–98

London was a dirty and unhealthy place, especially for vagrants, and especially in the famine years of the 1590s, as is shown in these extracts from the burial register of the London parish of St Botolph's without Aldgate, 1593–98.

Edward Ellis a vagrant who died in the street.
A young man not known who died in a hay-loft.
A cripple that died in the street before John Awsten's door.
A poor woman, being vagrant, whose name was not known, she died in the street under the seat before Mr. Christian Shipman's house called the Crown ... in the High Street.
A maid, a vagrant, unknown, who died in the street near the Postern [Gate].
Margaret, a deaf woman, who died in the street.
A young man in a white canvas doublet ... being vagrant and died in the street near Sparrow's corner being in the precinct near the Tower.
A young man vagrant having no abiding place ... who died in the street before the door of Joseph Hayes, a brazier dwelling at the sign of Robin Hood in the High Street ... He was about 18 years old. I could not learn his name.

From A. L. Beier, *Masterless Men: the Vagrancy Problem in England 1560–1640*, 1985, p. 46.

Artificers and Apprentices

107 Regulating wages, 1561, 1563

(a) Even before the great Statute of Artificers of 1563, JPs had an obligation to lay down wage rates for the various categories of wage earners. Here, this duty is fulfilled by the Justices for Buckinghamshire in 1561.

The Queen Majesty's Justices of Peace within her Grace's county aforesaid, by her special commandment assembling themselves for the reformation of wages, and other misdemeanours as well of artificers[†], husbandmen[†], as also of labourers, with others, have, upon great consideration, set forth the rates and orders for the same severally as hereafter followeth, requiring and straightly charging and commanding in her Majesty's name all mayors, bailiffs, constables, officers and ministers ... to see the same executed. And if any person or persons shall refuse to yield himself to this order, then the same to be brought to the next Justice and to be by him committed to the gaol. And there to remain for one whole year, or else to be sent to the Council, if the quality of the person do so require ... And also the said Justices, in her said Grace's name, do command and charge that the said rates and orders shall be read and published in every parish church once in every month, upon a Sunday or holyday.

Rates for days wages during the time of harvest.

	With meat & drink	Without meat & drink		
A mower	v d.	viii d.	Mowers by the acre	
A man reaper	iiii d.	vii d.	oats	iiii d.
A woman reaper	iii d.	vi d.	grass	viii d.
A common labourer	iiii d.	vii d.	barley	v d.
Women rakers & cockers[x] & such like	} ii d.	v d.	{ And whereas cause is to give less, less to be given	

And for wheat or rye reaped by the acre xvi d.

	With meat & drink	Without meat & drink
Labourers From harvest to Hallowtide [*the first week in November*]	iii d.	vi d.
From Hallowtide to Easter	ii d.	v d.
From Easter to harvest	iii d.	vi d.

Artificers from Easter to Michaelmas [*29 September*]

	With meat & drink	Without meat & drink
The master carpenter & sawyer	vi d.	ix d.
Other men	iiii d.	vii d.

Bricklayers, tylers & thatchers
| | v d. | viii d. |
| Other men | iii d. | vi d. |

Artificers from Michaelmas to Easter
The master carpenter & sawyer
| | iiii d. | vii d. |
| Other men | iii d. | vi d. |

With meat & drink — Without meat & drink

Bricklayers, tylers & thatchers
| | iii d. | vi d. |
| Other men | ii d. ob [$^1/2d$.] | v d. |

From R. H. Tawney and Eileen Power (eds), *Tudor Economic Documents*, vol. I, 1924, p. 334.

*A 'cocker' was someone who raked the hay into small heaps or 'cocks'.

(b) The Statute of Artificers (5 Elizabeth I, cap. 4) 1563, made more specific the procedure for setting out maximum wages in each county, as prescribed in clause 11.

And for the declaration and limitation what wages servants, labourers and artificers[†], either by the year or day or otherwise, shall have and receive: Be it enacted by the authority of this present Parliament that the Justices of Peace of every shire...shall have authority by virtue hereof, within the limits and precincts of their several commissions, to limit, rate and appoint the wages, as well of such and so many of the said artificers, handicraftsmen...or any other labourer, servant or workman...and shall yearly, before the 12th day of July next after the said assessment and rates so appointed and made, certify the same...into the Queen's most honourable Court of Chancery[†], whereupon it shall be lawful to the Lord Chancellor...to cause to be printed and sent down, before the first day of September next after the said certificate, into every county...ten or twelve proclamations or more, containing in every of them the several rates appointed...Upon receipt whereof the said Sheriffs, Justices of Peace, and the Mayor and head officer in every city or town corporate, shall cause the same proclamation to be entered of record...and...shall forthwith in open markets, upon the market days before Michaelmas then ensuing, cause the same proclamation to be proclaimed...and the same proclamation to be fixed in some convenient place...

From *The Statutes of the Realm*, vol. IV, 1819, p. 417.

108 Compulsory apprenticeship, 1563, 1593

(a) Clause 24 of the Statute of Artificers (5 Elizabeth I, cap. 4) 1563, is concerned with tightening up the rules of apprenticeship.

Be it further enacted by the authority aforesaid that after the first day of May next coming it shall not be lawful to any person or persons, other than such as now do lawfully use or exercise any art, mystery[†] or manual occupation, to set up, occupy, use or exercise any craft...except he shall have been brought up therein seven years at the least as apprentice, in manner and form abovesaid, nor to set any person on work in such...occupation, being not a workman at this day, except he shall have been apprentice as is aforesaid, or else, having served as an apprentice...will become a journeyman[†] or be hired by the year: Upon pain that every person willingly offending or doing the contrary shall forfeit and lose for every default 40s. for every month.

From *The Statutes of the Realm*, vol. IV, 1819, p. 420.

(b) Here the State (that is, the Privy Council) is seeking to modify the effect of its own legislation in a particular case (1593).

A letter to the mayor and jurats [*justices*] of the town of Sandwich. There is one Repent Hubbard of that town who (as we are given to understand) has been heretofore a man of good substance and ability and become very poor by great losses at sea and otherwise; and not being able to follow his trade which before his decay he did use, having (as it should seem) a very honest care to live to maintain himself, his wife and children, has betaken himself to the occupation of a baker, and has used baking almost for these two years; and because he was never bound apprentice to that science he is threatened (as it is alleged unto us) to be sued upon the statute made in the 5th year of her Majesty's reign concerning apprentices. We have thought good, considering this poor gentlemen has an honest intent to live by his handy labour, and not meaning to charge or burden the town with his wife or children, to pray you to call such persons before you that have, or shall have at any time hereafter, any purpose to sue him upon the foresaid statute; and to entreat and require them in our names that they will be contented to tolerate him, and not to trouble or molest him by course of law, but that in respect of his great losses he may be permitted to use the said faculty, whereby he may be better able to maintain him, his poor wife and children. And so not doubting but they will show themselves herein conformable, being for so charitable a cause as this is, we bid, etc.

From J. R. Dasent (ed.), *Acts of the Privy Council of England*, new series, vol. XXIV, *AD 1592–93*, 1901, pp. 352–3.

109   Compulsory husbandry, 1563

(a) One aim of the Statute of Artificers (5 Elizabeth I, cap. 4) 1563, was to ensure a supply of labour for farmers. The following extract is taken from clause 5.

Be it further enacted by the authority aforesaid that every person between the age of twelve years and the age of three score years, not being lawfully retained...nor being a gentlemen born, nor being a student or scholar in any of the universities or in any school, nor having lands...of the clear yearly value of 40s...being worth in goods and chattels to the value of £10, nor having a father or mother then living, or other ancestor whose heir apparent he is, then having lands of the yearly value of £10 or above, or goods or chattels of the value of £40 ... nor being otherwise lawfully retained according to the true meaning of this statute, shall ... be compelled to be retained to serve in husbandry[†] by the year with any person that keepeth husbandry, and will require any such person so to serve within the same shire where he shall be so required.

From *The Statutes of the Realm*, vol. IV, 1819, p. 415.

(b) The provisions of the Statute of Artificers which made it compulsory for all persons not gainfully employed to serve in husbandry might be used by an unscrupulous employer as a threat, as the following extract (1563) illustrates.

Robart Myller, of the city of Norwich, tanner, of the age of 16 years or there about, examined before Mr William Farrow, mayor of the city of Norwich [and others] ... on Wednesday, 14th April, anno 1563, sayth: that he was in service with one William George of Hempton, tanner, and dwelt with him by the space of three years. And upon a time about seven-night before Candlemass [*2 February*] last past, the wife of the said William George did fall out with this examinate and rebuked him for his work very much. And this examinate said unto his dame: 'I am sorry that I cannot please you, but if my service may not please you, if you and my master will give me leave to depart I shall provide me of a service in some place, I trust'. And hereupon his said dame declared unto her husband the same night that the said Robart Myller could be content to go from him and to place himself in some other service. And thereupon he called this examinate unto him and asked him whether he would go from him or not. And he said: 'For that my service cannot please you nor my dame, if you will give me leave to depart I can be contented to depart'. And then the said William George, his master, said: 'With a good will you shall depart, and provide yourself of a master so well as you can'. And thereupon he drew to his purse and paid to this examinate seven shillings in money that he owed him for certain calf skins that he had sold of his. And on the Sunday morning this examinate came to his said master to take his leave. And then his said master said unto him saying: 'You will go away? You shall not go out of the hundred[†], but you shall serve either Mr Clyfton or else Mr Raymer in husbandry[†]'. And this deponent said: 'Master, I have served these three years in your occupation and can no skill in husbandry, and I will be loath to lose all this time that I have served in the occupation'. And then the said William George said: 'Tarry till Sunday and you shall have a new pair of shoes'; and so this examinate tarried still there with the said William George till the Tuesday next following, and in that time he had understanding that there was a warrant procured for him to serve in husbandry, and thereupon he came from his said master the said Tuesday ...

From a deposition in the Norwich Municipal Archives; printed in R.H. Tawney and Eileen Power (eds), *Tudor Economic Documents*, vol. I, 1924, pp. 350–1.

Enclosures and the Land

110 Farming regions in England

This is what its compiler describes as a very tentative map of farming regions, which may require amendment in the light of further local research. It shows the two main categories into which English farming was divided, which were: (i) the lowland area, roughly south and east of a line joining Teesmouth in the north east and Weymouth in the south west, in which mainly mixed farming under the medieval open field system predominated; (ii) the highland area to the north and west of this line, dominated by pasture farming, and where much of the land was enclosed without commotion before, during, or shortly after the Tudor period. An attempt has also been made here to refine further the two basic types into sub-divisions.

From Joan Thirsk, 'The Farming Regions of England', in Joan Thirsk (ed.), *The Agrarian History of England and Wales*, vol. IV, *1500–1640*, Cambridge, 1967, p. 4.

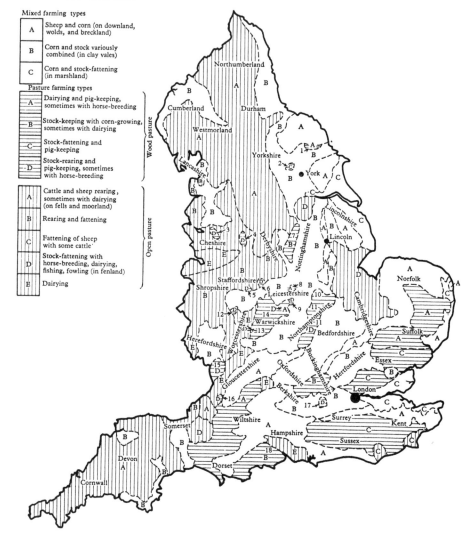

Mixed farming types

A Sheep and corn (on downland, wolds, and breckland)

B Corn and stock variously combined (in clay vales)

C Corn and stock-fattening (in marshland)

Pasture farming types

A Dairying and pig-keeping, sometimes with horse-breeding

B Stock-keeping with corn-growing, sometimes with dairying

C Stock-fattening and pig-keeping

D Stock-rearing and pig-keeping, sometimes with horse-breeding

Wood pasture

A Cattle and sheep rearing, sometimes with dairying (on fells and moorland)

B Rearing and fattening

C Fattening of sheep with some cattle

D Stock-fattening with horse-breeding, dairying, fishing, fowling (in fenland)

E Dairying

Open pasture

111   'Sheep eat men', 1516

Sir Thomas More's discussion at the beginning of *Utopia* represents the popular contemporary view of enclosures.

Your sheep, that were wont to be so meek and tame, and so small eaters, now, as I hear say, be become so great devourers and so wild that they eat up and swallow down the very men themselves. They consume, destroy and devour whole fields, houses and cities. For look in what parts of the realm doth grow the finest and therefore dearest wool, there noblemen and gentlemen, yea and certain abbots, holy men no doubt, not contenting themselves with the yearly revenues and profits that were wont to grow to their fore-fathers and predecessors of [*from*] their lands, nor being content that they live in rest and pleasure – nothing profiting, yea much annoying the weal public [*the public good*] – leave no ground for tillage [but] enclose all into pastures...

Therefore, [so] that one covetous and insatiable cormorant and very plague of his native country may compass about and enclose many thousand acres of ground together within one pale or hedge, the husbandmen[†] be thrust out of their own, or else either by covin [*deceit*] and fraud, or by violent oppression they be put besides [*deprived of*] it, or by wrongs and injuries they be so wearied that they be compelled to sell all. By one means, therefore, or by other, either by hook or crook, they must needs depart away, poor, silly [*simple*], wretched souls...All their household stuff, which is very little worth, though it might well abide the sale, yet being suddenly thrust out, they be constrained to sell it for a thing of nought. And when they have wandered abroad till that be spent, what can they then else do but steal   and then justly, pardy [*by God*], be hanged – or else go about a-begging?

From Sir Thomas More's *Utopia* (1516), translated into English by Raphe Robynson (1551), 1898 edn, pp. 18–19.

112   Intervention by the State, 1528, 1549

Lord Protector Somerset's attempts to restrict enclosure are part of a long paternalist tradition going back through Cromwell and Wolsey to the Middle Ages.

(a) The Bishop of Lincoln congratulates Wolsey on his efforts to reverse enclosures.

30 Sept. 1528. There was never thing done in England more for the Commonweal than to redress these enormous decays of towns and making of enclosures; 'for if your Grace did at the eyes see as I have now seen, your heart would mourn to see the towns, villages, hamlets, manor places, in ruin and decay, the people gone, the ploughs laid down, the living of many honest husbandmen[†] in one man's hand, the breed of mannery by this means suppressed, few people there stirring, the commons in many places taken away from

From J. S. Brewer (ed.),
Letters and Papers, Foreign and Domestic, of the reign of Henry VIII, vol. IV, part II, 1872, no. 4796, pp. 2076–7.

the poor people, whereby they are compelled to forsake their houses, and so wearied out and wot [*know*] not where to live, and so maketh their lamentation.' Never saw people so glad as they are now, hoping the King and Wolsey will see reformation made. They pray for the King and your Grace everywhere.

(b) The following extract comes from Somerset's instructions to the enclosure commissioners whom he appointed in 1549.

First, you shall enquire what towns, villages, and hamlets have been decayed and laid down by enclosures within the shire contained within your commission, since the fourth year of the reign of King Henry VII.

Item, what land was in tillage at the time of the said enclosures, and what was then in pasture.

Item, how many ploughs, by reason of the said enclosures, be decayed and laid down.

Item, how many meses [*habitations*], houses, cottages, and dwelling houses be fallen in decay, any the inhabitants of the same departed from their habitation there, by reason of enclosures taken away of the lands, or otherwise, and how much land belonged to the same.

Item, if any person have severed the lands from any house of husbandry[†], whereby it is made a cottage, a sheep house, a dairy house, or otherwise converted to any other use than for a dwelling place of an husbandman.

Item, by whom the said enclosures and decays were made, and how long ago, and if they were made within the same time, and of what yearly rents and profits they be.

From Paul L. Hughes and James F. Larkin (eds), *Tudor Royal Proclamations*, vol. I, New Haven, 1964, no. 338, p. 471.

Item, who hath now the state of inheritance and the profits of the same enclosure and houses decayed, and of whom the lands be holden ...

113   Forcible enclosure

One reason for the government's dislike of enclosure was that it threatened to reduce the military potential of the population. The following account of the activities of a grasping landlord in the 1590s stresses this angle.

Seaton Delavale [*near Alnmouth, Northumberland*] being a lordship and the inheritance of Robert Delavale esquire, whereof on his demesne[†] there he had 2 ploughs going to ancient time; and since or about the tenth year of the Queen, there was in Seaton Delavale town 12 tenements, whereon there dwelt 12 able men, sufficiently furnished with horse and furniture to serve her Majesty at all times when they were called upon ... who paid 46s. 8d. rent yearly apiece, or thereabouts. All the said tenants and their successors, saving 5, the said Robert Delavale either thrust out of their fermolds [*holdings*], or wearied them by taking excessive [entry] fines, increasing of their rents unto £3 apiece, and withdrawing part of their best land and meadow from their tenements; and by not permitting them to malt their malt corn they grew of their farms, for [fear of] hindering the vent or sale of their said landlord's; by taking their good land from them and compelling them to win moorish and heath ground; and after their hedging heath ground to their great charge, and paid a great fine, and bestowed great reparations on building on their tenements, he quite thrust them off [*out*] in one year, refusing either to repay the fine or to repay the charge bestowed in diking or building, as the tenants do bitterly exclaim. The said seven fermolds displaced had to every one of them 60 acres of arable land, *viz.*, 20 in every field at the least, as the tenants affirm, which amounteth to 480 acres of land yearly or thereabouts, converted for the most part from tillage to pasture, and united to the demesne of the lordship of Seaton Delavale. So that where there was 12 tenants with sufficient horse and furniture able to serve, they are now brought to 5... who have not one serviceable horse amongst them all for the causes aforesaid.

From H.H. E. Craster, *A History of Northumberland.* vol. IX, 1909, p. 201.

114 The advantages of enclosure

Thomas Tusser was an influential advocate of improved agricultural methods. His doggerel poem, *Five Hundred Points of Good Husbandry*, went through several editions during Elizabeth's reign.

The country enclosed I praise,
    The t'other delighteth not me;
For nothing the wealth it doth raise,
    To such as inferior be.
How both of them partly I know,
Here somewhat I mind for to show.

    . . .

Example by Leicestershire,
    What soil can be better than that?
For any thing heart can desire,
    And yet it doth want, ye see what.
Mast [*acorns, etc, for swine*], covert, close pasture, and wood,
And other things needful as good.

All these doth enclosure bring,
    Experience teacheth no less:
I speak not, to boast of the thing,
    But only a truth to express.
Example, if doubt ye do make,
By Suffolk and Essex go take.

More plenty of mutton and beef,
    Corn, butter, and cheese of the best,
More wealth anywhere, to be brief,
    More people, more handsome and prest [*willing*],
Where find ye? (go search any coast,)
Than there, where enclosure is most.

More work for the labouring man,
    As well in the town as the field;
Or thereof (devise if ye can)
    More profit, what countries do yield?
More seldom, where see ye the poor,
Go begging from door unto door?

From Thomas Tusser, *Five Hundred Points of Good Husbandry* (1557), ed. William Mavor, 1812, pp. 203–6.

CHAPTER 6   ORDER AND DISORDER

In a society in which lawlessness and violence were never far from the surface, rebellion was seen by many as the worst of evils. The State had no standing army, not even a proper police force, to deal with rebels, so that any local movement could very easily develop into a major threat. To prevent rebellion starting, the authorities had to rely on censorship and informers, and above all on the idea, which was proclaimed tirelessly from the pulpit and the magistrates' bench, that it was wicked to oppose one's God-given rulers.

The first section is concerned with the Pilgrimage of Grace, which was in some ways the archetypal protest movement of the century. One typical feature was the importance of local rumour, in an age when communication between regions was weak. The Lincolnshire rebels believed, for instance, that their parish churches were about to be pulled down like the monasteries. Another aspect was the crucial leadership role of the gentry in the Pilgrimage; but it is also significant that no great magnates participated, though some of their close relations did. It was characteristic that few of the Pilgrims wanted to rebel against the King himself. They combined a conservative loyalty to the established order with a hatred of Henry's 'evil councillors'.

The second section looks at rebellion which had economic roots. Throughout the century there were frequent small-scale outbreaks of discontent against price rises, rack renting or enclosures. Such riots were especially common in the mid-century and again in the 1590s, both periods of economic dislocation, inflation and war. However, with the possible exception of Kett's rebellion of 1549 they were never serious enough to pose a real threat to the Tudor State. Considering the increase in the cost of living during the century it is surprising there was not more violence than there was, and this reflects the deeply conservative nature of society. Even enclosure riots were not mere orgies of destruction but were attempts, through the pulling down of hedges and fences, to return to what was seen as a juster form of land distribution and cultivation.

The third section covers three major rebellions in the second half of the century. Of these, Wyatt's perhaps came nearest to success, but with hindsight we can see that none of them really managed to shake the government of the day. On the whole, sixteenth-century rebellions probably strengthened the authorities' hand, rather than causing them to alter course. The 1569 Northern rebellion led to the eclipse of feudalism in the North, with the fall of the Percies, Nevilles and Dacres. Essex's rebellion achieved little, except to confirm the power of his rival, Robert Cecil.

The Pilgrimage of Grace

115 Causes of the Pilgrimage, 1536

(a) The causes of the rebellion are still controversial. It used to be seen as a spontaneous rising of the North against Henry's regime generally, and especially his religious policy; this is the impression given by Robert Aske's replies to his examination after the failure of the rising.

To the statute of suppression* he did grudge against the same and so did all the whole country, because the abbeys in the north parts gave great alms to poor men and laudably served God; in which parts of late days they had but small comfort by ghostly [*spiritual*] teaching. And by occasion of the said suppression the divine service of almighty God is much [di]minished, great number of masses unsaid, and the blessed consecration of the sacrament[†] now not used and showed in those places, to the distress of the faith and spiritual comfort to man's soul; the temple of God russed [*injured*] and pulled down, the ornaments and relics of the church of God unreverent used, the tombs and sepulchres of honourable and noble men pulled down and sold, none hospitality now in those places kept...

And the profits of these abbeys yearly goeth out of the country to the King's highness, so that in short space little money, by occasion of the said yearly rents, tenths[†] and first fruits[†], should be left in the said country, in consideration of the absence of the King's highness in those parts, want of his laws and the frequentation of merchandise. Also divers and many of the said abbeys were in the mountains and desert places, where the people be rude [*primitive*] of conditions and not well taught the law of God; and when the said abbeys stood, the said people not only had worldly refreshing in their bodies but also spiritual refuge... Also the abbeys were one of the beauties of this realm to all men... Also all gentlemen were much succoured in their needs with money, their young sons there succoured, and in nunneries their daughters brought up in virtue... And such abbeys... were great maintainers of sea walls and dykes, maintainers and builders of bridges and highways, and such other things for the commonwealth.

*The 1536 Act for the dissolution of the lesser monasteries.

From M. H. and R. Dodds, *The Pilgrimage of Grace 1536–1537*, vol. I, Cambridge, 1915, pp. 348–9.

(b) Recently, emphasis has been put on the leaders of the 'Aragonese' faction at Court, such as Hussey and Darcy, who sought the restoration of the Princess Mary to the succession (see **Doc. 116c**) and who undoubtedly had been in touch with foreign powers with a view to rebellion. The following is from a letter to Charles V from the Imperial Ambassador, Eustace Chapuys, 30 September 1534.

The lord Hussey, chamberlain of the Princess, who for his good sense and prudence was one of the principal councillors of Henry VII, desiring of late to go home to the North, sought a secret interview with me before his departure, when he told me plainly what he had before expressed more covertly, that he and all the honest men of the kingdom were very much dismayed that your majesty did nothing to remedy affairs here, as it could be done so easily – that the thing concerned the lives and interests of the Queen [Catherine] and Princess [Mary] and the honour of your majesty, and that it was God's cause, which you, as a Catholic prince and chief of other princes, were bound to uphold, especially out of pity for all this people, who regard you with as much affection as if they were your own subjects . . .

Yesterday, just after this interview, I sent to lord Darcy by one of my confidential servants, who, after conversing about other things, began to speak of the above matters, conjuring him to keep it secret, as it might cost him his life. He said he considered himself as one of the most loyal vassals the King had in matters which did not injure his conscience and honour, but that the things treated here were so outrageous against God and reason that he could not hold himself for an honest man or good Christian if he consented to them, especially in matters which concern the faith, and that in the North he knew well there were 1,600 earls and other great gentlemen who are of his opinion . . .

From James Gairdner (ed.), *Letters and Papers, Foreign and Domestic, of the Reign of Henry VIII*, vol. VII, 1883, no. 1206, pp. 466–7.

116   The Pontefract Articles, 1536

The clearest statement of the aims of the Yorkshire Pilgrims was made at their council held at Pontefract between 2 and 4 December. The Articles' blend of religious, economic and political demands has much exercised historians as to the real nature of the Pilgrimage.

(a) Examples of religious demands.

I. Touching our faith, to have the heresies of Luther, Wyclif [and others], the works of Tyndal [and others], and such other heresies of Anabaptists[†], clearly within this realm to be annulled and destroyed.

II. To have the supreme head, touching *cura animarum* [*care of souls, i.e. the priestly function*], to be reserved unto the see of Rome, as before it was accustomed.

IV. To have the abbeys suppressed to be restored – houses, lands and goods.

VII. To have the heretics . . . and their sect to have condign punishment by fire . . .

XVIII. That the privileges and rights of the Church be confirmed by act of Parliament.

(b) Examples of economic demands.

IX. That the lands in Westmorland [and other places] may be by tenant right, and the lord to have at every change two years' rent for gressom [*entry fine*] and no more . . .

XIII. Statutes for enclosures and intacks [*intakes from wastes or commons*] to be put in execution, and that all intacks and enclosures since the fourth year of King Henry VII be pulled down, except on mountains, forests, or parks.

XIV. To be discharged of the Fifteenth[†] and taxes now granted by act of Parliament.

(c) Examples of political demands.

III. We humbly beseech our most dread sovereign lord that the Lady Mary may be made legitimate and the former statute* therein annulled . . . This to be in Parliament.

VIII. To have the Lord Cromwell, the Lord Chancellor [*Sir Thomas Audley*], and Sir Richard Rich [*Privy Councillor and Chancellor of the Court of Augmentations*] to have condign punishment as subverters of the good laws of this realm and maintainers of the false sect of these heretics and first inventors and bringers in of them.

XV. To have the parliament in a convenient place at Nottingham or York, and the same shortly summoned.

XX. To have the Statute of Uses** repealed.

XXI. That the statutes of treasons for words [*26 Henry VIII, cap. 13*] . . . be in like wise repealed.

*The succession Act of 1534, which affirmed that Henry had never been married to Catherine of Aragon, Mary's mother.
**This Statute limited the right of landowners to leave their property in trust for their heirs, thereby evading the feudal dues or 'incidents' which were payable to the crown when the property changed hands.

From J. A. Froude, *History of England*, 3rd edn, vol. III,1864, pp. 156–8.

117   An ideology of rebellion, 1536

Contemporaries' deeply conservative view of society, and especially the analogy customarily made between the community and a human body (**a**), made it extremely difficult for any sixteenth-century revolt to justify itself. Nevertheless, the Pilgrims' oath (**b**), probably devised by Aske himself, was a brilliant attempt to do so. Latimer's sermon (**c**), however, clearly reveals the contradictions of their position.

(a)

A commonwealth is like a body, and so like that it can be resembled to nothing so convenient as unto that. Now, were it not, by your faith, a mad hearing if the foot should say, I will wear a cap with an ouche [*brooch*], as the head doth? If the knees should say, we will carry the eyes another while: if the shoulders should claim each of them an ear: if the heels would now go before, and the toes behind? This were undoubtedly a mad hearing: every man would say, the feet, the knees, the shoulders, the heels make unlawful requests, and very mad petitions. But if it were so in deed, if the foot had a cap, the knees eyes, the shoulders ears, what a monstrous body should this be? God send them such a one, that shall at any time go about to

From Richard Morrison, *A Remedy for Sedition* (1536), reprinted 1933, pp. 20–1.

make as evil a commonwealth as this is a body. It is not meet, every man to do that he thinketh best.

(b) 'The Oath of the Honourable Men', 1536.

Ye shall not enter into this our Pilgrimage of Grace for the Commonwealth, but only for the love that ye do bear unto Almighty God his faith, and to Holy Church militant and the maintenance thereof, to the preservation of the King's person and his issue, to the purifying of the nobility, and to expulse all villein blood and evil councillors against the commonwealth from his Grace and his Privy Council of the same. And that ye shall not enter into our said Pilgrimage for no particular profit to yourself, nor to do any displeasure to any private person, but by counsel of the commonwealth; nor slay nor murder for no envy, but in your hearts put away all fear and dread, and take afore you the Cross of Christ, and in your hearts His faith, the Restitution of the Church, the suppression of these Heretics and their opinions, by all the holy contents of this book.

From M. H. and R. Dodds, *The Pilgrimage of Grace 1536–1537*, vol. I, Cambridge, 1915, p. 182.

(c) Hugh Latimer's sermon, preached at Paul's Cross, 29 October 1536.

These men in the north country, they make pretence as though they were armed in God's armour, girt in truth, and clothed in righteousness. I hear say they wear the cross and the wounds before and behind*, and they pretend [*claim*] much truth to the king's grace and to the commonwealth, when [in fact] they intend nothing less; and deceive the poor ignorant people, and bring them to fight against both the king, the church and the commonwealth. They arm them with the sign of the cross and of the wounds, and go clean contrary to him that bare the cross and suffered those wounds. They rise with the king, and fight against the king in his ministers and officers; they rise with the church, and fight against the church, which is the congregation of faithful men; they rise for the commonwealth and fight against it, and go about to make the commons each to kill other, and to destroy the commonwealth. Lo, what false pretence can the devil send among us! It is one of his most crafty and subtle assaults, to send his warriors forth under the badge of God, as though they were armed in righteousness and justice.

* The 'Pilgrims' wore on their sleeve an emblem of the Five Wounds of Christ with the name of Jesus in the middle.

From G. E. Corrie (ed.), *Sermons by Hugh Latimer*, Cambridge, 1844, pp. 29–30.

Social and Economic Revolts

118   A waiting game, 1497

The 1497 Cornish rebellion arose over resentment at having to pay a subsidy for a war against Perkin Warbeck in Scotland. Here Francis Bacon, in his history of the reign, analyses the factors leading Henry VII deliberately to delay before attacking the rebels, who had marched all the way to London.

But as for the King's forces, they were not only in preparation, but in readiness presently to set forth, under the conduct of Daubeny the lord chamberlain. But as soon as the King understood of the rebellion of Cornwall, he stayed those forces, retaining them for his own service and safety. But therewithal he dispatched the earl of Surrey into the north, for the defence and strength of those parts, in case the Scots should stir. But for the course he held towards the rebels, it was utterly differing from his former custom and practice; which was ever full of forwardness and celerity to make head against them, or to set upon them as soon as ever they were in action. This he was wont to do. But now, besides that he was attempered by years and less in love with dangers, by the continued fruition of a crown; it was a time when the various appearance to his thoughts of perils of several natures, and from divers parts, did make him judge it his best and surest way, to keep his strength together in the seat and centre of his kingdom ... Besides, there was no necessity put upon him to alter his counsel. For neither did the rebels spoil the country, in which case it had been dishonour to abandon his people: neither on the other side did their forces gather or increase, which might hasten him to precipitate and assail them before they grew too strong. And lastly, both reason of estate and war seemed to agree with this course: for that insurrections of base people [*not led by nobles or gentry*] are commonly more furious in their beginnings. And by this means also he had them the more at vantage, being tired and harassed with a long march; and more at mercy, being cut off far from their country, and therefore not able by any sudden flight to get to retreat, and to renew the troubles.

From Francis Bacon, *History of the Reign of King Henry VII* (1622), ed. J. Rawson Lumby, Cambridge, 1892, pp. 151–2.

119   An enclosure riot, 1514

Protests over enclosure were endemic during the whole century, though particularly rife at times of economic stress. And upheavals in London were especially dangerous for the government and needed tactful handling.

The towns about London (as Islington, Hoxton, Shoreditch, and others) had so enclosed the common fields with hedges and ditches that neither the young men of the city might shoot, nor the ancient persons might walk for their pleasure in the fields, except either the bows and arrows were broken or taken away, or the honest and substantial persons arrested or indicted[†], saying that no Londoner should go out of the city but in the highways. This saying sore grieved the Londoners, and suddenly this year a great number of the city assembled themselves in a morning, and a turner in a fool's coat came crying through the city, 'Shovels and spades!', and so many people followed that it was wonder, and within a space all the hedges about the towns were cast down, and the ditches filled, and everything made plain, the workmen were so diligent. The King's Council hearing of this assembly came to the Greyfriars, and sent for the mayor and the council of the city to know the cause, which declared to them the nuisance done to the citizens, and their commodities and liberties taken from them, [and said that] though they would not, yet the commonality and young persons, which were damnified [*harmed*] by the nuisance, would pluck up and remedy the same. And when the King's Council had heard the matter, they dissimuled [*passed over*] the matter, and commanded the mayor to see that no other thing was attempted, and to call home the citizens; which when they had done their enterprise, came home before the King's Council and the mayor departed, without any harm more doing, and so after the fields were never hedged.

From Edward Hall, *The triumphant reigne of Kyng Henry the VIII*, ed. Charles Whibley, vol. 1, 1904, p. 119.

120   Reporting seditious words, 1534

In the absence of a national police force or bureaucracy any reports of disaffection from up and down the country were given careful consideration by Tudor governments. Thomas Cromwell (Secretary, 1534–40) received many such reports.

Chester Herald to Cromwell, 7 March 1534.

On Saturday, 7 March, 25 Hen. VIII, I was with Dr Claybrooke at Thorgurton Abbey, Notts., where Sir William Dragley*, prebendary[†] of Southwell, took hold of a gold scutcheon on my breast and asked me what it was. I said, 'It is the King's arms'. 'Marry,' said he, 'I love it the worse.' 'Sir,' said I, 'wot [*know*] ye what you say?' 'By God's Passion,' said he, 'I love him not, for he taketh our goods from us, and maketh us to go to the plough. I have been at the plough this day myself.' 'Sir,' said I, 'ye need not for no necessity, for ye have enough if ye can be content; but I fear that ye will rather [im]pair than mend [*get worse rather than better*], so much have you said now. The King's grace covets no man's goods wrongfully.' 'God's Passion,' said he, 'I think no harm. God save the King.' 'Marry, amen,' said I, 'But whatsoever you think, your saying is naught.' 'I pray you, master Chester,' said he, 'Be content, for if ye report me I will say that I never said it.' 'Sir,' said I, 'that will not serve you, for I am one of the King's heralds; wherefore I must needs report all such things as is contrary to his honour.' Whether he were overcome with drink or no, I cannot tell; but the bearer,

From James Gairdner (ed.),
*Letters and Papers, Foreign and
Domestic, of the Reign of Henry
VIII*, vol. VII, 1883, no. 298, p. 129.

Dr Claybrooke, will inform you of his quality. I have been servant to king Henry VII and the present King 30 years and more, and never till now heard any of their subjects rail upon them, except one in the late King's days...

*Clerics were frequently given the courtesy title of 'Sir'.

121   Martial law against rioters, 1549

Protector Somerset appointed commissions to investigate enclosures, but their failure to produce effective reforms only stimulated further popular unrest.

Forasmuch as the King's majesty hath of late, for the redress of unlawful enclosures and such like enormities, directed his several commissions with large instructions for the same into every his counties...which commissions be now part in execution and part ready to be executed, and delayed only by the folly of the people seeking their own redress unlawfully; so that no subject can any more require of any prince, than by his majesty, his said uncle, and council, hath been devised, ordered, and commanded.

Yet nevertheless his majesty understandeth that divers of his subjects...do attempt and travail...to make assemblies, riots [etc.]...and...presume to do and attempt that which ought only to be done by the authority of the King and his majesty's laws...

For the which causes his majesty...by the advice of his said dear uncle and Lord Protector...chargeth...all manner his subjects...[to] cease forthwith, upon this proclamation proclaimed, from all manner their unlawful assemblies, riots and uproars...and that also no manner of subject...shall from henceforth by drum, taboret, pipe, or any other instrument striking and sounding, bell or bells ringing, open crying, posting, riding, running, or by any news, rumours, and tales inventing...congregate, and muster...any number of people, whatsoever they be...to pluck down any hedge, pale, fence, wall, or any manner of enclosure...upon pain of death presently to be suffered and executed by the authority and order of law martial.

From Paul L. Hughes and James
F. Larkin (eds), *Tudor Royal
Proclamations*, vol. I, *The Early
Tudors (1485–1553)*, 1964,
no. 341, pp. 475–6.

122   Kett's demands, 1549

The twenty-nine articles submitted by the Norfolk rebels in 1549 were not a coherent programme but a random list of grievances mainly concerned with tenant and common rights. They included measures to reform the clergy, but there is no evidence of anti-Protestantism. Generally, the demands were conservative and localised, and made from the point of view of men of moderate means.

1.   We pray your grace that where it is enacted for enclosing that it be not hurtful to such as have enclosed saffron* grounds, for they be greatly chargeable to them, and that from henceforth no man shall enclose any more...

3.   We pray your grace that no lord of no manor shall common [*put livestock to graze*] upon the commons...

5.   We pray that reedground and meadowground may be at such price as they were in the first year of King Henry VII...

8.   We pray that priests or vicars that be not able to preach and set forth the word of God to his parishioners may be thereby put from his benefice, and the parishioners there to choose another, or else the patron or lord of the town.

14.   We pray that copyhold† land that is unreasonably rented may go as it did in the first year of King Henry VII and that at the death of a tenant or [at] a sale the same lands to be charged with an easy [entry] fine, [such] as a capon [*chicken*] or a reasonable sum of money for a remembrance...

15.   We pray that no priest shall be a chaplain nor no other officer to any man of honour or worship, but only to be resident upon their benefices, whereby their parishioners may be instructed with the laws of God.

16.   We pray that all bondmen† may be made free, for God made all free with his precious blood shedding.

17.   We pray that rivers may be free and common to all men for fishing and passage...

20.   We pray that every proprietory parson or vicar having a benefice of £10 or more by year shall either by themselves or by some other person teach poor men's children of their parish the book called the catechism and the primer [*prayer book*]...

23.   We pray that no man under the degree of esquire shall keep any conies [*rabbits*] upon any of their own freehold or copyhold† unless he pale [*fence*] them in so that it shall not be to the commons nuisance...

29.   We pray that no lord, knight, esquire, nor gentlemen do graze nor feed any bullocks or sheep if he may spend forty pounds a year by his lands but only for the provision of his house.**

From Frederick William Russell, *Kett's Rebellion in Norfolk*, 1859, pp. 48–56.

*Saffron was an important local crop.
**This is the most far-reaching of all the articles; in effect it put an upper limit on the size of sheep and cattle farms.

Later Rebellions

123   Wyatt's proclamation, 1554

The considerable support which Sir Thomas Wyatt's opposition to Mary's Spanish marriage received is an indication of the growing strength of nationalism at this time. Wyatt's revolt came as close to success as any during the century.

A Proclamation agreed unto by Thomas Wyatt, George Harper, Henry Isleye, knights, and by divers of the best of the shire [*Kent*], sent unto the commons of the same.

Forasmuch as it is now spread abroad and certainly pronounced by the Lord Chancellor and other of the Council, of the Queen's determinate pleasure to marry with a stranger. We therefore write unto you because ye be our neighbours, because ye be our friends, and because ye be Englishmen, that ye will join with us as we will with you unto death in this behalf, protesting unto you before God that no other earthly cause could move us unto this enterprise but this alone, wherein we seek no harm to the Queen, but better counsel and counsellors, which also we would have forborn in all other matters, saving only in this. For herein lies the health and wealth of us all. For trial hereof and manifest proof of this intended purpose, lo, now, even at hand, Spaniards be now already arrived at Dover at one passage, to the number of an hundred, passing upward to London in companies of ten, four and six, with harness, arquebuses[†] and morians [*moors*], with match light, the foremost company whereof be already at Rochester. We shall require you therefore to repair to such places as the bearers hereof shall pronounce unto you, there to assemble and determine what may be best for the advancement of liberty and commonwealth in this behalf, and to bring with you such aid as you may.

From John Proctor, *The Historie of Wyattes Rebellion*, 1554; printed in Alfred J. Kempe (ed.), *The Loseley Manuscripts*, 1836, p. 127.

124   The Northern Rebellion, 1569

Northumberland describes the conspirators' original aim, before they were frustrated by the removal of Mary, Queen of Scots, from Tutbury to Coventry at the end of November 1569.

From the interrogation of the Earl of Northumberland in 1572, after he had been handed over to the English authorities by the Scots.

What was the intent and meaning of the said rebellion . . . ?

The intent and meaning of us upon our first conferences and assemblies was only and specially for the reformation of religion, and the preservation of the second person [*the heir apparent*], the Queen of Scots, whom we accounted by God's law and man's law to be right heir, if want should be of issue of the Queens Majesty's body. Which two causes I made full account was greatly favoured by the most part of noblemen within this realm, and especially for God's true religion...

What was the devices or means that you devised...for the taking away of the Scots Queen; and how many were privy to those devices: and how should the same have been executed?

My cousin Leonard Dacres, Francis Norton and Markinfeeld did confer with me whether the Queen of Scots might be by any means possibly gotten to liberty. My said cousin and Francis Norton seemed to give [approval to] the attempt, if they could find any likelihood of good success; and agreed that my said cousin and F. Norton should repair so near as they could to the Earl of Shrewsbury [*Mary's gaoler*], and to practise the matter with such acquaintance as my said cousin had in that house; and if he saw towardness and likelihood to get her conveyed from thence, then should he have twenty spare geldings sent him, with as many men of the principal of our household servants conveyed unto them two, secretly, by twos and threes, and so upon their advertisement we to meet them in the half way. My said cousin and F. Norton were departed about this matter, and as the matter was suddenly talked of, so were they suddenly returned again, and but two days absent; reporting that they could not bring it to pass...

What conference have you had with any touching the marriage of the said Scottish Queen ... And with whom did you or any other of your confederates purpose that she should have married?

Some liked her marriage one way, and some another way. As the Earl of Westmoreland, his uncles, and some of the Northons [*northerners*] liked well the match to be with the Duke [of Norfolk]. My cousin Dacres, I and some others wished her bestowed on a sound Catholic; yea, and if it were with some other foreign Prince...

From Sir Cuthbert Sharp, *Memorials of the Rebellion of 1569*, 1840, pp. 202–3, 192–3.

125   Essex's revolt, 1601

Essex's ambition to establish a monopoly of power and favour, and his rivalry with Burghley's political heir, Sir Robert Cecil, led him to attempt a *coup d'état* in February 1601. The citizens of London gave him no support and he was arrested together with his accomplices.

From the examination of Sir William Constable, February 1601.

On Saturday the 7th inst. he with Lord Mounteagle, Sir Christ. Blount, Sir Gelly Merrick, Sir Chas. Percy, Hen. Cuffe, Edw. Bushell, Ellis Jones, and Sir Jo. Davies met, for all he knows by chance, at one Gunter's house, over against Temple gate, where they dined, after which Thos. Lea came to the play*, where they were all assembled, at the Globe on the Bankside, saving Cuffe. After the play, examinate and Edw. Bushell went to Essex House, where they supped and lay all night, which he had never done before; the reason was that after supper the Earl signified to those assembled in the withdrawing chamber, where Lord Mounteagle, Sir Gelly Merrick, Sir Robt. Vernon and others were, that there was a plot laid by his enemies to draw him to the lord Treasurer's, and to take his life, as he was then called to the Council, which he had not been before since his disgrace. The Earl moved examinate to lie there all night, which he did with Sir Robt. Vernon...

Was there on Sunday morning, when the Lord Keeper and other Lords came to Essex House, when Sir Christ. Blount gave him command from the Earl to have a care of the gate, lest his enemies should assail him unawares; did so, finding there six partisans [*spears*], and when my Lord Keeper and the other Lords came, opened the gate to them, and would have suffered their company to enter, but Owen Salisbury shut the gate after the Lord Chief Justice, whom he had like to have hurt thereby, if examinate had not helped him. Thinks there were about 100 people in the court, weaponed only with swords; stayed at the gate until the Earl went into the city; went with him first to Sheriff Smythe's house, then back towards Ludgate, where they were encountered and resisted by force; examinate with Sir Christ. Blount, seeking to clear the way over the chain**, was thrust through the doublet in three places. Returning back with the Earl till he came to Bow Lane, was there forced to take a house, and hearing of the alderman's deputy being at the next house, yielded to him, who brought him to prison. Thinks 200 men went with the Earl into the city; he declared in his court, before he went, that because he could not hold himself safe in his house, he would put himself to the city.

*This was a special performance of Shakespeare's *Richard II* organised by Essex. In the play Richard is deposed and subsequently murdered.
**The City authorities had put up a chain in an attempt to close Ludgate to the rebel forces.

From M. A. E. Green (ed.), *Calendar of State Papers Domestic, 1598–1601*, 1869, no. 278, p. 573.

CHAPTER 7   WAR AND FOREIGN AFFAIRS

This chapter contains sections on foreign policy, the army, the navy, and exploration and trade.

Tudor foreign policy was set in the context of rivalry between the leading European powers, France and Spain. For England, a much weaker nation than either of these, the most important considerations were national security and the balance of power. But there were discontinuities in English policy. Henry VII aimed at recognition by neighbouring states, peace, and the elimination of challenges to his throne. He successfully fostered alliances, cemented by dynastic marriages, with Spain, and later with Scotland. The policies of Henry VIII, Wolsey and Somerset were more ambitious and aggressive, involving several short wars, mainly against France and Scotland. Mary, too, owing to her Habsburg marriage, took part in a brief, unsuccessful war against France. But after 1559 France and Scotland were less of a threat. France was torn by civil war, and Scotland, like England, had turned towards Protestantism. Hence, the early years of Elizabeth's reign were a time of relative security. But the growing power of Philip II forced England into a diplomatic revolution and, finally, events in the Netherlands brought about open war with Spain. The war dragged on for the remainder of the reign but produced little result, except vastly to increase Elizabeth's financial problems. In the 1590s, too, France emerged from its religious wars and England was once more confronted with the old problem of how best to maintain a balance between France and Spain.

The army was never England's strong point. Tudor armies sent abroad tended to become less impressive as the century went on. Henry VIII led a force of 35,000 men to France in 1513, and throughout his reign he was served by capable generals such as the Dukes of Norfolk and Suffolk. Elizabeth, on the other hand, saw the much smaller armies which she sent to the Netherlands and France in the 1580s and '90s as auxiliary forces only, and some of her generals, such as Leicester in the Netherlands and Essex in Ireland, proved disastrous choices.

Nevertheless, arrangements for recruitment did improve during the century, especially in respect of the home militia which was created to meet the growing threat of foreign invasion. Henry VII and Henry VIII had relied on the magnates to provide them with trained men, but, at least since the thirteenth century, the germ of an alternative system had existed, in the duty of all Englishmen between sixteen and sixty to bear arms for their King. As the techniques of warfare became more complex, and particularly as pikes and firearms gradually replaced bows and billhooks, more specialised training was needed and after 1573 the 'trained bands', selected from the general mass of the militia, formed the core of every county's defence forces. By 1588 26,000 men had received such training, but the cost was high and the demands much resented by those called on to supply men and equipment.

Henry VII passed on only five royal ships to his son in 1509, but after that the size of the navy steadily increased. Just as important was a great improvement in naval administration, with the setting up of the Navy Board in 1546. After 1578, Sir John Hawkins, as Treasurer, brought to the Board his seafaring experience which enabled him to set about improving the design of new ships, and also their fire power. In the campaign of 1588 Hawkins' new, long-range cannon proved decisive. But English sea power depended only partly on the official navy; many ships were privately owned and were drawn into service by the hope of profit. In the war against Spain English merchantmen turned increasingly towards privateering, a private-enterprise system which, although saving the government money, had its drawbacks. There was the further disadvantage that naval expeditions organised on a joint-stock basis, which provided for any profits to be split between the Queen and private investors, suffered from lack of unity in their command structure and lack of clarity in their objectives.

This was an age of commercial growth. Henry VII initially did much to stimulate both trade and exploration. Cloth remained far and away England's most important export, but the trade's prosperity, and in partic-ular its concentration on the Netherlands, was badly shaken in the mid-century by the decline of Antwerp as well as by drastic fluctuations in the quality of the English coinage. However, in the second half of the century there followed an expansion of geographical horizons, brought about by the new confidence of England's seamen as well as the growing mercantile rivalry with Spain. This in turn encouraged the development by merchants of new markets – in Russia, southern Europe, Turkey, and as far afield as India and the Far East. In this somewhat haphazard and disjointed manner, the foundations of the future British Empire were laid.

Foreign Policy

126   Anglo–Spanish relations under Henry VII, 1489

The Treaty of Medina Campo marked the acceptance of Henry's claim to the English throne by the rulers of Spain, one of the major states in western Europe.

1.   A true friendship and alliance shall be observed henceforth between Ferdinand and Isabella, their heirs and subjects, on the one part, and Henry, his heirs and subjects, on the other part. They promise to assist one another in defending their present and future dominions against any enemy whatsoever.

The subjects of one of the contracting parties are allowed to travel, stay and carry on commerce in the dominions of the other contracting party, without general or special passport, and will be treated on the same footing as the citizens of the country in which they temporarily reside.

The Customs [duties] are to be reduced to what they were in time of peace thirty years ago.

2. Neither party shall in any way favour the rebels of the other party, nor permit them to be favoured or stay in his dominions.

3. Mutual assistance to be given against all aggressors within three months after the assistance has been requested ...

4. Henry is not permitted to assist Charles, King of France, or any other prince at war with Spain. Ferdinand and Isabella promise the same to Henry.

5. Henry is not to conclude peace, alliance, or treaties with France without the sanction of Ferdinand and Isabella, who, on their side, bind themselves to the same effect with respect to Henry.

6. As often as and whenever Ferdinand and Isabella make war with France, Henry shall do the same, and conversely.

7. As Henry, however, has concluded a truce with France till the 17th of January next, he is not to call upon Spain, during this truce, to undertake a war with France. For the term of one year after the expiration of the said truce, either party shall be at liberty to conclude a new truce with the King of France, but the other contracting party must be included in it ...

13. All letters of marque[†] and reprisal are revoked. Any Spanish or English vessel sailing from a Spanish or English port is to give security for good behaviour at sea ... If during the voyage it causes damage to Spanish or English vessels, the injured party shall be indemnified from the said security ...

17. In order to strengthen this alliance the Princess Katharine is to marry Prince Arthur ...

18. The marriage shall be ... consummated as soon as the Prince and the Princess attain the necessary age for it. Henry and Ferdinand and Isabella shall swear to employ all their influence with their children that the marriage be contracted as stipulated.

Medina del Campo, 27th of March 1489.

From G. A. Bergenroth (ed.), *Calendar of Letters, Dispatches, and State Papers relating to the Negotiations between England and Spain*, vol. I, *Henry VII, 1485–1509*, 1862, no. 34, pp. 21–3.

127   The futility of invading France, 1525

With the King of France a prisoner in the hands of Charles V after the battle of Pavia, Henry VIII saw an ideal opportunity for military conquest and Wolsey sought to provide him with funds through the so-called 'Amicable Grant'. He met opposition, however, and the following letter to Wolsey from William Warham, Archbishop of Canterbury, written on 15 April 1525, provides a rarely voiced critique of royal policy.

Also it is spoken abroad, as I understand by relation, that it shall be the uttermost impoverishing of this realm, and the greatest enriching of the realm of France, if the Kings Grace should have all this money that is required and should spend it out of this realm in

France, where his Grace must continually make his abode a long season and keep it, if it fortune him to win it, or else it shall be soon lost again. Which the Kings Grace's long continuance there would be to the great decaying and desolation of this realm . . .

I have heard say moreover that where the people be commanded to make fires and tokens of joy for the taking of the French king, divers of them have spoken that they have more cause to weep than to rejoice thereat. And divers (as it hath been shown me secretly) have wished openly that the French king were at his liberty again, so as there were a good peace, and the Kings Grace should not attempt to win France. The winning whereof should be more chargeful to England than profitable: and the keeping thereof much more chargeful than the winning.

Also it hath been told me secretly that divers have recounted and repeated what infinite sums of money the Kings Grace hath spent already invading France; once in his own royal person, and two other sundry times by his several noble captains; and little or nothing (in comparison of his costs) hath prevailed: in so much that the Kings Grace at this hour hath not one foot of land more in France than his most noble father had, which lacked no riches or wisdom to win the kingdom of France if he had thought it expedient.

From H. Ellis (ed.), *Original letters, illustrative of English history, 1824–46*, 3rd series, vol. I, pp. 373–4.

128   Protector Somerset and the Scots, 1547

In 1543 Henry VIII concluded the Treaty of Greenwich with the Scottish government. Its principal provision was that the baby Mary, nominal Queen of Scots, should in due course be married to Henry's only son, Prince Edward. However, the pro-English Protestant group of Scottish nobles who had made this agreement were ousted by their pro-French Catholic rivals, who denounced the treaty. Henry was determined to enforce it, and sent an army into Scotland, under the command of the Earl of Hertford. After Henry's death, Hertford, now Lord Protector Somerset, continued the same policy of armed intervention.

The Lord Protector and the rest of the Council, calling to mind the evil dealing and crafty dissimulation of the Scots, concerning the matter of marriage betwixt the King's Majesty and the Queen of Scotland (which marriage, as ye have heard, in the five-and-thirtieth year of King Henry the Eight, was by authority of parliament in Scotland fully concluded) thought it not to stand with the King's honour to be in such manner by them deluded, and withal considering how greatly it should turn to the quietness and safety of both realms to have these two princes conjoined in matrimony, they did devise sundry ways and means how the same might be brought to pass; and the rather (as some do write) for that King Henry (before his death) had given them in special charge by all endeavours to procure that the said marriage might take place, as wholly wishing by the conjunction of those two young princes the uniting of the two kingdoms in perpetual amity and faithful league of love...

But the lords of Scotland were so inveigled and corrupted by the French king, and abused by Cardinal Beaton, Archbishop of St. Andrews, and other of their clergy, that they not only shrank from that which they had promised, but also sought to destroy those that favoured the King of England's part. Whereupon a great and puissant [*powerful*] army was now prepared to pass by land into Scotland, and likewise a navy to pass by sea to attend upon the same... Ye shall understand that first the Duke of Somerset, Lord Protector, took upon him to go himself in person, as general of the whole army...

[When the English army reached Newcastle] a proclamation with sound of trumpet was made by an herald in three several places of the camp, signifying the cause of the coming of the King's army at that present into Scotland. Which, in effect, was to advertise all the Scottish nation that their coming was not to deprive them [*the Scots*] of their liberties, but to advance the marriage already concluded and agreed upon betwixt the King's Majesty of England and their Queen, and no hostility meant to such as should show themselves furtherers thereof...

From Holinshed's Chronicles of England, Scotland and Ireland, 1577, vol. III, 1808 edn, pp. 867–8.

129   The loss of Calais, 1558

Calais was the last survival of the English Empire in France. Its capture by the French was a great blow to the prestige of Mary Tudor and her husband, King Philip of Spain. The following account comes from the report which the Venetian Ambassador at Brussels sent home on 8 January 1558.

Today, at noon, news arrived of the entry into Calais of the French, which in like manner as it is of greater importance than any other intelligence that could be heard at this present time, so has it very greatly troubled everybody here, both on account of the actual loss and the subsequent detriment; the French, on the other hand, having made the greatest possible acquisition in these parts, well nigh expelling the English from Flanders, and depriving them of that port which rendered them masters of the Channel, and of a fortress which they held in such great account, and giving them such vast repute, they being thus enabled to harass France and Flanders and all these States at any time. There still remain to the English Hammes and Guisnes, two small inland fortresses, whose security depended entirely on Calais, so through the loss of that place they will easily share the same fate...

From Rawdon Brown (ed.), Calendar of State Papers...in the Archives...of Venice, vol. VI, part III, 1557–1558, 1884, no. 1129, p. 1415.

130   Intervention in France, 1562

A statement by Sir William Cecil of the reasons for sending an English force to France to assist the Prince of Condé and his fellow Protestants, the Huguenots.

Why the Queen puts her subjects in arms.

1.   In arming her subjects she means only the peace of Christendom. At the beginning of these troubles she sent thither large offers of friendship, but the Guises would not accord without the ruin of the Prince of Condé, who requires nothing but the maintenance of the honour of God, the repose of the realm, and liberty of the King.

2.   The Duke [of Guise]'s proceedings will best appear by the following: – Soon after the peace of 1559 the Guises stirred up a quarrel in the name of the Queen of Scots, contrary to the treaty of peace. When they had employed all their practices in France and Scotland, and were wearied, they were content that their niece [*Mary, Queen of Scots*] should make peace, which was concluded at Edinburgh; yet they would not permit their niece to confirm the same. By the death of Francis II [*Mary's husband*], the governance which they had being taken from them, they sought the Queen's [*Elizabeth's*] goodwill, which she was willing to show them. An edict was made to retain all parties in peace who differed in matters of religion, but the Duke, not allowing these ordinances, of private authority broke the edict, and persecuted to death such as observed it.

3.   The Prince of Condé and a great number of the people have assembled only for their defence, and have offered themselves to serve the King.

4.   The cause has now become a manifest enterprise, not by teaching but by the sword, to force men's consciences. The quarrel cannot continue long in France, but will spread into adjoining countries. If they do not intend to force any men's consciences but their own countrymen, why are they so busy to compass a great league, which they would call Catholic? Why do they suffer their people to spoil and kill the English, who come only in trade into Brittany and Normandy? They call those whom they list to spoil Huguenots. Paris gives daily testimony how they destroy their own people with a cry of Huguenots.

From Joseph Stevenson (ed.), *Calendar of State Papers, Foreign Series, of the Reign of Elizabeth, 1562,* 1867, no. 667, p. 311.

131   Whether to aid the Dutch rebels, 1585

In a letter written on 11 January 1585, Secretary Walsingham, who had long been advocating a more active policy of support for the Protestant cause in Europe, tried to persuade Lord Burghley of the urgent need to aid the Dutch, following the assassination of William of Orange some six months earlier. By the end of the year Elizabeth had taken the plunge and despatched an army to the Netherlands.

I find that her Majesty is loath that the French king should have any absolute interest in the Low Countries not presently possessed by the Spaniard, in respect of some future peril that might grow thereby to this Crown – a matter worthy of good consideration were it not that time hath wrought a necessity of speedy resolution, considering the perilous state that those countries do presently stand in. For now it groweth to be a question whether it were more perilous to have those countries in the hands of the French or of the Spaniard, which can no other way be prevented but by her Majesty's taking into her hands the protection of the said countries, with a determination to be at the charges of two hundred thousand pounds by the year for two years' space, a burden I suppose would be willingly borne by this realm rather than it should come into the hands either of the French or of the Spaniard . . .

I conclude (always referring myself to your Lordship's better judgement) that the direction presently given to both her Majesty's ministers in France and the Low Countries, tending to impeach [*prevent or hinder*] that the French king shall have no full footing in those countries, can be but most perilous unto her Majesty unless she shall resolve to take the protection of them herself, which would be most profitable for the cause, the most surest course for herself, and the only and likeliest way to draw the Malcontents [*a group of Dutch Catholic nobles*] to revolt from the Spanish course, which would work more furtherance to the cause than a million of pounds.

From Conyers Read, *Mr Secretary Walsingham and the policy of Queen Elizabeth*, vol. III, Oxford, 1925, pp. 87–8.

132   The prohibition of trade with Spain, 1591

The following royal proclamation, issued on 16 September 1591, is a reminder that the war with Spain continued long after the Armada. Attempts to deprive Spain of the guns and munitions which it bought from abroad were of limited effectiveness since English merchants, like their Dutch counterparts, were skilful in evading embargoes, and frequently put profits before patriotism.

Forasmuch as it is manifestly seen to all the world how it hath pleased Almighty God of his most singular favour to have taken this our realm into his special protection these many years . . . with a special preservation of our own person, as next under his almightiness supreme governor of the same, against many malicious and violent attempts ... it behoveth us in very duty first to continue our own perpetual thanks to his goodness for so wonderful a favour, and next to employ all the forces of those his good people which He hath committed to our rule and government in defence of themselves and all our realms and dominions against such our potent and violent enemies as ... have these many years made open wars against us; and consequently also not to be negligent, but to foresee and provide by all good, politic and lawful means that our said enemies be not aided, strengthened, and made more able to increase and extend their forces against us and our people by sufferance of provisions for the war, as corn and other victual, munition of sundry kinds of artillery, shot and powder and other furniture for shipping, to be carried out of any our dominions ... into Spain, Portugal, and other dominions of the King of Spain, who, of any monarch or prince in Christendom, is at this day the only enemy to our estate and hath longest continued in mortal war against us, manifestly violating the treaties of peace and refusing to live in such peace with us as hath been by solemn contracts and leagues anciently established and continued betwixt our predecessors and his ... notwithstanding we even at the beginning of our reign did offer by a noble embassage to have faithfully observed and confirmed the same, which by the said King was refused.

From Paul L. Hughes and James F. Larkin (eds), *Tudor Royal Proclamations*, vol. III, *The Later Tudors (1588–1603)*, 1969, no. 737, pp. 83–4.

133   England and France, 1595

Henry IV of France, the former Huguenot warrior who turned Catholic in order to confirm his claim to the French throne, had to defend himself from the continuing threat of his Catholic rivals at home and their Spanish supporters. In January 1595 he declared war on Spain, and appealed to Elizabeth for help against the common enemy. The following report of divisions within the English Council comes from the despatch which the Venetian Ambassador in France sent to the Doge and Senate on 9 December 1595.

There reigns a division in the councils of the Queen, and her two principal ministers are secretly in disaccord ... One of these great ministers, the Lord Treasurer [*Burghley*], is very ill-disposed towards the crown of France, and uses all his influence to prevent the Queen from taking an active part in this direction. There is a strong suspicion that he has been bought with Spanish gold. The other great nobleman, a prime favourite with the Queen [*the Earl of Essex*], is of the contrary opinion ... These facts cause the Queen the greatest perplexity. The Lord Treasurer, in addition to all his other arguments, urges the plea of economy, to which women by their nature are more inclined than men ... The Queen is quite well aware that the French will be beaten if they are not helped; on the other hand, she is very much afraid that if she declared herself entirely on the French side, the only result in the end would be that, under the pressure of necessity and of their actual poverty, the French could make peace or a long truce with Spain and so divert the full force of the tempest upon her . . . She has recently asked the King [*Henry IV*] to give her Calais; and the French think it a strange request, almost indicating that she would like to make herself mistress of the country. She, however, knows quite well that if the Spanish attacked Calais in force the French are incapable of holding the place as she could do. This daily demand for help, without making any equivalent return, is not the way to obtain their end. The Queen is seriously alarmed lest the great Spanish fleet, which is already at Corunna, one hundred and sixty strong, is intended for Ireland . . . All these considerations keep the mind of the Queen in grave perplexity. She has at present a fleet ready which is far more powerful than the one that routed the Duke of Medina Sidonia [*the Armada*]; she has armed the whole kingdom; every day there are musters and reviews; all the ports are placed in a state of defence . . . The English agent told me that there is news that Drake has burned Cadiz, and that now he will go to the Indies to fortify the positions captured from the Spaniards last year, in order to prevent the arrival of so many gold fleets. A design they have often projected with ease but effected with difficulty.

From Horatio F. Brown (ed.), *Calendar of State Papers . . . in the Archives . . . of Venice*, vol. IX, *1592–1603*, 1897, no. 384, pp. 174–6.

The Militia and the Army

134   Military qualities and resources, 1513, 1519

(a) Ferdinand of Spain writes to his Ambassador in England, in February 1513, about a projected joint invasion of France.

Another circumstance which must be taken into consideration is that the French have a considerable number of German troops in their pay. Spanish soldiers are superior to French, but they are incapable of breaking the rank and file of the German veterans. English soldiers are strong and courageous, but for a long time past they have not been accustomed to warlike operations. Thus, it is probable that if the French army, reinforced by German troops, had to fight with exclusively Spanish and exclusively English armies, the victory would remain on their side. In order to be sure of victory it is necessary to employ a certain number of German troops in the Spanish as well as in the English army. The strength of the infantry lies in the art of using the pike and musket. The principal use to which they can be put is to defend the artillery, now in general use. If English archers were intermixed with German pikemen, they would certainly render good service; but it is not probable that English archers alone could resist German troops in a pitched battle. German infantry has deservedly acquired a high reputation.

From G. A. Bergenroth (ed.), *Calendar of Letters, Despatches, and State Papers relating to the Negotiations between England and Spain*, vol. II, *Henry VIII, 1509–1525*, 1866, no. 86, p. 94.

(b) The former Venetian Ambassador to England, reporting on his mission before the Doge and Senate on 10 September 1519, gives his opinion of English military capacities.

In England they did not make use of men-at-arms, so that they could not raise 100 in the whole island. The real military force of the country consisted in its infantry, which was supposed to amount to 150,000 men, whose peculiar weapon was the long bow. When they took the field, their arms consisted of a breast-plate, bow, arrows, sword, and two stakes – one before and one behind – with which they made their pallisadoes or stockade; but all their prowess was in the bow. They insisted on being paid monthly, and did not choose to suffer any hardship; but when they had their comforts, they would do battle daily, with a courage, vigour, and valour that defied exaggeration.

From Rawdon Brown (ed.), *Calendar of State Papers ... in the Archives ... of Venice*, vol. II, *1509–1519*, 1867, no. 1287, p. 562.

135   English military resources, 1554

The following report was made to the Venetian Senate by the Republic's former Ambassador to England, on 18 August 1554.

From her whole realm of England ... the Queen might easily raise 100,000 men, taking at the muster those deemed fit for military service, and who would perform it spontaneously; but in case of war, it is not the custom to enrol every sort of person present at the muster ... but merely those nearest the scene of action. Besides this mode of enrolment, it is usual to order noblemen to collect such an amount of troops as required, which is done when the Crown does not trust everybody; and the third mode of mustering forces – in case of foreign invasion, or some sudden insurrection of the natives – is to place a light on the top of certain huge lanterns fixed on heights in all the villages, on appearance of which signal anywhere, all the neighbouring places do the like, and the forces muster at the first sight. So in a short time the general muster is made, the remedy and assistance proving alike efficient.

From the muster aforesaid some 15,000 horse might be raised, but the native English horse is not good for war, and they have not many foreign horses. The weapons used by the English are a spear, and not having much opportunity for providing themselves with body-armour, they wear, for the most part, breast-plates, with shirts of mail, and a skull-cap, and sword. The rest would be footmen, of which they have four sorts. The first, which in number and valour far excels the others, consists of archers, in whom the sinew of their armies consists, all the English being as it were by nature most expert bowmen, inasmuch as not only do they practise archery for their pleasure, but also to enable them to serve their King, so that they have often secured victory for the armies of England. The second sort consists of infantry, who carry a sort of bill[hook]; and there are some of these likewise who would make good soldiers.

The other two sorts are harquebusiers[†] and pikemen, of which weapons they have little experience.

The Crown has occasionally subsidised German troops, taking them for the most part from the sea towns, from which they have sometimes had as many as 10,000...About four years ago it was determined to raise a cavalry force of 1,000 men-at-arms in the French fashion, but after keeping them for a year, at a cost to the King of 80,000 crowns, they were disbanded, it having been found impossible to make the plan answer. They have no commanders of note in their pay, either English or foreign, but merely give a few pensions to some who served them on former occasions.

From Rawdon Brown (ed.), *Calendar of State Papers ... in the Archives ... of Venice*, vol. V, *1534–1554*, 1873, no. 934, pp. 547–8.

136   The Northamptonshire Militia, 1588

The 'trained bands', selected from the county militias, were regularly mustered during the period of war with Spain. However, the cost of this was a heavy burden upon the local communities. And at times of emergency, as in 1588, when the entire county militias were called up, there were additional charges for providing for the men, suitably equipped, to be conducted to the designated rendezvous.

(a) Sir Christopher Hatton, Lord Chancellor and Lord-Lieutenant of Northamptonshire, to the Deputy-Lieutenants of Northamptonshire, 19 July 1588.

After my very hearty commendations: Yesterday, by direction from her Majesty, I wrote unto you signifying her pleasure that the 400 men which are to attend her here [at London] should be in a readiness. Since which time it hath been resolved that the whole forces of that county, both of horse and footmen, should be called up and furnished for that purpose. I pray you let present order be taken for it, and see them in a readiness to march hither about the end of next week at the farthest.

Touching the charge of coat-and-conduct money, since all the other shires of the realm are to bear the same (as in like case hath been always accustomed heretofore), and that our shire hath been specially favoured both in expense and number of men, I hope they will not think it much to yield to this contribution, especially in a service of this weight and importance; and this the rather through your good persuasions, as also that so soon as the men shall be delivered here into her Majesty's army, that charge shall cease.

(b) Captain Nichols' accounts.

Paid unto Captain Nichols for his allowance, the 30th day of July 1588, at Northampton, as followeth:

First, for 150 coats at 15s. the coat	£112.	10.	0.
For conduct money for 150 men at 10s. a man	75.	0.	0.
Item. Allowed and paid to the captain for the leading of them	20.	0.	0.

Item.	Paid more unto him for the repairing of his armour, shot and weapons	10.	0.	0.
Item.	Given to his lieutenant, Mr John Goodfellow, in reward		1.	0.
Item.	Given more to his serjeants, drummer and corporals	5.	0.	0.
Sum total		£222.	11.	0.

From Jeremy Goring and Joan Wake (eds), *Northamptonshire Lieutenancy Papers.* Northamptonshire Record Society, 1975, pp. 58, 63.

137   The uses of the bow

During Elizabeth's reign the musket and arquebus[†] gradually took the place of the bow, but the latter still had its advocates.

First in the field against horsemen, though it be shot at the highest random, only with the weight of the fall it galleth both horse and man, and though the wound be not mortal, yet both horse and man are made unserviceable then and long after, if so be they escape death. Secondly, in rainy weather and when men come near together, it is a very good weapon. Thirdly, in the night it is both a ready and secret shot, and doth not discover itself as doth the arquebusier[†] both with his fire and blow; and the use of it is good when it be in forcing the enemy's trenches, in sallying out of town, or otherwise. Fourthly, at an assault, when all the defences of a town are taken away, you deliver your arrows over the walls and rampires [*ramparts*] with its fall only. The like use we have of them out of the town, when an assault is given, in delivering them into the enemy's trenches, and among men at their approach to an assault, though they be shot over the wall by chance. Fifthly, to shoot arrows with wildfire, to burn a gate or drawbridge, to fire thatched or shingled houses. In France when we were before Paris and divers other towns that we besieged, bows would have stood us in good stead and I did then wish that we had brought some bowmen with us. Surely we have no reason to give over the bow as we have done, for I hold . . . the worst bowman that can draw but his bow to be far better than a bad fire-shot.

From Sir Thomas Wilford, *A Military Discourse* . . . , (c. 1589); quoted in C. G. Cruickshank, *Elizabeth's Army*, Oxford, 1966, pp. 107–8.

138   The medical service, 1591

Sixteenth-century surgery was a grim affair, without anaesthetic or antiseptic.

You shall have in readiness a good strong form and a steady, and set the patient at the very end of it. Then shall there bestride the form behind him a man that is able to hold him fast by both his arms. Which done, if the leg be to be taken off beneath the knee, let there be also another strong man appointed to bestride the leg that is to be taken off, and he must hold fast the member above the place where the incision is to be made, very steadily without shaking, and he that doth so hold should have a large hand and a good grip, whose hand may the better stay the bleeding... In like manner there must be another skilful man that hath good experience and knowledge to hold the leg below, for the member must not be held too high, for staying and choking of the saw, neither must he hold down his hand too low for fear of fracturing the bones in the time it is a-sawing off. And he that doth cut off the member must be sure to have a sharp saw, a very good caitlin [*a double-edged knife*], and an incision knife, and then boldly with a steady and quick hand cut the flesh round about to the bones without staying... then set your saw as near the sound flesh as easily you may, not touching it, and with a light hand speedily saw it off.

From William Clowes, *A Prooved Practice for All Young Chirurgians* (1591); quoted in C. G. Cruickshank, *Elizabeth's Army*, Oxford, 1966, pp. 177–8.

139   Lack of equipment, 1594

Country gentlemen were often reluctant to provide the military hardware needed to equip the trained bands. Their reasons are illustrated in the following letter written by Sir Henry Cocke, a Hertfordshire JP, to Lord Burghley, on 18 June 1594.

Right honourable, and my very good Lord, having of late fully performed our general musters of the Shire and therewith also taken a perfect view of all the Trained Bands, we found many defects in them, both of men, armour and other furniture...

Under your Honour's favour it were very fit and necessary that for so much (at the least) as every of them [*the Justices of the Peace*] ought of right to find (according to their easy taxations in the Subsidy) they should both make show of them and employ them also amongst their neighbours in those her Majesty's necessary services, which will now, and hereafter also, spare the Country a great deal of money in these kind of provisions; and for the rest of their armour and furniture, above these proportions, they may at their pleasures keep them privately to themselves, whereof in that dangerous time of '88 I saw no great use: for many men kept their armour and furniture close shut up in their Armories without any offer of employment of them. This error hath grown upon this weak conceit, that if men should once deliver in writing what number of horses, armours and other such furniture they have in a readiness to serve her Majesty, it should still remain as a record ever after to charge them with the finding of them. This strange conceit and fancy, no doubt of it, doth keep secret and concealeth the knowledge of a very great strength both of horse and armour within the Realm, which, being not in time made known, can never be orderly employed, nor to any good purpose used.

From Henry Ellis (ed.), *Original letters illustrative of English history*, 2nd series, vol. 3, 1827, pp. 175–7.

Naval Warfare

140   Henry VIII's naval laws, c. 1530

From the start of his reign Henry VIII pursued a vigorous naval policy and by his death there were 53 naval vessels, large and small, which carried between them some 8,000 men in time of war.

Orders to be used in the King's Majesty's Navy by the Sea.

First, the laws which be written what every man ought to do in the ship towards his captain to be set in the main mast in parchment to be read as occasion shall serve.

If any man kill another within the ship, he that doth the deed shall be bound quick [*alive*] to the dead man, and so be cast into the sea, and a piece of ordnance shot off after they be thrown into the sea.

If any man draw a weapon within the ship to strike his captain, he shall lose his right hand . . .

If any man within the ship draweth any weapon or causeth tumult or likelihood of murder or bloodshed within the ship, he shall lose his right hand as is before said.

If any man within the ship steal or pick money or clothes within the ship duly proved, he shall be three times dipped at the bowsprit, and let down two fathoms within the water, and kept on live, and at the next shore towed aland bound to the boat's stern, with a loaf of bread and a can of beer, and [be] banished the King's ships for ever.

If any man within the ship do sleep his watch 4 times and so proved, this be his punishment: the first time he shall be headed at the main mast with a bucket of water poured on his head. The second time he shall be armed, his hands haled up by a rope, and 2 buckets of water poured into his sleeves. The third time he shall be bound to the main mast with certain gun chambers tied to his arms and as much pain in his body as the captain will. The fourth time and last punishment, being taken asleep he shall be hanged on the bowsprit end of the ship in a basket, with a can of beer, a loaf of bread, and a sharp knife, choose to hang there till he starve or cut himself into the sea . . .

From 'A Book of Orders for the War both by Sea and Land', written by Thomas Audley at the command of Henry VIII (c. 1530); printed in H. W. Hodges and E. A. Hughes (eds), *Select Naval Documents*, Cambridge, 1927, p. 4.

141   The sinking of the *Mary Rose*, 1545

In July 1545, during a naval engagement with the French off Portsmouth, the *Mary Rose*, the pride of Henry's fleet, sank. There are different versions of the cause of the disaster.

(a) A French account.

The Admiral being arrived off the Isle of Wight . . . sent the Baron de la Garde, with four galleys[†] . . . to see in what posture the English lay, it being his resolution to attack them. He returned with the report that their fleet consisted of sixty tall ships, excellently well equipped for war, fourteen of which had taken the opportunity of a land-wind to get out of Portsmouth with as much alacrity, good order, and seeming unconcern as if their design was to stand the brunt of our whole fleet. But our Admiral advancing, with the rest of the galleys, the whole English fleet came out of the harbour and faced him. After a long, but distant fight, the English began to retreat under shelter of the land to a place where they were secured on the one side by the cannon of certain forts...and on the other side by blind sands and rocks...This retreat, and the approaching night, put an end to the battle for that day...

During the night, the Admiral disposed the order of battle for the next day...In consideration of the advantageous situation of the English, it was ordered that at daybreak the galleys should advance towards their fleet, while at anchor, and, by firing at them with all possible fury, provoke them to an engagement, and then, retreating, endeavour to draw them out of their hold, towards the main battle. This order was executed with a great deal of intrepidity, and the weather favoured our attempt beyond our wishes; for it proving, in the morning, a perfect calm, our galleys had all the advantages of working which they could desire, to the great damage of the English, who, for want of wind not being able to stir, lay exposed to our cannon. And being so much higher and bulkier than our galleys, hardly a shot missed them; while they [*the galleys*], with the help of their oars, shifted at pleasure, and thereby avoided the danger of the enemy's artillery. Fortune favoured our fleet in this manner for above an hour, during which time, among other damages which the English received, the *Mary Rose*, one of their principal ships, was sunk by our cannon, and of five or six hundred men which were on board, only five and thirty escaped.

From T. Lediard, *The Naval History of England*, 1735, vol. I, p. 107.

(b) An account by the chronicler Raphael Holinshed.

The twentieth of July, the whole navy of the Englishmen made out, and purposed to set on the Frenchmen; but in setting forth, through too much folly, one of the King's ships called the *Mary Rose* was drowned in the midst of the haven, by reason that she was overladen with ordnance, and had the ports [*portholes*] left open, which were very low, and the great artillery unbreached; so that when the ship should turn, the water entered, and suddenly she sunk. In her was Sir George Carew, knight, and four hundred soldiers under his guiding. There escaped not past forty persons of all the whole number...

From *Holinshed's Chronicles of England, Scotland and Ireland*, 1577, vol. III, 1808 edn, p. 848.

(c) From the memoirs of Sir Peter Carew.

Sir George Carew being entered into his ship, he commanded every man to take his place, and the sails to be hoisted. But the same was no sooner done, but that the *Mary Rose* began to heel – that is to say, lean on the one side. Sir George Carew being then in his own ship, and seeing the same, called for the master of his ship, and told him thereof, and asked him what it meant; who answered that if she did heel she was liked to be cast away. Then the said Sir Gawain* passing by the *Mary Rose*, called out to Sir George Carew, asking him how he did; who answered that he had a sort of knaves whom he could not rule. And it was not long after but that the said *Mary Rose*, thus heeling more and more, was drowned with 700 men which were in her, whereof very few escaped ... He had in his ship a hundred mariners, the worst of them being able to be a master in the best ship within the realm; and these so maligned and disdained one the other, that refusing to do that which they should do, were careless to do that which was most needful and necessary; and so contending in envy, perished in frowardness [*perversity*].

From *The Life and Times of Sir Peter Carew, Kt.*, ed. John Maclean, 1857, pp. 33–4.

*Sir George Carew's uncle, and captain of another ship.

142 Hawkins' first contract, 1579

After the death of Henry VIII the navy suffered a period of neglect. Under Elizabeth worsening relations with Spain meant it would be vital to have a strong navy, with ships able to fight far from home waters. The process of modernisation started when John Hawkins made his first contract for the navy's maintenance.

The Bargain of John Hawkins for the Navy, viz:

Conditions in the behalf of her Majesty

First all that which was ordinary in such time as it was £5714 yearly John Hawkins shall perform...

Item to keep in repair all her Majesty's ships so as upon a grounding [*grounding in low water for small repairs*] they may be ready to serve at the seas until some one of them come to be new made in a dry dock.

Item to moor the navy sufficiently so that the ships may ride without danger.

Item to repair all manner of storehouses and wharves at Chatham, Woolwich, Deptford and Portsmouth until any of them shall fall into such decay as they must be new built.

Item to continue all her Majesty's navy in serviceable order and every year to do such reparations as shall be needful either in making of a new ship, repairing in dry docks, or any way otherwise that shall be needful so that the full number be kept as they are now at this present, if any ship be decayed another to be put new in the place of like length and breadth sufficiently builded...

From N. A. M. Rodger, *The Armada in the Public Records*, 1988, pp. 28–9.

143   Sickness and mortality, 1588

Although the English fleet had fended off the Armada, it was in no great shape itself, as is shown in the following despatch from the English commander, Lord Howard of Effingham, to Lord Burghley. It is dated 10 August 1588.

My good Lord:- Sickness and mortality begins wonderfully to grow amongst us; and it is a most pitiful sight to see, here at Margate, how the men, having no place to receive them into here, die in the streets. I am driven myself, of force, to come a-land, to see them bestowed in some lodging; and the best I can get is barns and such outhouses; and the relief is small that I can provide for them here. It would grieve any man's heart to see them that have served so valiantly to die so miserably.

The *Elizabeth Jonas*, which hath done as well as ever any ship did in any service, hath had a great infection in her from the beginning, so as of the 500 men which she carried out, by the time we had been in Plymouth three weeks or a month there were dead of them 200 and above; so as I was driven to set all the rest of her men ashore, to take out her ballast, and to make fires in her of wet broom, three or four days together; and so hoped thereby to have cleansed her of her infection; and thereupon got new men, very tall and able as ever I saw, and put them into her. Now the infection is broken out in greater extremity than ever it did before, and the men die and sicken faster than ever they did; so as I am driven of force to send her to Chatham . . .

It is like enough that the like infection will grow throughout the most part of our fleet; for they have been so long at sea and have so little shift of apparel and so few places to provide them of such wants and no money wherewith to buy it, for some have been – yea the most part – these eight months at sea. My Lord, I would think it a marvellous good way that there were a thousand pounds worth or two thousand marks[†] worth of hose, doublets, shirts, shoes and such like sent down; and I think your Lordship might use therein the Controller of the navy and Waker, Mr Hawkyns his man, who would use all expedition for the providing and sending away of such things; for else in very short time I look to see most of the mariners go naked. Good my Lord, let mariners be pressed and sent down as soon as may be; and money to discharge those that be sick here; and so in haste I bid your Lordship farewell.

From H. W. Hodges and E. A. Hughes, *Select Naval Documents*, Cambridge, 1927, pp. 29–30.

144   Sir Richard Grenville and *The Revenge*, 1591

The exploits of Elizabethan seamen against Catholic Spain, repeated and magnified, contributed not a little to a potent and lasting myth of English nationhood which was also associated with Protestantism and with the cult of Elizabeth. One such exploit, later to be commemorated in Tennyson's famous ballad, was that of Sir Richard Grenville, who insisted on taking on an entire Spanish fleet with one small ship. But was Grenville a suitable role-model for English youth?

(a) From Tennyson's *Revenge*, published in 1878.

He had only a hundred seamen to work the ship and to fight,
And he sailed away from Flores till the Spaniard came in sight,
With his huge sea-castles heaving upon the weather bow,
'Shall we fight or shall we fly?
Good Sir Richard, tell us now,
For to fight is but to die!
There'll be little of us left by the time this sun be set.'
And Sir Richard said again: 'We be all good English men.
Let us bang these dogs of Seville, the children of the devil,
For I never turned my back upon Don or devil yet.'

Sir Richard spoke and he laughed, and we roared a hurrah, and so
The little Revenge ran on sheer into the heart of the foe,
With her hundred fighters on deck, and her ninety sick below;
For half of their fleet to the right and half to the left were seen,
And the little Revenge ran on through the long sea-lane between.

From *The Poems of Tennyson*, ed. Christopher Ricks, 1969, p. 1242.

(b) Grenville as described by a contemporary, John van Linschoten.

This sir Rich. Greenvil was a great and a rich gentleman in England, & had great yearly revenues of his own inheritance, but he was a man very unquiet in his mind, and greatly affected to war; insomuch as of his own private motion he offered his service to the Queen: he had performed many valiant acts, and was greatly feared in these lands and known of every man, but of nature very severe, so that his own people hated him for his fierceness, and spake very hardly of him: for when they first entered into the fleet or Armada [*when the Spanish fleet was first encountered*] they had their great sail in a readiness, and might possibly enough have sailed away, for it was one of the best ships for sail in England, and the master perceiving that the other ships had left them & followed not after, commanded the great sail to be cut that they might make away: but sir Rich. Greenvil threatened both him and all the rest that were in the ship that if any man laid hand upon it he would cause him to be hanged, and so by that occasion they were compelled to fight & in the end were taken. He was of so hard a complexion that, as he continued among the Spanish captains while they were at dinner or supper

From Richard Hakluyt, *The Principal Navigations Voyages Traffiques & Discoveries of the English Nation*, vol. VII, Glasgow, 1904, pp. 81–2.

with him, he would carouse three or four glasses of wine, and in a braverie take the glasses between his teeth and crash them in pieces & swallow them down, so that oftentimes the blood ran out of his mouth without any harm at all unto him: & this was told me by divers credible persons that many times stood and beheld him.

(c) A portrait of Sir Richard Grenville, aged twenty-nine.

From Roy Strong, *Tudor and Jacobean Portraits*, vol. 2 (Plates), HMSO, 1969, plate 256 (National Portrait Gallery no. 1612).

145 Privateering, 1603

In the years after the Armada the sea war with Spain continued, with varying degrees of success. Financial constraints meant that the government relied to a large extent on individual enterprise, but the activities of the privateers did little to enhance the reputation of England in foreign eyes. The following account was sent to Venice by Giovanni Scaramelli, the Republic's representative in England, on 20 March 1603. Scaramelli certainly underestimated the number of the Queen's ships.

While on this topic I must not omit to say that the English through their rapacity and cruelty have become odious to all nations. With Spain they are at open war and are already plundering her and upsetting the India trade; they are continually robbing with violence the French, whom they encounter on the long stretches of the open sea . . .

Hence both those who command, and those who execute here in England, see quite clearly how great, how universal, and how just is the hatred which all nations, nay all peoples we might say, bear to the English, for they are the disturbers of the whole world. And yet with all this they not only do not take any steps to remedy the mischief, but in a certain sense they glory that the English name should become formidable just in this way. For whereas the Kings of England, down to Henry VII and Henry VIII, were wont to keep up a fleet of one hundred ships in full pay as a defence, now the Queen's ships do not amount to more than fifteen or sixteen, as her revenue cannot support a greater charge; and so the whole of the strength and repute of the nation rests on the vast number of small privateers, which are supported and increase to that dangerous extent which everyone recognises; and to ensure this support, the privateers make the ministers partners in the profits, without the risk of a penny in the fitting out, but only a share in the prizes, which are adjudged by judges placed there by the ministers themselves.

From Horatio F. Brown (ed.), *Calendar of State Papers . . . in the Archives . . . of Venice*, vol. IX, *1592–1603*, 1897, no. 1160, pp. 556–7.

Exploration and Trade

146 Henry VII and the wine trade, 1485

Henry VII inherited a navy of some ten ships, built up by his Yorkist predecessors. He increased the size of the King's ships, while allowing the overall number to fall. He also developed dockyards at Portsmouth and on the Thames, and, as the following extract shows, attempted to encourage the growth of merchant shipping.

An Act against bringing in of Gascon wines, except in English, Irish or Welshmen's ships. 1 Henry VII, cap. 8.

Item, in the said Parliament it was called to remembrance of the great [di]minishing and decay that hath been now of late time of the Navy within this realm of England, and idleness of the mariners within the same, by the which this noble realm, within short process of time, without reformation be had therein, shall not be of ability and power to defend itself. Wherefore at the prayer of the said Commons, the King our sovereign lord, by the advice of the Lords spiritual and temporal in this said present Parliament assembled, and by authority of the same, it is enacted, ordained and established that no manner person of what degree or condition that he be of, buy nor sell within this said realm...any manner wines of the growing of the Duchy of Guyenne or of Gascony, but such as shall be...brought in an English, Irish or Welshman's ship or ships, and the mariners of the same English, Irish or Welshmen for the more part...This Act and ordinance to endure betwixt this and the beginning of the next Parliament...

From *The Statutes of the Realm*, vol. II, 1816, p. 502.

147   John Cabot, 1496–97

John Cabot, an Italian who appeared in Bristol in about 1495, is thought to have made at least two voyages of exploration across the Atlantic. He may have landed on Newfoundland during the first, but disappeared during the second, in 1498. However, his son, Sebastian, who also became a famous explorer, seems to have deliberately obscured his father's achievement.

(a) From Henry VII's *Letters Patent*[†], granted to John Cabot and his sons, 5 March 1496.

The King, to all to whom, etc. Greeting: Be it known and made manifest that we have given and granted as by these presents we give and grant, for us and our heirs, to our well-beloved John Cabot, citizen of Venice, and to Lewis, Sebastian and Sancino, sons of the said John, and to the heirs and deputies of them, and of any one of them, full and free authority, faculty and power to sail to all parts, regions and coasts of the eastern, western and northern sea, under our banners, flags and ensigns, with five ships or vessels of whatsoever burden or quality they may be, and with so many and with such mariners and men as they may wish to take with them in the said ships, at their own proper costs and charges, to find, discover and investigate whatsoever islands, countries, regions or provinces of heathens and infidels, in whatsoever part of the world placed, which before this time were unknown to all Christians...

From J. A. Williamson, *The Cabot Voyages and Bristol Discovery under Henry VII*, Hakluyt Society, 1961, p. 204.

(b) A foreign report.

Raimondo de Raimondi de Soncino, Milanese Ambassador in England, to Ludovico Maria Sforza, Duke of Milan

(*London, 18 December, 1497*) Perhaps amid the numerous occupations of your Excellency, it may not weary you to hear how his Majesty here has gained a part of Asia, without a stroke of the sword. There is in this Kingdom a man of the people, Messer Zoane Caboto by name, of kindly wit and a most expert mariner. Having observed that the sovereigns first of Portugal and then of Spain had occupied unknown islands, he decided to make a similar acquisition for his Majesty. After obtaining patents that the effective ownership of what he might find should be his, though reserving the rights of the Crown, he committed himself to fortune in a little ship, with eighteen persons. He started from Bristol, a port on the west of this kingdom, passed Ireland, which is still further west, and then bore towards the north, in order to sail to the east, leaving the north on his right hand after some days. After having wandered for some time he at length arrived at the mainland, where he hoisted the royal standard, and took possession for the king here; and after taking certain tokens he returned.

This Messer Zoane, as a foreigner and a poor man, would not have obtained credence, had it not been that his companions, who are practically all English and from Bristol, testified that he spoke the truth. This Messer Zoane has the description of the world in a map, and also in a solid sphere, which he has made, and shows where he has been. In going towards the east he passed far beyond the country of the Tanais [*the River Don*]. They say that the land is excellent and temperate, and they believe that Brazil wood [*a tree from which red dye was obtained*] and silk are native there. They assert that the sea there is swarming with fish, which can be taken not only with the net, but in baskets let down with a stone, so that it sinks in the water. I have heard this Messer Zoane state so much.

These same English, his companions, say that they could bring so many fish that this kingdom would have no further need of Iceland, from which place there comes a very great quantity of the fish called stockfish*. But Messer Zoane has his mind set upon even greater things, because he proposes to keep along the coast from the place at which he touched, more and more towards the east, until he reaches an island which he calls Cipango**, situated in the equinoctial region, where he believes that all the spices of the world have their origin, as well as the jewels.

*This was the name for cod and other fish, cured by drying in the open air.
**Cipangu was the name given by Marco Polo to Japan.

From Allen B. Hinds (ed.),
Calendar of State Papers and Manuscripts existing in ... Milan,
vol. I, 1912, no. 552, pp. 336–7.

(c) Sebastian Cabot's account.

When my father departed from Venice many years since to dwell in England, to follow the trade of marchandises, he took me with him to the city of London, while I was very young, yet having nevertheless some knowledge of letters of humanitie, and of the Sphere. And when my father died in that time when news were brought that Don Christopher Colonus [*Columbus*] Genuese had discovered the coasts of India, whereof was great talk in all the Court of king Henry the 7, who then reigned, insomuch that all men with great admiration affirmed it to be a thing more divine than human, to sail by the West into the East where spices grow, by a way that was never known before, by this fame and report there increased in my heart a great flame of desire to attempt some notable thing. And understanding by reason of the Sphere, that if I should sail by way of the Northwest, I should by a shorter tract come into India, I thereupon caused the King to be advertised of my devise, who immediately commanded two carvels [*caravels*[†]] to be furnished with all things appertaining to the voyage, which was as far as I remember in the year 1496, in the beginning of summer.

From Richard Hakluyt, *The Principal Navigations Voyages Traffiques & Discoveries of the English Nation*, Glasgow, vol. VII, 1904, pp. 147–8.

148   Overproduction of cloth, 1550

Cloth was easily England's greatest export and the cloth trade grew rapidly during the first half of the century. However, in 1550 the boom started to collapse, partly due to a general glut of cloth for sale in Antwerp, and partly owing to Northumberland's deflationary policy which was pricing English cloth out of the European market. A law limiting apprenticeship, as suggested here, was passed in 1552 and reinforced in the Elizabethan Statute of Artificers, 1563.

At the Star Chamber, the xxviiith of April, 1550.
Complaint was made by certain clothiers that the Merchant Adventurers by agreement had set such a price upon their cloths that without the loss of xxs. in a piece they could not utter [*sell*] them; for the more perfect knowledge whereof, all manner of clothiers that then were in London appeared at the Star Chamber by commandment, where the more part denied to be privy or of counsel with the said complaint, finding great fault with the multitude of clothiers lately increased in the realm, affirming that, as long as every man that would, had liberty to be a clothier, as they have now, it was impossible to have good cloth made in the realm, for he that is not bred up in that faculty must trust his factors [*agents*], and so is commonly deceived; and now the good making is decayed, the cloths are out of estimation, by reason whereof the prices must also decay; wherfore it was concluded that some device should be had for a law that none should meddle with cloth-making but such as had been prentices to the occupation.

For the clothiers' matter the Merchant Adventurers were called before the Council, for whom the Mayor of London with certain of the chiefest of the Company appeared, and to the complaint of the clothiers answered that they agreed not together to hinder the clothiers' prices, but the truth is that there lie at Antwerp such a number of our cloths unsold that till they were uttered these here would not well be bought; which, together with the naughtiness [*faults*] of the making, hindered the prices, and besides that it was commonly not used to ship any between Easter and Whitsuntide.

Further divers reasons were made by them touching the decay of our money by exchange, with other devices touching the commonwealth, which they were commanded to put in writing.

From J. R. Dasent (ed.), *Acts of the Privy Council of England*, New Series, vol. III, *1550–1552*, 1891, pp. 19–20.

149   Hakluyt's *Voyages*, 1589

In his massive quarto edition of 1589 (enlarged to three volumes in 1598–1600), the industrious Richard Hakluyt attempted to record the naval history of his times. In so doing he inspired his countrymen to further efforts, as well as providing future historians with a wealth of source material which might otherwise have vanished.

... to speak a word of that just commendation which our nation do indeed deserve: it can not be denied, but as in all former ages there have been men full of activity, stirrers abroad, and searchers of the remote parts of the world, so in this most famous and peerless government of her most excellent Majesty, her subjects through the special assistance and blessing of God, in searching the most opposite corners and quarters of the world, and to speak plainly, in compassing the vast globe of the earth more than once, have excelled all the nations and people of the earth. For, which of the kings of this land before her Majesty had their banners ever seen in the Caspian sea? Which of them hath ever dealt with the Emperor of Persia, as her Majesty hath done, and obtained for her merchants large & loving privileges? Who ever saw before this regiment [*rule*], an English Ligier [*ambassador*] in the stately porch of the Grand Signor at Constantinople? Who ever found English consuls & agents at Tripolis in Syria, at Aleppo, at Babylon, at Balsara, and, which is more, who ever heard of Englishmen at Goa before now? What English ships did heretofore ever anchor in the mighty river of Plate, pass and repass the unpassable (in former opinion) straight of Magellan, range along the coast of Chili, Peru, and all the backside of *Nova Hispania* [*the Pacific coast of South America*], further than any Christian ever passed, traverse the mighty breadth of the South sea, land upon the Luzones [*the Philippines*] in despite of the enemy, enter into alliance, amity and traffic with the princes of the Moluccaes and the isle of Java, double the famous Cape of *Bona Speranza* [*Good Hope*], arrive at the isle of Santa Helena, and last of all return home most richly laden with the commodities of China, as the subjects of this now flourishing monarchy have done?

From Richard Hakluyt, *The Principal Navigations Voyages Traffiques & Discoveries of the English Nation*, Glasgow, 1904: *Epistle Dedicatorie to Sir Francis Walsingham*, vol. I, p. xx.

150   The East India Company, 1599

The setting up of this company is an example of the beneficial use of a monopoly. This extract, which is from the Court Minutes of the East India Company, describes the joint-stock principle on which the company was based.

An assembly of the persons hereunder named holden the xxiiij of September 1599.
[Fifty-seven names]
Whereas the several persons abovenamed together with divers others whose names are Registered in the beginning of this book, by

the sufferance of almighty god after Royal assent of our Sovereign Lady the Queens most excellent Majesty first thereunto had and obtained, do intend for the honour of our native Country and for the advancement of trade of merchandise within this realm of England upon their several adventures according to the several proportions of the sums of money by them severally set down and inregistered under their own hands. To set forth a voyage this present year to the East Indies and other the Islands and Countries thereabouts, and there to make trade by the sale of such commodities as upon further deliberation shall be resolved to be provided for those parts or otherwise by buying or bartering of such goods wares jewels or merchandise as those Islands or Countries may yield or afford ... And therefore at this assembly it is agreed ordained and resolved as followeth.

First that no ship shall be received to be brought in by any adventurer in this voyage to be employed in the same as his stock or portion of adventure at any rate whatsoever.

Also that all shipping to be employed in this voyage shall be bought and provided by such as shall be thereto appointed for ready money only.

That no commodity shall be accepted in the said voyage to be brought in as any man's portion of adventure, but that all goods wares and other things shall be bought and prepared by such as shall be thereunto appointed as Committees and directors of the said voyage, for the buying and providing of shipping and merchandise ...

From R.H. Tawney and Eileen Power (eds), *Tudor Economic Documents*, 1924, vol. II, pp. 83–5.

It is resolved at this assembly that from henceforth no adventurer in this voyage shall be received to adventure in the same for a less sum than 200 pounds.

CHAPTER 8   CULTURE AND SOCIETY

This chapter presents documents on three separate aspects of sixteenth-century culture – the role of women; education and literacy; buildings and furnishings.

Although England was ruled by women during the second half of the century, there were still those who felt that a female was intrinsically unfit for such a role. In a thoroughly patriarchal society the husband and father was seen as possessing all authority within the household, as did monarch or nobleman within their respective spheres. The law reflected the subordination of wives, whose property was placed under their husbands' control. It was, too, the male's task to guard the 'honour' of his wife and daughters. Primogeniture made it important, among the better-off classes at least, that a child's paternity should not be in dispute. Hence, seduction and adultery were seen as a form of theft, and a woman's value was bound up with her chastity. Among the poor, bastardy was also likely to involve a charge on the parish; the magistrates' time was therefore much taken up with bastardy cases and paternity orders. No doubt there were many happy marriages in Tudor England, but in all except the lowest sections of society marriage was often considered first and foremost as an unbreakable financial contract. Divorce was not sanctioned by the Church, although separation might be condoned, especially in cases of adultery.

The century saw many improvements and considerable interest in education, as England came under the influence of Renaissance ideas. Books on the subject appeared, new schools were founded, and to some extent teaching techniques advanced beyond the rote learning typical of earlier ages. Nevertheless, contemporaries did not share the modern concept of the child as a being with special needs, such as play. The Tudor curriculum always involved long, tedious hours of formal education, starting at a very tender age. In the new grammar schools holidays were short, punishment frequent, and there was an almost exclusive emphasis on the classics. The two English universities expanded considerably in this period, with the foundation of several new colleges. They ceased to be primarily for the training of priests and it became fashionable for gentlemen to send their sons there for at least a year or two. After 1593 over half the House of Commons were graduates. Women, however, continued to lack proper education, apart from a very few upper-class girls.

The first English printing press was set up by William Caxton some eight years before the battle of Bosworth, and the Tudor period saw the output of books and other printed material steadily increasing. Both the Renaissance and the Reformation hastened this development. The revival of Latin and Greek literature created a demand for classical texts which only printing could satisfy. And Protestantism based its challenge to the Roman Church on the authority of the Bible, the word of God, which reformers claimed should be available to all men and women. Not only reading but also writing became highly desirable assets, and knowledge of these skills expanded among the population, particularly in the higher levels, during the reign of Elizabeth.

Patterns of consumption grew more extravagant during the century. Dress became elaborate and colourful, diet more varied, and houses larger and more comfortable. Such changes affected everyone except the very poor, whose condition probably deteriorated, especially in the harsh years of the century's last decade. At the upper end of society there appeared the new 'prodigy' houses of the nobility and leading gentry, often financed out of the profits of government service. Many middling gentry and yeomen also built themselves new houses, though on a much smaller scale, and their inventories in the second half of the century show that they possessed a variety of furniture, carpets and wall-hangings as well as bed linen and personal clothing. Pewter dishes were taking the place of wooden trenchers, and former luxuries such as glass windows and chimneys were becoming more common. These improvements in life-style made their contribution to the powerful growth of English self-confidence and nationalism at this time: the idea that of all peoples, God held the English in a special esteem.

The Role of Women

151   A farmer's wife, 1548

The myriad responsibilities of a farmer's wife made her in practice, if not legally, her husband's equal partner.

And when thou art up and ready, then first sweep thy house, dress up thy dishboard, and set all things in good order within thy house: milk thy kye [*kyne*], secle [*suckle*] thy calves, sye up [*strain*] thy milk, take up thy children, array them, provide for thy husband's breakfast, dinner, supper, and for thy children and servants, and take thy part with them. And to ordain corn and malt to the mill, to bake and brew withall when need is. And mette [*send*] it to the mill, and from the mill, and see that thou have thy measure again besyde the tolle [*the miller's portion*], or else the miller dealeth not truly with thee, or else thy corn is not dry as it should be. Thou must make butter and cheese when thou mayest, serve thy swine both morning and evening, give thy poleyn [*poultry*] meat in the morning, and, when time of the year cometh, thou must take heed how thy hens, ducks and geese do lay, and when they wax broody, set them there as no beasts, swine nor other vermin hurt them ... It is convenient for a husband to have sheep of his own for many causes, and then may his wife have part of the wool, to make her husband and herself some clothes...It is a wife's occupation to winnow all manner of corns, to make malt, to wash and wring, to make hay, shear corn, and in time of need to help her husband to fill the muck wayne or dung cart, drive the plough, to load hay, corn, and such other. And to go or ride to the market, to sell butter, cheese, milk, eggs, chickens, capons, hens, pigs, geese and all manner of corns. And also to buy all manner of necessary things belonging to the household, and to make a true reckoning and account to her husband, what she hath received and what she hath paid. And if the husband go to market, to buy or sell, as they oft do, he then to show his wife in like manner. For if one of them should use to deceive the other he deceiveth himself, and he is not like to thrive. And therefore they must be true either to other.

From John Fitzherbert, The boke of husbandrye, 1548, fols. 67–8.

152   Knox's *First Blast*, 1558

Shortly before Elizabeth's accession, John Knox published his notorious attack upon female rulers, *A First Blast of the Trumpet against the Monstrous Regiment* [Rule] *of Women* (**a**). This was hardly calculated to appeal to Queen Elizabeth, and a year later, when Knox needed her permission to travel through England on his way back to Scotland, he wrote her a letter in which he 'explained' his meaning (**b**).

(a) 1558.

To promote a woman to bear rule, superiority, dominion or empire above any realm, nation, or city, is repugnant to nature, contumely to God, a thing most contrarious to his revealed will and approved ordinance, and finally it is the subversion of good order, of all equity and justice...

For who can deny but it...repugneth to nature that the blind shall be appointed to lead and conduct such as do see? That the weak, the sick and impotent persons shall nourish and keep the whole and strong? And, finally, that the foolish, mad and frenetic shall govern the discreet and give counsel to such as be sober of mind? And such be all women compared unto man in bearing of authority. For their sight in civil regiment is but blindness: their strength, weakness: their counsel, foolishness: and judgement, frenzy, if it be rightly considered.

(b) 1559.

To the virtuous and godly Elizabeth...

As your Grace's displeasure against me most unjustly conceived hath been and is to my wretched heart a burden grievous and almost intolerable, so is the testimony of a clean conscience to me a stay and uphold that in desperation I sink not, how vehement that ever the temptation appear. For in God's presence my conscience beareth me record that [neither] maliciously nor of purpose I never offended your Grace, nor your realm...

I cannot deny the writing of a book against the usurped authority and unjust regiment of women, neither yet am I minded to retreat or to call back any principal point or proposition of the same...For, first, my book toucheth not your Grace's person in especial, neither yet is it prejudicial to any liberty of the realm, if the time and my writing be indifferently considered. How could I be enemy to your Grace's person?...And, as concerning your regiment [*government*], how could I, or can I, envy that which most I have thirsted [for], and [for] which...I render thanks unfeignedly unto God?...

But omitting the accusation of others, for my own purgation [*clearing myself of guilt*] and for your Grace's satisfaction I say that nothing in my book contained is, or can be, prejudicial to your Grace's just regiment, provided that ye be not found ungrateful unto God.

From David Laing (ed.), *The Works of John Knox*, Edinburgh, 1895: (**a**) vol. V, pp. 373–4; (**b**) vol. VI, pp. 47–9.

153   The marriage contract

Following the Church's teaching, sixteenth-century commentators were very clear about the purpose of marriage. However, their views conflicted with a widespread tendency, especially among the propertied classes, to look on the marriages of their own children primarily as financial and social contracts.

(**a**) From William Harrington's *Comendacions of Matrymony*, published in 1528.

Moreover this consent which doth make matrymony ought to be grounded of a good cause and intent, that is to say, those that will enter into this holy order must do it principally for one of three causes: that is to say, either to the intent for to bring forth children to be nourished in the laws & service of God, and that is the most principal cause...or else, secondarily, for remedy against sin, as such as ben [*those who are*] inclined naturally to the sin of the flesh and will not endeavour them self to live chaste may make matrymony for that cause, to avoid the sin of fornication...Or else, thirdly, for solace and help, which either may have of other without the act of fleshly medlynge.

Secondly, there be other causes which move rather to take one person than another, as riches, beauty, reforming of peace or such other...But such as doth not marry principally for one of the three causes afore said but rather principally for riches, beauty or friends or such other, do not marry godly or graciously, but they sin deeply and the devil hath great power of them.

(**b**) From Thomas Becon's *Boke of Matrimony*, c. 1562, on forced marriages of noblemen's children.

This kind of marrying hath ever been detested. And not without a cause. For when they come into the perfection of age, and see other whom they could find in their heart to fancy and love better, then many of them begin to hate one another and curse their parents even unto the pit of hell for the coupling of them together. Then seek they all means possible to be divorced one from another. But if it be so that they remain still together, what frowning, overwharting [*quarrelling*], scolding and chiding is there between them, so that the whole house is filled full of those tragedies even unto the top. What a wicked and hell-like life is this! The baser sort of people see this unquiet life that is used among the gentlemen and their wives, then go they home, and if any thing (be it never so little) displeases them, straight they are together by the ears with their wives, so that shortly after the whole town is in a roar ... What is the original cause of all these tragical and bloody dissensions but only the covetous affection [*desire*] of those parents which for lucre's [*money's*] sake so wickedly bestow their children in their youth, and yoke them with such as they can not favour in their age.

Both extracts printed in C. L. Powell, *English Domestic Relations 1487–1653*, New York, 1917: (**a**) Appendix C, pp. 232–3; (**b**) p. 125.

154 The condition of English women, 1565

Sir Thomas Smith's view of the state of women in sixteenth-century England. For details about the author, see **Doc. 52**.

The wife is so much in the power of her husband that not only her goods by marriage are straight made her husband's, and she loseth all her administration which she had of them: but also, where all English men have name and surname ... our daughters, so soon as they be married, lose the surname of their father, and of the family and stock whereof they do come, and take the surname of their husbands, as transplanted from their family into another ...

Although the wife be (as I have written before) *in manu et potestate mariti* [*in the hand and power of her husband*], by our law yet they be not kept so strait – as in mew [*confinement*] and with a guard – as they be in Italy and Spain, but have almost as much liberty as in France. And they have for the most part all the charge of the house and household ... which is indeed the natural occupation, exercise, office and part of a wife. The husband [is] to meddle with the defence either by law or force, and with all foreign matters, which is the natural part and office of the man, as I have written before. And although our law may seem somewhat rigorous toward the wives, yet for the most part they can handle their husbands so well and so dulcely [*sweetly*], and specially when their husbands be sick, that where the law giveth them nothing, their husbands at their death, of their goodwill, will give them all.

From Sir Thomas Smith, *De Republica Anglorum* (1583), ed. L. Alston, Cambridge, 1906, pp. 125–7.

155   Falling from virtue, 1547, 1583

(a) An unmarried daughter who became pregnant could expect little mercy from her family, as is shown in this letter from Christopher Breten to his brother-in-law, John Johnson, written in December 1547.

After all hearty commendations unto you and my sister your bed-fellow, and also my brother Laurence, with the same from my wife, I am very sorry my daughter – whom I would God had pleased to have taken before she had been fully one day old – hath given so much occasion towards the evil bruit [*rumour*] that hath been bruited and spoken of her, as I do now think by your writing (the more sorry therefore) to be true . . .

Brother, as against Rede [*the presumed father of the baby*] ye have so compelled me by your writing to suppose him to be an offender, that I shall desire you with other my friends to help to punish him as he shall be found worthy, being nothing glad I have or should have occasion so to do. And for my daughter, God amend her, if this be true [she] shall have for my part the broad world to walk in. I pray God give her grace and me also to repent and amend (as much as in us may be) all things that be amiss, and if any have misreported her, to give them like grace.

Brother, if you perceive the thing to be so great that she be not worthy to resort again into your service, I shall desire you till we may meet, that ye will see them where she hath been [staying] recompensed for their charges and pains she hath put them unto; and I shall, God willing, see you recompensed with most hearty thanks; and after, let God (if so may please him) and herself provide for her.

From Barbara Winchester, Tudor Family Portraits, 1955, pp. 87–8.

(b) Punishment for the offence of producing an illegitimate child was usually more severe for the woman than for the man.

24 December [1583]. Mr. Dr. William Lewyn and I [JPs] took order that Margaret Dutton should be first whipped at Gravesend and then sent to the house of correction for a bastard woman child there born and begotten on her by Robert Cole, as it is thought, whom also we committed till he give sureties to appear at the Easter sessions, for to stand to the order of the bench there, because he refused to perform the order set down against him by my Lord Cobham and Mr. Somer.

The same day also he and I took like order for the whipping of Abigail Sherwood for a bastard man child born by her at Chatham and for her like sending to the house of correction. But as touching the reputed father, we left the decision thereof to the ecclesiastical trial, for that she confessed herself to have been carnally known of many men. The child also was dead so that nothing was to be done in the parish.

From Conyers Read, William Lambarde and Local Government, Ithaca, New York, 1962, pp. 30–1.

156   Equal partners? c. 1599

In *Julius Caesar*, Portia, the wife of Brutus, asks why a wife should not be entitled to share her husband's problems.

PORTIA: Within the bond of marriage, tell me Brutus,
Is it excepted I should know no secrets
That appertain to you? Am I your self
But as it were in sort or limitation,
To keep with you at meals, comfort your bed,
And talk to you sometimes? Dwell I but in the suburbs
Of your good pleasure? If it be no more,
Portia is Brutus' harlot, not his wife.
BRUTUS: You are my true and honourable wife,
As dear to me as are the ruddy drops
That visit my sad heart.
PORTIA: If this were true, then should I know this secret.
I grant I am a woman; but withal
A woman that Lord Brutus took to wife.

From William Shakespeare, *Julius Caesar*, Act II, Scene i.

157   Offensive words

(a) Female vanity was a conventional theme for many contemporary writers, especially Puritan commentators on society.

Yet we see how proud many, especially women, be of such bables [*baubles*]: for when they have spent a good part of the day in tricking and trimming, pricking and pinning, pranking and pouncing, girding and lacing, and braving up themselves in most exquisite manner, then out they come into the streets with their pedlers shop about their back, and carry their crests very high, taking themselves to be little angels, or at least somewhat more than other women; whereupon they do so exceedingly swell with pride that it is to be feared they will burst with it as they walk in the streets. And truly we may think the very stones in the street and the beams in the houses do quake & wonder at their monstrous, intolerable and excessive pride: for it seemeth that they are altogether a lump of pride, a mass of pride, even altogether made of pride, and nothing else but pride, pride.

From Arthur Dent, *The Plaine Mans Path-way to Heaven*, 1601; quoted in Louis B. Wright, *Middle-Class Culture in Elizabethan England*, University of North Carolina Press, 1935, pp. 478–9.

(b) The fact that the following allegation, made in 1570, was taken seriously by the authorities says something about the unequal relationship between the sexes at this time.

The Bishop of Peterborough to a local magistrate.

I pray you at your convenient leisure to call before you, in my name, William Ellis, Robert Jower, the wife of one Mellish and also Tristram Griffith, inhabitants of Witley, and (upon their several oaths) to examine them severally whether that they heard Nicholas

From Keith Thomas, *Man and the Natural World. Changing attitudes in England 1500–1800*, 1983, p. 43.

Woodies of Witley say and affirm that women had no souls, or the like words, contrary to the creation of man. I pray you betwixt this and Friday come seven night certify me what you find in this matter. Let the vicar of Witley be present, the better to put the witness in mind of the words.

Education and Literacy

158   *The Boke Named the Governour*, 1531

Sir Thomas Elyot, a protégé of Wolsey who subsequently served Henry VIII as ambassador to the Emperor Charles V, was the author of the first treatise on education to be written in English. *The Boke Named the Governour* was first published in 1531 and thereafter went through many editions.

Some old authors hold opinion that before the age of seven years a child should not be instructed in letters. But those writers were either Greeks or Latins, among whom all doctrine and sciences were in their maternal tongues, by reason whereof they saved all that long time which at this day is spent in understanding perfectly the Greek or Latin. Wherefore it requireth now a longer time to the understanding of both. Therefore that infelicity of our time and country compelleth us to encroach somewhat upon the years of children, and specially of noblemen, that they may sooner attain to wisdom and gravity than private persons – considering, as I have said, their charge and example, which above all things is most to be esteemed.

Notwithstanding, I would not have them enforced by violence to learn, but . . . to be sweetly allured thereto with praises and such pretty gifts as children delight in. And their first letters to be painted or limned [*depicted*] in a pleasant manner, wherein children of gentle courage have much delectation. And also there is no better allective [*incentive*] to noble wits than to induce them into a contention with their inferior companions – they sometime purposely suffering the more noble children to vanquish, and, as it were, giving to them place and sovereignty, though indeed the inferior children [may] have more learning. But there can be nothing more convenient than by little and little to train and exercise them in speaking of Latin, informing them to know first the names in Latin of all things that cometh in sight and to name all the parts of their bodies; and giving them somewhat that they covet or desire, in most gentle manner to teach them to ask it again in Latin. And if by this means they may be induced to understand and speak Latin, it shall afterward be less grief to them, in a manner, to learn anything, where they understand the language wherein it is written . . .

From Sir Thomas Elyot, *The Boke Named the Governour*, vol. I, ed. H. H. S. Croft, 1883, pp. 31–3.

159   The example of Queen Elizabeth

The following extract comes from *The Scholemaster*, another English treatise on education, written this time by Roger Ascham, who was tutor to Elizabeth.

There is one example for all the gentlemen of this Court to follow that may well satisfy them, or nothing will serve them, nor no example move them to goodness and learning. It is your shame – I speak to you all, you young gentlemen of England – that one maid should go beyond you all, in excellency of learning and knowledge of divers tongues. Point forth six of the best given gentlemen of this Court, and all they together show not so much good will, spend not so much time, bestow not so many hours daily, orderly and constantly for the increase of learning and knowledge, as doth the Queen's Majesty herself. Yea, I believe that beside her perfect readiness in Latin, Italian, French, and Spanish, she readeth here now at Windsor more Greek every day than some prebendary[†] of this Church doth read Latin in a whole week. And that which is most praiseworthy of all, within the walls of her privy chamber she hath obtained that excellency of learning, to understand, speak and write, both wittily with head and fair with hand, as scarce one or two rare wits in both the universities have in many years reached unto. Amongst all the benefits that God hath blessed me withal, next the knowledge of Christ's true religion, I count this the greatest: that it pleased God to call me to be one poor minister in setting forward these excellent gifts of learning in this most excellent Prince. Whose only example, if the rest of our nobility would follow, then might England be for learning and wisdom in nobility a spectacle to all the world beside...

From Roger Ascham, *The Scholemaster* (1570), ed. J.E.B. Mayor, 1863, pp. 62–4.

160   Sir Thomas More's daughters

This portrait of Sir Thomas More and his family was painted in 1593 after an earlier portrait by Holbein, but purports to show the family in about 1530. In the centre of the picture are More's three highly educated daughters, Cecily, Elizabeth (standing) and Margaret. To the left, More himself is seated alongside his father.

From Roy Strong, *Tudor and Jacobean Portraits*, vol. 2, HMSO, 1969 (National Portrait Gallery no. 2765).

161   A day with one's tutor, c. 1530

Young upper-class boys received the attentions of a full-time tutor in order to turn them into gentlemen. Here, the tutor of Gregory Cromwell reports to Gregory's father, Thomas Cromwell.

After that it pleased your Mastership to give me in charge not only to give diligent attendance upon Master Gregory, but also to instruct him with good letters, honest manners, pastimes of instruments, and such other qualities as should be for him meet and convenient, pleaseth it you to understand that for the accomplishment thereof I have endeavoured myself by all ways possible to invent and excogitate how I might most profit him, in which behalf through his diligence the success is such as I trust shall be to your good contentation and pleasure, and his no small profit. But for cause summer was spent in the service of the wild goddess [*Diana, goddess of hunting*] it is so much to be regarded after what fashion youth is educated and brought up, in which time that that is learned (for the most part) will not all wholly be forgotten in the older years. I think it my duty to assertain your Mastership how he spendeth his time, so that if there be anything contrary [to] your good pleasure, after advertisement received in that behalf it may be amended.

And first, after he hath heard mass he taketh a lecture [*reading*] of a Dialogue of Erasmus' *Colloquium*, called *Pietas puerilis* [*youthful piety*], wherein is described a very picture of one that should be virtuously brought up, and for cause it is so necessary for him, I do not only cause him to read it over, but also to practise the precepts of the same, and I have also translated it into English, so that he may confer them both together, whereof (as learned men affirm) cometh no small profit; which translation pleaseth it you to receive by the bringer hereof, that ye may judge how much profitable it is to be learned. After that, he exerciseth his hand in writing, one or two hours, and readeth upon Fabian's *Chronicle** as long. The residue of the day he doth spend upon the lute and virginals. When he rideth (as he doth very oft) I tell him by the way some history of the Romans or the Greeks, which I cause him to rehearse again in a tale. For his recreation he useth to hawk and hunt, and shoot ... his long bow, which frameth and succeedeth so well with him that he seemeth to be thereunto given by nature ...

From Henry Ellis (ed.), *Original Letters, illustrative of English History*, 3rd series, vol. I, 1846, pp. 343–5.

*Robert Fabian (d. 1513) was the author of a popular *Chronicle* which covered the history of England from the (mythical) arrival of Brutus down to the death of Henry VII.

162   The grammar school

Dozens of grammar schools were founded by private charity during the century. Although nominally open to all those who could afford the small fees, these 'free' schools, with their almost exclusively classical curriculum, came to be dominated by pupils from the richer sections of society.

(a)

And the said master of the scholars shall teach freely in the said school of Jesus all scholars coming to learn ... and he shall have a register book and therein write the names of all his scholars with the day and year of their first coming and admission into the said school, taking therefore of every scholar only at his said first coming four pence, and never after anything ...

And to the intent the scholars of the said school may be placed in a seemly order whereby they may more quietly apply their learning, the said school shall be divided into four forms.

And in the first form shall be placed young beginners commonly called petties, until they can read perfectly, pronounce also and sound their words plainly and distinctly; the master himself shall not be bound to teach the same young beginners so long as they continue in their first form but only assign in order and course daily or weekly by his direction so many of his scholars placed in the third and fourth form as may sufficiently teach young beginners, and he himself to bestow two hours in teaching them...

In the second form shall be placed such scholars as can read and pronounce their words...and [the master] shall teach [them] the introduction of grammar, commonly called the eight parts of speech...And when they know these concords well he shall teach them the verses of manners made by William Lilly*; the *Precepts* of Cato; with such other little books wherein is contained not [only] the eloquence of the tongue, but also good plain lessons of honesty and godliness whereby they may be induced to perfect pronunciation.

In the third form...the master shall teach them the Latin grammar as it is set forth and used in this realm; Terence; also *Aesop's Fables*, Virgil and Tully's [*Cicero's*] *Epistles*...and as he shall perceive them [to] profit in learning so he shall place them in the fourth form and teach unto them there Sallust, Ovid, Tully's *Offices*, [and] the *Commentaries* of Caesar...And he shall teach them also the art of versifying (if he himself be expert therein) to such scholars as he shall perceive apt to learn the same, and the art of numbering by arithmetic...

The scholars of the third and fourth forms shall speak nothing in the school but Latin, saving only in their teaching of the lower forms.

*William Lily (d. 1522), the first headmaster of St Paul's School, was the author of the standard Latin grammar.

From the statutes of Guisborough Grammar School, 1561 (founder: Robert Pursglove); preserved in manuscript in the library of Prior Pursglove College, Guisborough, Cleveland.

(b) Francis Bacon was among those who criticised the non-vocational nature of the grammar schools when he wrote to James I in 1611 opposing the foundation of Charterhouse School.

Concerning the advancement of learning, I do subscribe to the opinion of one of the wisest and greatest men of your kingdom that, for grammar schools, there are already too many, and therefore no providence to add where there is excess. For the great number of schools which are in your Highness's realm doth cause a want, and likewise an overthrow; both of them are inconvenient, and one of them dangerous; for by means thereof they find want in the country and towns, both of servants for husbandry†, and apprentices for trade; and on the other side, there being more scholars bred than the State can prefer and employ, and the active part of that life not bearing a proportion to the preparative, it must needs fall out that many persons will be bred unfit for other vocations, and unprofitable for that in which they were bred up, which fill the realm full of indigent, idle and wanton people, who are but *materia rerum novarum* [*interested only in novelty*].

From James Spedding (ed.), *The Letters and the Life of Francis Bacon*, 1861–72, vol. IV, p. 249.

163   The universities

William Harrison describes the contemporary expansion of the universities which, like the grammar schools, had largely ceased to provide for the poor. (For details about the author, see **Doc. 21**.)

In my time there are three noble universities in England: to wit – one at Oxford, the second at Cambridge, and the third in London [*the Inns of Court*]; of which the first two are the most famous, I mean Cambridge and Oxford, for that in them the use of the tongues, philosophy, and the liberal sciences, besides the profound studies of the civil law, physic, and theology, are daily taught and had; whereas in the latter the laws of the realm are only read and learnt ...

   In most of our colleges there are also great numbers of students, of which many are found by the revenues of the houses and other by the purveyances and help of their rich friends, whereby in some one college you shall have two hundred scholars, in others an hundred and fifty, in divers a hundred and forty, and in the rest less numbers, as the capacity of the said houses is able to receive; so that at this present, of one sort and other, there are about three thousand students nourished in them both (as by a late survey it manifestly appeared). They were erected by their founders at the first only for poor men's sons, whose parents were not able to bring them up unto learning, but now they have the least benefit of them, by reason the rich do so encroach upon them. And so far hath this inconvenience spread itself that it is in my time an hard matter for a poor man's child to come by a fellowship (though he be never so good a scholar and worthy of that room [*place*]).

From William Harrison, *The Description of England* (1577), ed. Frederick J. Furnivall, 1877, pp. 70–1, 76–7.

164   The uses of literacy

(a) An early seventeenth-century author sums up the advantages of literacy.

[Through writing] all high matters of whatsoever nature or importance are both intended and prosecuted, secret matters are secretly kept, friends that be a thousand miles distant are conferred with and (after a sort) visited; the excellent works of godly men, the grave sentences of wise men, and the profitable arts of learned men, who died a thousand years ago, are yet extant for our daily use and imitation; all the estates, kingdoms, cities and countries of the world are governed, laws and printing maintained, justice and discipline administered, youth bred in piety, virtue, manners and learning at schools and universities, and that which is most and best, all the churches of God from the beginning established and always unto this day edified.

From David Brown, *The Introduction to the true Understanding of the whole Arte of Expedition in teaching to Write*, 1638; printed in David Cressy, *Literacy and the Social Order*, Cambridge, 1980, p. 9.

(b) Another seventeenth-century source. The speaker in this extract is a 'countryman'.

This is all we go to school for: to read common prayers at church and set down common prices at markets, write a letter and make a bond, set down the day of our births, our marriage day, and make our wills when we are sick for the disposing of our goods when we are dead. These are the chief matters that we meddle with and we find enough to trouble our heads withal.

From Nicholas Breton, *The Court and Country*, 1618; printed in David Cressy, *Literacy and the Social Order*, Cambridge, 1980,   p. 11.

165   Literacy and social status

The ability to read and write varied according to sex, social status, occupation and geographical location, as is shown by the tables in **(a)** and **(b)**, which are derived from the records of ecclesiastical courts. These dealt with wills, marriage licences and other documents which required either a signature or, in the case of the illiterate, a 'mark'.

(a) Illiteracy in the diocese of Durham, 1561–1631.

Social group	No. sampled	No. signing with mark	
Clergy/Professions	208	5	= 2%
Gentry	252	53	= 21%
Tradesmen/Craftsmen	727	470	= 65%
Yeomen[†]	1326	971	= 73%
Servants	18	14	– 78%
Husbandmen[†]	379	345	= 91%
Labourers	176	172	= 98%
Women	706	690	= 98%

(b) Illiteracy in the Diocese of London: Essex and Hertfordshire, 1580–1640.

Social group	No. sampled	No. signing with mark	
Clergy/Professions	177	0	= 0%
Gentry	161	5	= 3%
Yeomen	319	105	= 33%
Tradesmen/Craftsmen	448	188	= 42%
Husbandmen	461	337	= 73%
Labourers	7	7	= 100%
Women	324	308	= 95%

From David Cressy, *Literacy and the Social Order*, Cambridge, 1980, **(a)** Table 6.3, p. 120; **(b)** Table 6.4, p. 121.

Buildings and Furnishings

166   Hampton Court Palace

Although more survives today of Hampton Court than of any other Tudor palace, the architectural history of this great complex of buildings is far from certain. Wolsey began it, but after his fall from power it was completed by Henry VIII. Even in Wolsey's time the palace, built in late Gothic style, was calculated to give visitors a vivid impression of its owner's status and wealth.

(a) From John Skelton's contemporary poem attacking Wolsey.

Why come ye not to court?
To whiche court?
To the kinges court,
Or to Hampton Court?
Nay, to the kinges court.
The kinges court
Should have the excellence,
But Hampton Court
Hath the preeminence.
And Yorkes Place*,
With my lordes Grace!
To whose magnificence
Is all the confluence, . . .

From 'Why come ye not to Court?' in P. Henderson (ed.), *The Complete Poems of John Skelton*, 1959, p. 320.

*York Place, subsequently the royal palace of Whitehall, was Wolsey's London residence.

(b) Hampton Court: plan showing building attributed to Cardinal Wolsey, c. 1515–29.

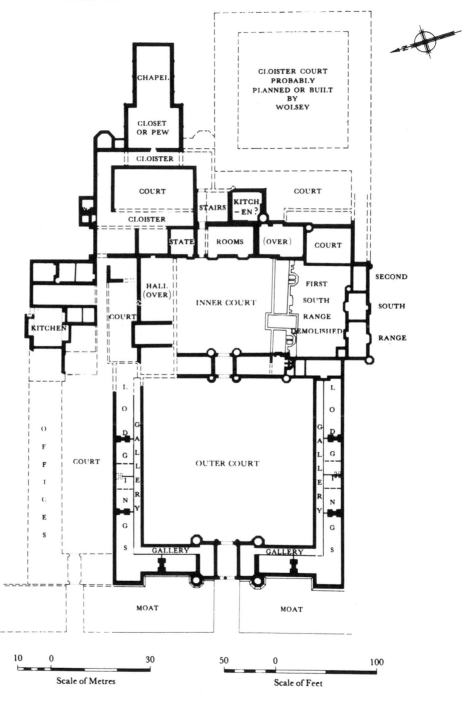

CHAPEL

CLOISTER COURT PROBABLY PLANNED OR BUILT BY WOLSEY

CLOSET OR PEW

CLOISTER

COURT

COURT

STAIRS

KITCH-EN?

CLOISTER

STATE

ROOMS

(OVER)

COURT

HALL (OVER)

FIRST

SECOND

INNER COURT

SOUTH

SOUTH

COURT

RANGE

KITCHEN

DEMOLISHED

RANGE

LODGINGS

OFFICES

COURT

GALLERY

OUTER COURT

LODGINGS

GALLERY

GALLERY

GALLERY

MOAT

MOAT

| 10 | 0 | 30 |

Scale of Metres

| 50 | 0 | 100 |

Scale of Feet

Work attributed to Cardinal Wolsey
(incorporating excavated evidence)

NB Windows, Doorways, etc are not shown

– – – Conjectural

Hampton Court: plan of the Tudor palace by the end of the sixteenth century.

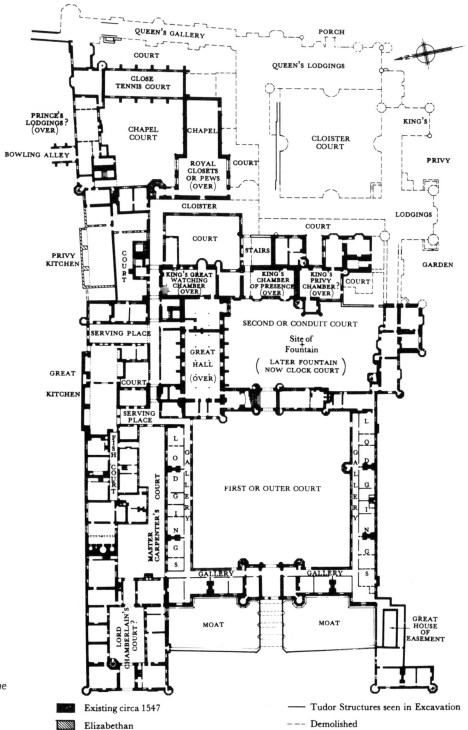

From H. M. Colvin (ed.), *The History of the King's Works*, vol. IV, *1485–1660*, part II, HMSO, 1982, pp. 130–1.

Existing circa 1547

Elizabethan

——— Tudor Structures seen in Excavation

- - - Demolished

From the Ashmolean Museum, Oxford; printed in H. M. Colvin (ed.), *The History of the King's Works*, vol. IV, *1485–1660*, part II, HMSO, 1982, plates 7 and 9.

(c) Two views of Hampton Court made by A. van den Wyngaerde in 1558: (above) from the south; (below) from the north, showing from left to right the Tudor tennis court, the great hall and the outer gatehouse.

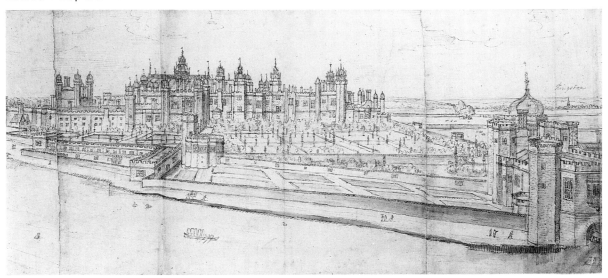

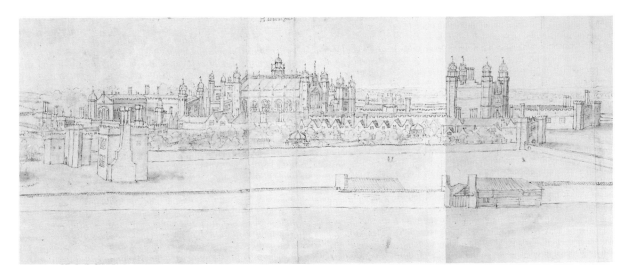

167   A changing world

The clergyman William Harrison, writing in 1577, provides one of the best contemporary accounts of Elizabethan England. The following extracts show how, for the better-off at any rate, life was steadily improving. (For details about the author, see **Doc. 21**.)

(a) Buildings.

The ancient manors and houses of our gentlemen are yet, and for the most part, of strong timber, in framing whereof our carpenters have been and are worthily preferred before those of like science among all other nations. Howbeit, such as be lately builded are commonly either of brick or hard stone, or both; their rooms large and comely, and houses of office further distant from their lodgings. Those of the nobility are likewise wrought with brick and hard stone, as provision may best be made; but so magnificent and stately, as the basest house of a baron doth often match, in our days, with some honours of princes in old time. So that if ever curious building did flourish in England, it is in these our years, wherein our workmen excel and are in manner comparable in skill with old Vitruvius, Leon Battista, and Serlio* . . .

   There are old men yet dwelling in the village where I remain which have noted . . . the multitude of chimneys lately erected, whereas in their young days there were not above two or three, if so many, in most uplandish towns of the realm (the religious houses and manor places of their lords always excepted, and peradventure some great personages), but each one made his fire against a reredos [*the back of an open hearth*] in the hall, where he dined and dressed his meat.

*Vitruvius, who lived in Rome in the 1st century BC, wrote a treatise on architecture which had an enormous influence on Renaissance architects – among them Leon Battista Alberti (1404–72) and Sebastiano Serlio (1475–1554).

(b) Furnishings.

The furniture of our houses also exceedeth, and is grown in manner even to passing delicacy; and herein I do not speak of the nobility and gentry only, but likewise of the lowest sort, in most places of our south country, that have anything at all to take to. Certes, in noblemen's houses it is not rare to see abundance of arras, rich hangings of tapestry, silver vessel and so much other plate as may furnish sundry cupboards, to the sum oftentimes of £1000 or £2000 at the least, whereby the value of this and the rest of their stuff doth grow to be almost inestimable. Likewise in the houses of knights, gentlemen, merchantmen, and some other wealthy citizens, it is not geson [*uncommon*] to behold generally their great provision of tapestry, Turkey work [*Turkish-style tapestry*], pewter, brass, fine linen, and thereto costly cupboards of plate, worth £500 or £600 or £1000, to be deemed by estimation. But as herein all these sorts do far exceed their elders and predecessors, and in neatness and curiosity the merchant all other, so in times past the costly furniture stayed there, whereas now it is descended yet lower, even unto the inferior artificers and many farmers, who, by virtue of their old and not of their new leases, have for the most part learned also to garnish their cupboards with plate, their joined beds [*good quality beds, made by a joiner*] with tapestry and silk hangings, and their tables with carpets and fine napery...

[Another improvement is] the great (although not general) amendment of lodging, for... our fathers... have lain full oft upon straw pallets, on rough mats covered only with a sheet, under coverlets made of dagswain or hop-harlots [*coarse, shaggy materials*]... and a good round log under their heads instead of a bolster or pillow... Pillows... were thought meet only for women in childbed. As for servants, if they had any sheet above them it was well, for seldom had they any under their bodies to keep them from the pricking straws that ran oft through the canvas of the pallet and rased their hardened hides.

[Yet another improvement] is the exchange of vessel, as of treen [*wooden*] platters into pewter, and wooden spoons into silver or tin...

From William Harrison, *The Description of England* (1577), ed. Frederick J. Furnivall, 1877, pp. 238–40.

168   A probate inventory, 1580

Wills and inventories from the second half of the century show fireplaces, changes of clothes and linen, and varied domestic utensils becoming increasingly common. This is the inventory of John Lawson of Chester, a gentleman who was comfortably, but not conspicuously, well-off. In this document the original spelling has been retained.

July 21, 1580. *In the hall.* One irone chymney [*fireplace*], with all the apperterances to it belonging, 6s. 8d. A drawinge table with a carpet, a forme, and iij buffett stooles 13s. 4d. One counter [*table*], j carpett, j forme, ij chayres, with a little chayre, and j salte kytt [*box*] for salte 13s 4d. One almerie [*cupboard*], with a Danske chiste, and j payre of tables 18s. xj qwyshinges [*cushions*] 4s. One raper [*dagger*] with a hanger 5s. *In the chamber.* One trussyng [*bundle of straw*], j leather bead, j bolster, j pillowe, ij hanginges, j coverlett, and ij blankettes 13s. One table, iij bolsters, and viij coodes [*pillows*] 10s. Two old chystes 2s. One chyste covered with leather, wherin iij payer of shettes is lying, 14s. v payer of straking shettes 13s 4d. iij payer of harden shettes 6s. [*types of linen sheets made from different parts of the flax plant*] ij payer of course shettes for servantes beddes 3s. 4d. xiiij pillowberes 13s. 4d. ix table cloths, whereof one is of dyaper [*linen*], with two course tabel clothes 20s. iiij lynnen towelles, iiij straking towelles, and j harden towell 6s. 8d. Two dozen and a halffe of tabel napthkens 6s. 8d. The painted clothes hanginges about the chamber, with a capcase 2s. 6d. *In the parler* One stand bedd with j feather bedd, j payer of blanketts of wollen, ij happynges [*coverlets*], j coveringe, j bolster, j pillowe, with hanginges of wollen

22s. v coverlettes, ij happinges and iij payer of wollen blankettes 13s. 4d. One long settell bedd, j chyste, j coffer, j other litle chyste, and j forme 13s. 4d. One peace of lynnen 10s. *The inner chamber.* One servantes bedde, ij happinges, j payer of shettes and j bolster 5s. One almerie 5s. xviij peace of putter [*pewter*] vessell, as plateres and dyshes, j basinge, iiij sawseres, j chamber pott, j quart pott, ij bountinge potts [*a type of short, wide pot*], j pynte poot and ij salte salleres 20s. The ketchinge vessell, viz., ij brase pootes, j posnett [*a metal pot with feet*], j yetlinge [*a cast iron pot*], v panes [*pans*], j morter with a pestell, j ladell, j grayt, j gyrdeiron, j fleshe knyfe, ij rackes, j payer of gybcrockes [*pot hooks*], and ij spettes [*Spits*] 20s. *In the butrye and ketchen* 10s. One greate arke for corne or bread 6s. 8d. iiij sylver sponnes 12s. The brewe vessell with a tappe stone 6s. 8d. One almerie 6s. 8d. Apperell geven by legacie to the value of 20l. Apparell not geven 30s. Two cappes, j sworde with a buckler, and a stafe with a sworde in it 30s. One steyle cape with a cover 5s. iiij shyrtes 20s . . .

From *Wills and Inventories from the Registry at Durham*, part II, Surtees Society, vol. XXXVIII, 1860, pp. 20–1.

169 Diagrams of yeomen's houses

Some examples of three-roomed houses, possibly appropriate to yeomen and built in the late sixteenth, or early seventeenth, century. They are similar to, or slightly smaller than, the house inhabited by John Lawson (see **Doc. 168**).

(a) Bispham, Lancashire. Cruck built with mud walls and only one entrance, on to a lobby by the side of back-to-back fireplaces.

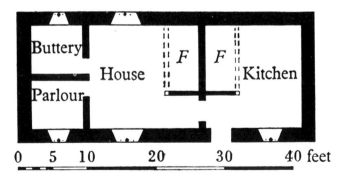

(b) Billingshurst, Sussex. Timber framed with a brick chimney stack and front entrance at the lower end of the hall.

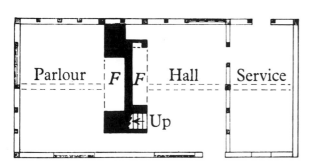

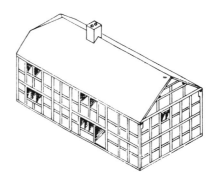

(c) Nutfield, Surrey. Also timber framed, with an outshot or cove, used in this case to house the staircase.

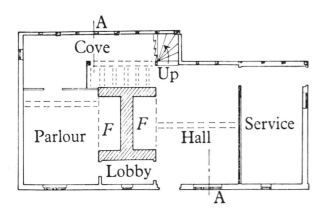

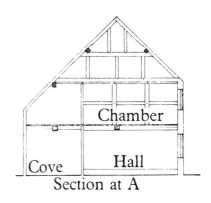

From M. W. Barley, 'Rural Housing in England', in Joan Thirsk (ed.), *The Agrarian History of England and Wales*, vol. IV, *1500–1640*, Cambridge, 1967, p. 753.

170 Great wealth, 1592

Francis Bacon, still only an aspiring courtier, published a propagandist account of the achievements of Elizabeth's reign, which shows the optimistic mood of the time.

The benefits of Almighty God upon this land, since the time that in his singular providence he ... placed in the kingdom his servant our Queen Elizabeth, are such as ... are worthy to be both considered and confessed, yea and registered in perpetual memory ... And first for grain and all victuals, there cannot be more evident proof of the plenty than this; that whereas England was wont to be fed by other countries from the east, it sufficeth now to feed other countries ... Another evident proof thereof may be, that the good yields of corn ... hath of late time invited and enticed men to break up more ground and to convert it to tillage, than all the penal laws for that purpose made and enacted could ever by compulsion effect.

A third proof may be, that the prices of grain and victual were never of late years more reasonable.

Now for arguments of the great wealth and plenty in all other respects, let the points following be considered.

There was never the like number of fair and stately houses as have been built and set up from the ground since her Majesty's reign; insomuch that there have been reckoned in one shire that is not great to the number of three and thirty, which have been all new built within that time; and whereof the meanest was never built for two thousand pounds.

There were never the like pleasures of goodly gardens and orchards, walks, pools and parks, as do adorn almost every mansion house.

There was never the like number of beautiful and costly tombs and monuments, which are erected in sundry churches in honourable memory of the dead.

There was never the like quantity of plate, jewels, sumptuous movables and stuff, as is now within the realm.

There was never the like quantity of waste and unprofitable ground inned [*taken in*], reclaimed and improved.

There was never the like husbanding of all sorts of grounds by fencing, manuring and all kinds of good husbandry[+].

The towns were never better built nor peopled; nor the principal fairs and markets never better customed nor frequented . . .

There was never so many excellent artificers[+], nor so many new handicrafts used and exercised, nor new commodities made within the realm; as sugar, paper, glass, copper, divers silks, and the like.

From *The Letters and the Life of Francis Bacon*, ed. James Spedding, vol. I, 1890, pp. 153–9.

171 Lord Burghley's defence of his building operations

William Cecil, Lord Burghley, Queen Elizabeth's principal minister, frequently protested that he had made little or nothing out of the royal service. Nevertheless, he managed to build two of the largest houses in England – Theobalds, in Hertfordshire, and Burghley House in Lincolnshire. The former was completed by 1585 and the latter by about 1589.

Theobalds was subsequently exchanged by Burghley's son, Robert Cecil, for the royal manor of Hatfield, and has now completely disappeared. Burghley House survives and is still in the possession of the Cecil family.

My house at Theobalds was begun by me with a mean measure, but increased by occasion of her Majesty's often coming; whom to please I never would omit to strain myself to more charges than building is. And yet not without some special direction of her Majesty upon fault found with the small measure of her chamber, which was in good measure for me, I was forced to enlarge a room for a larger chamber. For my house in Westminster, I think it so old as it should not stir any, many having of later times built larger by far, both in city and country. And yet the building thereof cost me the sale of lands worth an £100 by year in Staffordshire, that I had of good King Edward [VI]. My house of Burghley is of my mother's inheritance, who liveth and is the owner thereof, and I but a farmer [*tenant*]. And for the building there, I have set my walls upon the old foundation. Indeed I have made the rough stone walls to be of square, and yet one side remaineth as my father left it me. I trust my son shall be able to maintain it, considering there are in that shire a dozen larger, of men under my degree.

From John Strype, *Annals of the Reformation*, vol. III, part II, Oxford, 1824, p. 381.

172   Two prodigy houses: Theobalds and Holdenby, 1579

Burghley's great house was an inspiration to Sir Christopher Hatton, a favourite of Elizabeth who became Lord Chancellor in 1587. He was in attendance on the Queen in August 1579, and was therefore unable to be present when Burghley paid a visit to Holdenby, Hatton's palatial seat in Northamptonshire. Two archways, set on a lawn, are all that survive of Hatton's mansion.

(a) Hatton to Burghley, 9 August 1579.

... I fear me that as your Lordship shall find my house unbuilt and very far from good order, so through the newness you shall find it dampish and full of evil air; whereof I pray God your health be not impeached [*damaged*]. Before God, Sir, I take great comfort of your most honourable courtesy to visit your poor friend in so kind manner. I pray God I may deserve it by my true service towards you. I humbly beseech you, my honourable Lord, for your opinion to the surveyor of such lacks and faults as shall appear to you in this rude [*rough*] building, for as the same is done hitherto in direct observation of your house and plot [*plan*] at Tyball's, so I earnestly pray your Lordship that by your good corrections at this time, it may prove as like to the same as it hath ever meant to be. I beseech you, Sir, use patience in your too too rude entertainment, and think how much he doth honour and love you that would have wished it to have been much better and fit for so honourable a personage...

(b) Burghley to Hatton, 10 August 1579.

Sir, I may not pass out of this good house without thanks on your behalf to God, and on mine to you, nor without memory of her Majesty, to whom it appeareth this goodly, perfect, though not perfected work is consecrated; and all this I do in mind largely conceive, and in writing do mean but to touch, because I am hastened to Northampton, and I will reserve matter to enlarge at my return, to yourself... Approaching to the house, being led by a large, long, straight fair way, I found a great magnificence in the front or front pieces of the house, and so every part answerable to other, to allure liking. I found no one thing of greater grace than your stately ascent from your hall to your great chamber; and your chambers answerable with largeness and lightsomeness, that truly a *Momus* [*the god of mockery and censure*] could find no fault. I visited all your rooms high and low, and only the contentation of mine eyes made me forget the infirmity of my legs. And where you were wont to say it was a young Theobalds, truly Theobalds I like as my own; but I confess it is not so good as a model to a work, less than a pattern, and no otherwise worthy in any comparison than a foil. God send us both long to enjoy Her, for whom we both meant to exceed our purses in these. And so I end with my prayer for her health, and thanks humbly for her Majesty's remembrance of me, her weak spirit*.

From a monument of her Majesty's bountifulness to a thankful servant: that is, from Holdenby, Queen Elizabeth's memory, by Sir Christopher Hatton, her faithful servant and counsellor.

*Elizabeth's nickname for Burghley was 'Spirit'.

From Sir Harris Nicolas, *Memoirs of the Life and Times of Sir Christopher Hatton, K.G.*, 1847, pp. 124–6.

TOPIC INDEX

This is a list of suggested topics which can be followed up as an alternative to studying the book section by section. The numbers refer to particular documents.

GLOSSARY

anabaptists   Radical Protestants who refused to have their children baptised, and who were universally persecuted.

apostolic   Descended from the apostles.

arquebus   Early type of portable gun.

artificer   Craftsman.

benefit of clergy   Exemption from trial in secular courts for clergy in **felony** cases, and by extension to those who could read.

bondmen   Tenants who were bound to perform services for their lord.

canon law   System of church law, as used in the church courts.

caravel   Small, fast merchant ship with triangular sails.

chalice   Cup used for communion or mass.

chancel   The eastern part of a church. Before the Reformation it was reserved for the clergy and separated from the rest by a screen (see **rood**).

Chancery, Court of   Lord Chancellor's court, in which **equity** was used.

chantry   Endowment for the singing of masses for the souls of the dead.

conventicle   Presbyterian religious meeting, often secret and illegal.

Convocation   The representative assembly of the Church of England. Its meetings coincided with those of Parliament.

cope   Coloured vestment worn by priest when celebrating mass.

copyhold   Land tenure by custom of the manor, as proved by a copy of the manorial roll.

corrody   Provision for someone's maintenance, usually by a monastery.

demesne   Land held by landlord himself, and not rented out to tenants.

equity   System of law based on fair play, which could in certain courts take precedence over the common law.

felony   Capital crime below treason.

Fifteenth   Parliamentary tax on personal, movable property.

First Fruits   Part of the first year's income of a benefice, paid in tax.

galley   Low, sea-going ship propelled by sails and oars.

harquebus   See **arquebus**.

homily   Sermon printed by the government for parish clergy to read out.

hundred   Sub-division of a county, made up of several parishes.

husbandry, husbandman   Farming, farmer.

indenture   Legal deed or agreement.

indictment   Charge or accusation in a jury court.

injunctions   Orders, e.g. by a bishop to his clergy.

journeyman   Someone qualified at a trade, having served an apprenticeship.

larceny   Theft.

Letters Patent   Royal order under the Great Seal, e.g. for a grant of land or monopoly.

livery   Distinctive suit or badge worn by retainers or servants.

Lollards, Lollardy   Followers of doctrines of John Wyclif (c. 1320–84). They had their own English translation of the Bible and were highly critical of many aspects of the Church.

mark   13 shillings and 4 pence, or two-thirds of a pound.

Marque, Letters of   Licence to be a privateer, i.e. to capture enemy merchant shipping.

mystery   Handicraft or trade, or the guild controlling one.

praemunire   The crime of introducing into England foreign (usually papal) jurisdiction. See **Doc. 13**.

prebendary   A canon of a cathedral or collegiate church holding a prebend, i.e. receiving an income.

Presbyterians   Extreme **Puritans** who disapproved of the government of the Church of England by bishops, deans, etc., and favoured the pattern established by Calvin in Geneva.

procuration   Giving legal authority to someone else to act for one.

purgatory   A state intermediate between Heaven and Hell, in which souls were prepared for Heaven by being purged through suffering.

Puritan   Rather over-worked term, basically meaning one who wanted to make the Church of England more Calvinist.

quorum   Justices of the Peace with special qualifications, whose attendance at sessions was required in order to make them valid.

recognizance   Sum of money pledged as security, e.g. for good behaviour.

recusant   Someone (usually Catholic) who refused to attend Church of England services.

rochet   Linen vestment worn by bishops.

rood (screen)   Wooden screen, usually with a crucifix and images on it, which separated the **chancel** from the nave in a pre-Reformation church.

sacraments   Certain rites of the Church held to be necessary for salvation. **The Sacrament** means the consecrated elements in the mass or communion service.

schism, schismatic   Split in the Church; someone who has split away from the Church.

sectary   Member of a religious sect which refused to acknowledge the authority of the Church of England.

seminary   College for the training of priests (seminarists).

signet   Small seal used by monarch for certain official documents.

sureties   Persons who agreed to be liable at law for the performance of an action by someone else.

Tenth   Tax, originally paid to the pope, involving the tenth part of the annual profit of a benefice. (But for the Parliamentary '**Fifteenth and Tenth**', see **Doc. 95**.)

tithingman   Constable of a tithing, i.e. a local government unit similar to a **hundred**.

usury   Lending money at interest, a practice condemned by the medieval Church.

yeoman   Farmer of respectable standing.